HURRICANE WATCH

University Of Miami Football

MIAMI ORANGE BOWL

HURRICANE WATCH

University Of Miami Football

By Jim Martz

THE STRODE PUBLISHERS
HUNTSVILLE, ALABAMA   35801

Acknowledgments

Photographs Courtesy Of:
University of Miami Sports Information Department
Micki and Richard Lewis
Walt Kichefski
The *Miami Herald*

Dedication

To my parents,
Ira and Liz Martz,
And to the late George Gallet,
The prototype sports information director

Contents

Foreword

The devastating hurricane of September 16, 1926, forced the University of Miami to delay opening its classes for the first time until October 18. Just five days later, on Friday, October 23, the new university's football team played its first game, resulting in a victory against the Rollins College freshmen. From that slim beginning until January 2, 1981, when the team, dubbed "Hurricanes" early during the first stormy fall, defeated the Gobblers of Virginia Tech in the Peach Bowl in Atlanta, football at the University of Miami has scaled peaks of success and descended into valleys of disappointment. This book by Jim Martz is the saga of the highlights and lowlights of all the seasons from 1926 on.

Every president of a university where "big time" football is played has reason to contemplate the value of the sport. To some members of the faculty and student body it represents misplaced emphasis. Such criticism has surfaced in the history of this young university. Only recently a faculty member, chiding the university for the merry-go-round that took on and threw off head coaches with abandon during the seventies, exclaimed that for fifteen years football at the University of Miami had been "one coach away from greatness." At least in our troubled football fortunes of the last decade, no one could claim, as one American university president is supposed to have said about his university, that all we needed here in Coral Gables was a university worthy of the football team.

Football, holding the center of the stage in varsity sports, has provided the university with more plus than minus factors, according to Professor Emeritus Charlton W. Tebeau, who authored the *Golden Anniversary History of the University of Miami*, published in 1976. I am inclined to agree. Football, particularly during its victorious years, has brought a unifying, enlivening influence upon campus and community alike. Also, given the obsessive penchant of most Americans for watching or reading about sports, the football team has provided the university with much local and national publicity. Thanks to athletics, the nation became aware of this fledgling, independent, private institution in South Florida that was beginning its own shaky, but steady march toward an academic rendezvous with greatness.

I commend heartily Jim Martz's exciting story of how the Hurricanes, having developed into a great storm on occasions and a zèphyr on others, are now blowing with renewed intensity. Hurricane fans everywhere believe that football greatness is not now "one coach away." Howard Schnellenberger is at the helm.

Henry King Stanford
President
University of Miami
March 16, 1981

A Peach Of A Time

Bill Bruce, the droll master of ceremonies for numerous sports banquets in South Florida, has attended University of Miami football games since the 1930s when he would sneak into old Moore Park Stadium on Thirty-Sixth Street. For years he would say, "Watching University of Miami football is like watching a friend drown."

At the Miami Touchdown Club's annual banquet honoring the team early in 1981, Bruce felt compelled to throw out that line.

"It's better watching the Hurricanes now," he said. "I don't have to look through my fingers."

A few years earlier, Bruce almost could count the number of persons attending the Touchdown Club's banquet on his fingers. On this night, however, 820 persons jammed into the dining hall of Miami Springs Villas to honor the 1980 Hurricanes who had compiled the school's best record (9-3) in 30 years and had played in a bowl game for the first time since 1967. The crowd was double the size of the previous year's.

Coach Howard Schnellenberger sat at the dais with Bruce and surveyed the mob scene with an air of satisfaction. After two standing ovations, he gave his State of the Hurricanes message.

"As I was eating, I saw some people in the back of the room standing," Schnellenberger said. "In the back of my mind, I could see the same thing happening slightly north of Mark Light Baseball Stadium and south of the Hecht Athletic Center in a cozy little football stadium."

Schnellenberger's reference to the long-dreamed-of campus stadium was received warmly by the audience. A year earlier, many would have snickered at the audacity of such a statement. Pro-

11

Cheerleader Kathy Jones hailed Peach Bowl champions.

Miami's Tim Flanagan (90) leaped in celebration of Peach Bowl victory over Virginia Tech.

posals for a stadium on campus have come and gone like tropical storms since classes began in 1926. Invariably they were a lot of hot air.

What made Schnellenberger's statement less than outlandish was his track record at the UM. He had accomplished more in his first two years on the job than any of the 14 men preceding him accomplished in the same span. He was the first to take his team to a bowl and the first to win 13 games within two years.

Moreover, his team had made good on its implausible statement at the start of the 1980 season: "A bowl is our goal."

"Few in this room thought that would happen," Schnellenberger said. "But this team accomplished something more—it turned the program around and established it as a national contender. And it left for the teams to follow the ability and promise to be in the top echelon of college football for a long, long time to come.

"I remember the 1979 season that ended with a 5-6 record and sort of digressed-regressed from the 6-5 season under Lou Saban in 1978," Schnellenberger added. "The beginning of '79 had been a crushing thing—they lost a coach they respected and they struggled with a new coach. They had to somehow pull this thing together.

"Eventually, they accepted the new staff and a difficult schedule. In the last four games, they won at Penn State, they fought Alabama tooth and nail for a half. They lost to Notre Dame under not very conducive conditions in Tokyo, and they beat Florida.

"Rather than going out down and disillusioned, they came out with pride. That was the spark and catalyst of what we were able to do in 1980. With all but two starters back, they knew they could go out and challenge the same teams that had been better than them on that day.

"They went to the weight room and did something that's uncomfortable and has no glamour to it. They made themselves bigger, stronger, faster, and in some cases littler. And they continued it over the summer. When they came back August 17, they did the things necessary not only to talk about a bowl but to do something about it."

Most of the 1980 Hurricanes were in the first or second grade the last time the UM played in a bowl. Since then, the school had managed only two winning seasons (6-5 in both 1974 and 1979) and had changed coaches six times.

It is no wonder fans were skeptical when the Hurricanes predicted a bowl in 1980. En route to it, though, they went through three seasons in one: a 4-0 start, a 0-3 skid, and a 5-0 finish. The start was culminated by a 10-9 victory over ninth-ranked Florida State in the Orange Bowl before 50,000 fans, the largest crowd to see a home game since 1971. In victory, the defense upheld its ranking as the top team in the nation against the rush.

"The town was sky high with Hurricane Fever and everything was going fine through four games," Schnellenberger said as he continued his State of the Hurricanes message. "Then they had to take a trip to South Bend to face a tough Notre Dame team. On that day, they made too many mistakes.

"They came back home and played a great Mississippi State team, but nobody knew for sure the Bulldogs were great. We charged into the Orange Bowl and were greeted by 18,000 stout-hearted fans and couldn't knock the ball two-and-a-half yards at the end and didn't win. A similar thing happened at Penn State.

"Then this team came to the turning point. Either it was going to be like most Miami teams, beat some great teams but not be able to sustain it, or it was going to be different.

"And this is what I'm most proud of. With no tradition in their lifetime, no connection except themselves, they picked themselves up and won five straight. At the end of the third game in that streak, they reached their goal. They were invited to a bowl. At the end of the fourth, they beat a very good Florida team. At the end of the fifth, they beat a very good Virginia Tech team and became Peach Bowl champions."

Schnellenberger concluded, "We may not always win, but I assure you that's only because the clock runs out on us. If we have time, we'd catch them. We set a milestone here at tonight's banquet. There must be a lot of interest to draw 820 people. We're on our way."

If there was a particular moment which sent the Hurricanes on their way in 1980, it occurred with 39 seconds left in the Florida State game. That was when they resembled a man clinging to the top of a ledge. Most University of Miami teams the previous decade would have let go and fallen to death. This one pulled itself up to victory.

The scene: quarterback Rick Stockstill had just thrown an

11-yard pass to cap the Seminoles' only touchdown drive. Then he stepped into the pocket to throw a pass for a two-point conversion that would win the game. But the secondary left few openings. Then middle guard Jim Burt shed one blocker, leaped over another, and batted away Stockstill's pass to seal the triumph and snap Florida State's regular-season winning streak at 19 games.

That triggered a celebration seldom witnessed at UM games in the Orange Bowl since the MIRAcle days of George Mira in the early 1960s.

"This is the first time I really feel like I'm in college," said a student.

Added another, "The Hurricanes are the most talked-about thing on this campus since they raised tuition."

Only a year earlier, the UM had trouble giving away tickets. In fact, not one customer showed up at the two ticket outlets in Palm Beach County during the 1979 season. Attendance had shrunk from an average of 50,000 in 1965 to 17,000 in 1976, and it had improved only slightly by 1980.

Many of the 50,000 fans at the Florida State game were curiosity seekers wondering if the Hurricanes were a mirage or if they could finally compete week after week with the gorillas on the schedule. Many were Seminole fans, who had suffered through some dismal seasons of their own in the 1970s. And there were the faithful few who had endured so many UM seasons of mediocrity and broken promises.

Schnellenberger said he could not blame South Florida fans for not getting enthused in the seventies. "When a team has no hope of winning or really getting better, how do you expect someone to get involved with them?" he asked after the Florida State game. "Now the students almost seem starved. They want to win as much as the players do themselves.

"That's what it's all about. Football wouldn't be worth it if it was just 44 guys going out and getting tired. It means something when 50,000 people come out to watch and suddenly you're all involved. Everyone goes home exhausted and satisfied. They know they were a part of it. It's a great feeling to know that the spirit that has been dormant so long is alive and well."

Schnellenberger's diagnosis was premature. After the 32-14 loss to Notre Dame in the next game, the fans seemed to go back into hibernation. Some figured this was just another flash-in-the-pan Hurricane team, a tease like the 1973 squad that started with a 3-1 record incuding an upset of Texas and a near upset at Oklahoma. That team finished 2-5. Then there was the 1974 team that began 4-1 and finished 2-4.

Only 17,806, including 1,500 high school band members, showed up to see the eighteenth-ranked Hurricanes face a Mississippi State squad that eventually would win nine games, including an upset of Alabama.

"This is like being invited to a party and nobody shows," said Schnellenberger.

Hurricane parties lacked punch in 1980 until late in the season. In the first seven games, the offense had little trouble zipping between the 20-yard lines behind the passing of Jim Kelly, the receiving of Jim Joiner, Larry Brodsky, and Pat Walker, and the running of scatbacks Smokey Roan and Chris Hobbs.

But an inability to ram the ball into the end zone proved costly in the losses to Notre Dame, Mississippi State, and Penn State and elicited criticism that the line was not big enough, strong enough, or good enough.

Then the schedule softened and the line toughened with maturity. Suddenly, Roan and Hobbs found big holes to dart through. The week after the Penn State setback, Roan amassed a school-record 249 yards in 33 carries to spark a 23-10 victory over East Carolina.

Yet only 11,048 showed up in the Orange Bowl, and there were no bowl scouts.

"If there were any, I would have been able to see them," grumbled Schellenberger.

The next week at Nashville, Tennessee, the Hurricanes struggled to a 24-17 triumph over a Vanderbilt team which had lost 29 straight Southeastern Conference games. That was hardly the way to impress the bowls on the first day bids could be issued. But they had not bothered to send scouts anyway.

So here were the Hurricanes all dressed up with a 6-3 record on a schedule rated the second-toughest in the nation. But no one came calling.

In fact, several teams with less impressive records but more impressive traditions received bids, including 5-4 Houston that had lost at home to Miami, 14-7.

The bowls, obviously, were wary of the Hurricanes' erratic

attendance. Would they bring any fans? Would anyone watch on television? Moreover, would they defeat Tangerine Bowl-bound Florida in Gainesville in two weeks after playing North Texas State at home in the Orange Bowl?

Schnellenberger returned to Miami after the Vanderbilt game frustrated with the feeling the Hurricanes probably would get no closer to a bowl than their television sets. Late that night, however, he learned that the Peach Bowl in Atlanta had invited Virginia Tech but still was looking for an opponent. North Carolina had backed out at the last minute of its commitment to play in the Peach Bowl.

A crack was open, and Schnellenberger was determined to get his foot in the door. He called longtime friend Charley Thornton, the assistant athletic director at Alabama who had been Miami's athletic director briefly early in 1980 (he said he resigned because of his wife's health).

"How do I arouse interest in the Peach Bowl?" Schnellenberger asked.

"Call them," said Thornton.

Schnellenberger reached a Peach Bowl official and said, "You're about to make a terrible mistake. We may have one of the best teams in the country, and we're not even on your list."

Soon, Peach Bowl officials told the press the Hurricanes had been added to their list "as an afterthought." The prime candidates remained Stanford, Indiana, Louisiana State, and Kansas.

Schnellenberger then dispatched athletic director Dr. Harry Mallios, a running back in the Hurricanes' glory days in the 1950s, and administrative assistant Billy Proulx to Atlanta the following Monday morning to lobby with Peach Bowl brass. Mallios and Proulx pointed out that Miami's record was better than that of the other contenders and of many teams which had received bids. And it had been accomplished against stronger competition, on the basis of opponents' records. Moreover, the UM promised to sell 10,000 tickets.

Meanwhile, Schnellenberger took his case to South Florida, beseeching fans to come to the North Texas State game in the Orange Bowl Saturday afternoon to show Peach Bowl scouts their support.

"I'm hollering for help," he said at a press conference as four cans of peaches were perched in front of him. "This is the most important week the football department has had in a long time."

The response was not overwhelming, but it was significant by University of Miami standards. Businessmen bought about $5,000 worth of tickets to be given to area youth groups. Emerson Allsworth, an alumnus from Fort Lauderdale, sent a certified check for $5,000 to the Peach Bowl for tickets if Miami got a bid. Alumni rented a plane that flew over downtown Atlanta toting a sign that said: "UM Alumni Thinking Peach Bowl." Dade County Metro Mayor Steve Clark proclaimed Saturday "Support the Hurricanes Day."

Meanwhile, good news for the football program began to come in from several sources. ABC said it would regionally televise the Miami-Florida game—a $211,000 bonanza for an athletic department budget that had been strapped by million-dollar deficits. LSU withdrew from Peach Bowl consideration because of a rash of injuries. And the executive committee of the UM's board of trustees finally made a move on Schnellenberger's 18-month-old proposal for a 42,000-seat stadium on campus. It authorized a feasibility study to be undertaken by a professional consulting firm. This marked the first time money outside the athletic department would be used in regard to the proposal.

Schnellenberger, keeping an eye on all details, instructed the head of the UM Young Alumni Association, Ron Stone, to make sure Peach Bowl selection committee chairman Art Gregory received VIP treatment on his trip to the North Texas State game. VIP in this case stood for Very Important Propaganda, and it no doubt enhanced the Hurricanes' chances of receiving a bid.

Stone called Delta Airlines and had Gregory's ticket upgraded from coach to first class. He asked airline officials to give Gregory red-carpet service. The moment Gregory arrived at the Delta ticket counter, he was whisked into the VIP lounge and served cocktails.

Stone met Gregory at Miami International Airport. As they drove down the exit road, they passed a huge electric sign which usually says something like "Welcome to Miami." This time it read: "Welcome Peach Bowl Committee. We Want It!" Stone pretended not to notice the sign but slowed to be sure Gregory would not miss it. He did not.

"Stop the car! I don't believe this!" Gregory exclaimed.

The sign was just an appetizer. At the Marriott Hotel,

Gregory was quartered in the VIP suite, naturally. At dinner that night, he was joined by Peach Bowl selection committee member Bill Brigman. They dined on hors d'oeuvres and lobster at an exclusive restaurant, where matchbooks with their names inscribed in gold were placed at their table. Gregory and Brigman also received Hurricane football jerseys with their names sewn on.

It was breakfast with Schnellenberger the next morning. Then Gregory was taken by state trooper escort to the Omni Hotel where, to his surprise, the Orange Bowl Committee lobbied on behalf of the Hurricanes. This reportedly marked the first time a member of another bowl committee was allowed to attend a closed-door meeting of the Orange Bowl Committee.

Perhaps Gregory did not have the heart not to give the Hurricanes the bid after their 26-8 victory over North Texas State before 20,293. Or did he?

While Miami was winning, Indiana and Kansas lost and Stanford trailed California. But Gregory was not going to make any announcement until the Stanford game was over.

For 53 agonizing minutes after Miami's game, Schnellenberger and his players and coaches fidgeted and paced in the locker room.

"I don't know whether to stand up, sit down, cry, or pray," Schnellenberger said as he flipped a small plastic peach in his hand. "Someone get me my pipe and tobacco. I'm about to have a fit."

Somebody entered the room and announced that Stanford had gone ahead, 28-21, with three minutes left. That was wrong but nobody in the room knew it.

Finally, Stone, who had been escorting Gregory and Brigman, appeared and signaled Schnellenberger to follow him into the locker room. The Hurricanes erupted at the sight of the coach.

Gregory and Schnellenberger met in the middle of the room. Players crowded around and Schnellenberger asked for silence. Then Gregory said, "On behalf of the Peach Bowl, I extend an invitation to...." You could not hear the rest through the shouts of "Peach! Peach!"

Later, Schnellenberger was asked if peaches would be served more often at the training table. "We always serve peaches at our pregame meal," he said. "They're a fine source of extra sugar. Thank God we didn't get invited to the Gator Bowl."

Mark Rush dove for a touchdown in 31-7 rout of Florida in 1980.

Gators, nevertheless, were on the minds of the Hurricanes. Peach Bowl hoopla had to be put aside for a week because Miami had a date with bitter-rival Florida in Gainesville.

Mentioning Gators around the UM is like waving a red flag in front of a bull. Not only did the Hurricanes beat Florida for the third straight year, they did it by the widest margin in the 42-year-old series, 31-7.

The offensive line of tackles John Canei and Frank Frazier, guards Art Kehoe and Jim Pokorney, and center John Fenton opened holes that Hurricane alumni Chuck Foreman and Ottis Anderson were seldom fortunate enough to see in their UM careers. The rushing game netted 194 yards, and Jim Kelly completed 13 of 21 passes for 191 yards. The defense, meanwhile, shut down the Gators after allowing a game-opening drive of 80 yards for a touchdown.

Tangerine Bowl officials wore the look of someone who had just swallowed a rotten tangerine whole. Peach Bowl officials looked like proud papas in a maternity ward.

Seldom has there been a Miami-Florida game void of controversy, and this was no exception. Florida fans heaved tangerines, oranges, ice, and other debris at the Hurricane bench throughout the game. Assistant coach Chris Vagotis was struck in the side of the head by an orange, and a student photographer from the UM was hit in the stomach by fruit and was doubled up. In retaliation, Schnellenberger ordered Danny Miller to kick a 25-yard field goal on the final play of the game.

"Normally I wouldn't do that," Schnellenberger said. "But it was a reaction to all the crap that was going on. I felt this would draw attention to a problem they've got to solve up there."

Not to mention drawing attention to the next Miami-Florida game which would open the 1981 season in the Orange Bowl.

Miami's victory at Gainesville erased the flash-in-the-pan tag for 1980. Not only did the Hurricanes finish with their best regular-season record since 1966, they set school records for total points (258) and total yardage (3,732).

Jim Burt became the UM's twenty-seventh All-American when he was named to the Newspaper Enterprise Alliance first team and the Associated Press third team. And Schnellenberger won the AP Coach of the year honor for Southern independents over five other coaches going to bowls, including FSU's Bobby Bowden.

For a school that received the last of 30 bowl bids, and that one as "an afterthought," the Hurricanes did not fare badly. The Peach Bowl's payoff of $330,000 was higher than half the other bowls. And the game was telecast nationally by a major network (CBS).

But the Peach Bowl's January 2 date, requested by CBS because it was a Friday afternoon and there would be no other sports events on television, was weird. Coming the day after the glut of four major bowl games on the tube, the Peach Bowl earned such labels as The Red Eye Bowl and the Anticlimactic Bowl. Or for bettors, the Get Even Bowl. In Atlanta, it was the Ho Hum Bowl.

The Hurricanes should have felt right at home. They were playing second fiddle to a pro team, this time the Atlanta Falcons, who would play their first National Football League playoff game in history two days after the Peach Bowl in the same Atlanta Stadium.

Actually, the Peach Bowl played third fiddle because the Georgia Bulldogs were top "dawgs" in town. Their successful bid to defeat Notre Dame in the Sugar Bowl and win the national championship for the first time overshadowed the Falcons.

It was a chilly, windy afternoon when the Peach Bowl was played before a half-empty stadium. About 50,000 tickets had been sold, but the game was carried live on local TV and there were 20,000 no-shows.

The Hurricanes played adequately, but were not domineering, in downing Virginia Tech, 20-10. Kelly completed 11 of 22 passes for 179 yards, including a 15-yard touchdown pass to Brodsky. Miller hit two field goals, and Hobbs ran 12 yards through a mammoth hole for a touchdown.

"Ho hum, just another bowl game. Ha ha!" crowed offensive guard Art Kehoe as he strutted into the locker room.

Schnellenberger, whom CBS commentator Frank Glieber once called Harold Schnellenbarger, clutched the Peach Bowl trophy and said, "This is as good a place as any to stop and rest on our journey to the national championship. What we have to figure out now is whether we have a chance right away—next year—or whether we will need, well, intermediate steps."

Later at a victory party at the Peachtree Plaza Hotel, he told Hurricane fans: "I guarantee we're on a collision course with the best teams in the country. This is not only our first victory of 1981,

Coach Howard Schnellenberger beamed while holding Peach Bowl trophy.

but a new plateau toward challenging for the No. 1 spot. We were not outclassed by anybody this year. We lost to Notre Dame and Penn State but weren't outclassed.''

While seniors such as Burt and defensive end Mike Goedeker lamented the fact that their UM careers were ending just when the program was moving forward, split end Pat Walker took a more philosophical outlook.

"I feel like this is forever," Walker said. "I'm going out a winner. I feel like a champion. And I'll always be an alumnus. I'll always come back, because it has been a great four years. What I really appreciate, though, is being a part of progress from a team that couldn't do anything to a team that could do almost everything."

Meanwhile, Proulx went to work on a new bumper sticker: "You Ain't Seen Nothing Yet."

Pipedreams And Traditions

Howard Schnellenberger thought he was in a time warp when he first saw the 1927 *Ibis*, the University of Miami's first yearbook. There on page 143 was an artist's rendition of a huge stadium to be built on campus.

The accompanying story revealed plans for a 50,000-seat bowl suitable for football, soccer, baseball, and track. The board of regents already had authorized a fund board composed of prominent South Florida citizens to raise money.

But the bowl turned out to be nothing more than a pipedream, just as were many other stadium proposals over the years. Yet Schnellenberger had to wonder if he was dreaming as he read the *Ibis* account referring to thousands of fans who would ride on trains to the stadium on tracks that were going to be built. Schnellenberger had envisioned fans coming to his stadium via the metrorail which was being built a block from campus.

"The entire project has been endorsed by the bankers and businessmen of South Florida," said the *Ibis*. "And the railroad companies have made arrangements to run spur lines from neighboring towns to the stadium. Every citizen has a whole-hearted interest in the great bowl as the success of the community will be measured, in a way, by the success of the stadium.

"Imagine, if you can, the first football game of next season! All roads leading to the stadium jammed with traffic; people pouring into the huge bowl; flags flying; the band marching down the field; yells and songs, echoing to the sky; the shrill blast of the referee's whistle; the kickoff—and the great game is on! That game will live long in the memories of those who are fortunate enough to attend, for it will be more than a contest between two

Stadium planned for Miami campus in 1926 was patterned after the Rose Bowl.

teams, more than songs, yells and enthusiasm displayed by the spectators—it will be a splendid example of the cooperation of citizens in a community project; it will be the reincarnation of the ancient Greeks' idea of perfect physical manhood.''

There was never any doubt among the UM's founders that the school should have a first-rate intercollegiate athletic program, according to Charlton W. Tebeau, author of the *Golden Anniversary History of the University of Miami*. Bowman F. Ashe, the university's first president, said well-known coaches would be sought and players recruited for football, baseball, and track. He also mentioned the possibility of a postseason football game.

But the lofty thoughts of the *Ibis* and Dr. Ashe had to take a back seat to reality. The great bowl the Hurricanes would play in would be the Orange Bowl in Miami. And that would not be built for a decade.

Even plans for a temporary, 8,000-seat stadium on campus went awry. Work started on September 15, 1926, one day before a hurricane leveled much of South Florida, but never went any farther. The storm killed more than 130 people in the Miami area and damaged more than 10,000 homes.

A makeshift grandstand was built, however, with lumber from a dismantled stadium in Coral Gables. It was set up at University Drive and Avenue Levante east of the present Faculty

Dr. Bowman F. Ashe, president of the University of Miami from 1926 to 1952.

Club. The grassless field consisted of coral rock overlaid with mulch, and players jokingly referred to it as Sandspur Stadium.

The "name" coach the UM hired to assemble the first team was Howard (Cub) Buck, a two-time All-American at Wisconsin who had been an assistant coach at his alma mater. He organized a team about two weeks before the opening of classes.

"He instilled into his men the fighting spirit that spread to everyone at the university," reported the *Ibis*. "His men loved him and would die fighting for him."

Before they could die for him, though, many had to be taught the basic fundamentals of blocking and tackling. Among his novices was Larry Catha, a 190-pounder who was dubbed "Big Boy" because he was the biggest player on the team.

The UM's first football field in 1926.

"There was no such thing as a scholarship," Catha recalled. "Everybody on the team was working. The depression had already started in Florida. I was working on the Florida East Coast Railroad when the coach spotted me.

"I was big from working, so he asked me what position I played. I said tackle, though I had never been in a football uniform in my life. The only protection we used to wear was a leather strap to keep the other team from biting your ears."

The Hurricanes apparently kept their ears intact because they went undefeated in eight games—playing a freshman schedule—and outscored the opposition, 122-13.

The first game was played October 23, five days after classes began, against visiting Rollins College of Winter Park, Florida. The UM won the ragged contest, 7-0, on a touchdown by quarterback Cliff Courtney before 304 spectators and curiosity seekers. Florida Southern, Mercer, Stetson, and Loyola were next to fall, then the Hurricanes won a pair of games over the University of Havana by identical 23-0 scores. The first was played Thanksgiving Day on campus and the second on Christmas Day at Havana. The season ended against visiting Howard College of Alabama in a New Year's Day contest that served as a forerunner to the Orange

The first gridiron contest in 1926 led to an undefeated year and a Miami total of 122 points to the oppositions' 13.

Bowl Classic.

The 36-man squad included players with such colorful nicknames as Sag (Cliff Courtney), McGoogan (Johnny McGuire), Old Folks (Jimmy O'Brien), Pug (Everett Ellis), Half Pint (Henry McLendon), and Pee Wee (Peter White). Most of the players came from out of state but many settled in South Florida after graduation, including center and captain Bill Kimbrough, who became Coral Gables' chief of police, and fullback Ted Bleier, who became director of physical education in the Dade County school system.

Bleier, from Appleton, Wisconsin, is the uncle of Rocky Bleier, who nixed Ted's efforts to lure him to the UM and became captain at Notre Dame and a star with the Pittsburgh Steelers following a comeback from wounds suffered in the war in Vietnam.

"Our field was nothing but rocks and boulders," recalled Kimbrough. "It was right where the practice field is now. The hurricane did a lot of damage and the depression knocked the hell out of everything. But school spirit was excellent."

Roy Weakley, a guard, recalled the early days of the program as times when "you could walk down the street in Miami and if you were a football player you would know 75 per cent of the people you would meet. We used to have a snake dance after the game where we would dance down Flagler Street to the Olympia Theater, and they would stop the movie while we sang the UM song."

The fight song, "Hail to the Spirit of Miami U," was composed and written by students Ted Kennedy (class of 1930) and Dale Clark (class of 1929). Here are the not-so-immortal words:

> Hail to the spirit of Miami U,
> Hail to her pride and glory free,
> Hail to her orange, green, and white so true,
> Hail to her fighting varsity!
> Long may her banners wave o'er vanquished foe,
> In our hearts may she always be;
> Hail to the spirit of Miami U.
> We pledge our faith and loyalty.

Porter Norris, a member of the first football team, is said to be the first to use the nickname Hurricanes. Though it caught on quickly, there occasionally were detractors.

The *Miami Herald* reported on November 22, 1926, that the name was offensive to many people in the area who felt all reference to hurricanes should be eliminated "in word and thought." But on December 14, the *Herald* conceded that the name had not really been given. It had happened and probably could not be changed.

In the 1930s, a local journalist campaigned to get rid of the nickname because he felt it was bad public relations in the area's efforts to lure tourists and new development. But he gave up when UM students threatened to hang him, and not in effigy.

And in 1960, Chicago financier and Florida real estate developer John D. MacArthur tried to whip up another campaign to change the nickname.

"Shivers ran up and down my back every time they mentioned the 'Hurricanes' during the telecast of the Miami-Pitt game last week," billionaire MacArthur complained. "Why keep reminding people there are Florida hurricanes? This hurricane business is played up beyond all proportions.''

South Florida realtors and UM officials were not impressed with his reasoning. Said a university spokesman: ''Does anyone think that Chicago is full of bears just because the town has a football team by that name?''

The UM's school colors were selected in 1926 by a committee consisting of Ruth Bryan Owens (daughter of famed attorney William Jennings Bryan), Harry Provin, and Bertha Foster. Owens was a member of the board of regents and taught speech, and it was through her persuasion that the colors from the orange tree of Florida were selected—orange for the orange itself, white for the blossom, and green for the leaves.

Sebastian the Ibis, the UM mascot, was the brainchild of the late Norman A. (Chink) Whitten and was named after the old San Sebastian dorms. The ibis is a large wading bird related to the heron, with long legs and a long, slender, curved bill. They can be seen in the Everglades where they make their homes during the fall and winter months.

In the mid-1950s, the football team had a second mascot, a boxer dog named Hurricane. He received national publicity when he became the proud papa of a football team—11 boxer pups.

The UM band was not organized until 1933 by Walter E. Schaeffer, solo clarinetist and concertmaster with the United States Marine Band under John Philip Sousa. The band's name, the Band of the Hour, was given in 1949 as it played Henry Fillmore's march ''The Man of the Hour'' during a halftime show in the Orange Bowl. The public address announcer said, ''Here's 'The Man of the Hour' played by the 'Band of the Hour,''' and the name caught on.

Few traditions, however, have caught on in Hurricane football. Perhaps that is because the university is relatively young and located in a transient community. Perhaps, as is often said, the area is too blase.

Probably the most noted tradition that has survived over the years is Touchdown Tommy, the cannon which signals the scoring of touchdowns and field goals in the Orange Bowl. The cannon idea originated in 1935 when a cheerleader named Ernie Duhaime borrowed a toy gun to fire during games.

The original cannon disappeared when taken to a road game in 1936, but it was replaced before the next season when Erl Roman, then fishing editor of the *Herald,* started a crusade to buy a new cannon.

First Miami team scored a winning season.

Twice just before Florida games, Touchdown Tommy was stolen, but it turned up safely after each game. For several years after that, the cannon was locked in the coaches' offices after games.

A ship's bell atop the student union has heralded the opening of homecoming. The 175-pound bell was given to the school by the navy department. It had been the bell of the U.S.S. *Bulmer* and had called sailors to their battle stations in both the Atlantic and South Pacific theaters during World War II.

The Hurricanes and Florida Gators used to play for a Seminole war canoe, reportedly the only authentic one in the world. The Hollywood, Florida, Chamber of Commerce donated the canoe in 1955 to serve as a trophy to the winning team. It had been handmade by Seminole craftsmen from a 200-year-old Everglades cypress.

But the tradition died over the years. When a reporter asked whatever happened to the canoe, one UM employee thought it was stored at the student union, another thought it was stored in the Hecht Athletic Center, and another thought the Florida State Seminoles had absconded with it.

The Good, The Bad, And The Indifferent

"There has always been an element of crisis, even something of a gamble, in the story of the University of Miami," wrote Tebeau in his *Golden Anniversary History*. "It has moved from crisis to crisis, growing in stature all the while.... The university has always been overextended and underfinanced. It opened with a debt of a half-million dollars and few off-setting tangible assets."

The school was born during a land boom. George Merrick, a land developer, pledged $4 million in cash and 160 acres on the outskirts of Coral Gables for a university. A realtor offered $1 million for a building to the memory of William Jennings Bryan. And in the spring of 1926, framework for the first building was dedicated. But nine months later the boom was a bust. The pledges could not be filled and a hurricane turned the fledgling South Florida into a land of torn trees, broken dreams, and shattered buildings.

Nevertheless, the school opened on schedule, not on "an artificial hill 200 feet high, which will be the highest spot in Dade County," but in an unfinished abandoned hotel. To form classrooms, wallboard partitions were set up at intervals, which led students to jokingly call it "Cardboard College."

Coral Gables and the university, in a sense, were born twins. The school received its charter three weeks ahead of the city, but the city had a head start in construction.

Dr. Ashe, the first president, had been an administrator at the University of Pittsburgh. His daughter Dorothy married Eddie Dunn, who in the late 1930s became the Hurricanes' first football hero. Dunn later was a coach at the UM, and his sons Bo and Gary played for the Hurricanes in the 1970s, and Gary went on to play for the Pittsburgh Steelers.

Though 5,000 were expected, only 125 students registered at the new school on a September morning. The first student was Francis Houghtaling, a 19-year-old Miami Senior High graduate who later became manager of the basketball team.

Financial aid for players was limited basically to a tuition scholarship. Players were expected to earn their own room and board and personal expenses, but several jobs were made available to assist them. Many worked for the school's maintenance department or at local race tracks. The latter prompted Dunn to suggest that degrees of football players might well be called "Masters of Hounds."

When varsity competition began in 1927, the Hurricanes rolled to a 39-3 victory over Rollins in their first game. Coach Buck "pulled a Rockne" by starting practically the entire second team, then making wholesale substitutions resulting in a rout.

But after a 49-0 romp the next week over Piedmont, the UM discovered it was not ready to compete equally with most schools on the schedule. The Hurricanes scored only three touchdowns the rest of the year in losing to the likes of Spring Hill, Stetson, Howard, Oglethorpe, and Millsaps and finishing with a 3-6-1 record. The guarantee to visiting schools totaled $16,000. (Guarantees now average $100,000 per game.)

Efforts in the spring and summer of 1927 to construct a stadium similar to the original plans failed to succeed. "The field, or what there was of it, was in the wrong place at the time," wrote Tebeau. "The only other university symbols on the original campus were the unfinished administration building and the men's dormitory, where the students ruefully gave their address as 'East Tampa.' The Anastasia Building, where university operations were being conducted temporarily, was two miles away and the fans in Miami much farther."

After Buck's 1928 team went 4-4-1, a group of area business and professional men offered support in the form of management and financial backing for football. They wanted a well-known new coach and they promised equipment, which was badly lacking. They also thought the games should be transferred to a downtown Miami stadium, and this led to the eventual move to Moore Park. The group also guaranteed the university and visiting teams that all bills would be paid.

J. Burton Rix, who had coached at the University of Texas,

In 1930 Coach Ernest Brett added a mechanical bucking machine to the Miami training schedule.

Southwestern Louisiana, and Southern Methodist, was the so-called ''well-known'' coach hired to replace Buck.

But Rix's 3-2 season in 1929 was not impressive. Both losses came on the first road games ever for the varsity—to Southwestern Louisiana and Stetson. The team traveled in the City of Miami's private car, ''The Spirit of Miami,'' on the Seaboard Airline Railroad. Home games were played at Miami High because the makeshift stadium on campus was condemned by safety officials.

The stock market crash in October of 1929 doomed whatever chances the off-campus management group had of lending support. The national depression extended the three-year-old Florida depression several years.

When the season ended, Rix quit and was replaced by Ernie Brett, who had been an assistant at UM since the first season. Brett inherited an ambitious schedule which featured one of the first night games ever played in the nation, plus a road trip that bordered on suicide—three games in eight days, the first being indoors on a field as hard as cement.

Home games that season were played at the new Moore Park stadium at Seventh Avenue and Thirty-Sixth Street, which was closer to the downtown fans but too remote from campus to interest many students. On October 31, the Hurricanes introduced night games to the area in a game against Bowden State College. The field was lighted by unprotected, high-watt bulbs, and old-timers recall that when it rained, exploding bulbs could be heard as the field gradually grew darker.

The hectic road trip began against Temple University of Philadelphia and was played in the auditorium at Atlantic City, New Jersey. It was the UM's first intersectional game and was only the second college football contest played indoors.

One account says an estimated three million square feet of Pennsylvania black dirt was brought to the Atlantic City auditorium to make the grassless field. But Bill Kimbrough, center on the team, recalls that, "They had held a hockey game in the auditorium the night before and put this reddish brown substance—clay or whatever it was—over the frozen surface, I suppose. Anyway, it was as hard as a rock."

The UM players carried coconuts to the game and presented them to the Temple players. Temple, in return, handed the Hurricanes a 34-0 defeat. Wilbert Bach, who was to become the UM's first paid football publicity man ($15 a week for 12 weeks) around 1935, recalls hearing parts of the game on his crystal radio while he was a newspaperman in Toledo, Ohio.

"The big teams frowned on night football then as such a commercial exhibition," Bach said. "But Miami was struggling and saw a chance to pick up some money and grabbed it."

The game drew 25,000, the largest to see the Hurricanes to date, and was played on Saturday night. Then the team traveled to Dothan, Alabama, to face Howard the following Tuesday afternoon and lost, 24-0. Then it was on to Lafayette, Louisiana, where they salvaged the trip with a 6-0 victory over Southwest Louisiana on Saturday.

As if the gruelling travel was not enough (remember there were no jet planes then), the Howard game was played in rain on a makeshift field, and after the first two plays the players were covered with lime that burned through their jerseys and caused painful burns before the second half. According to the *Ibis*, the Hurricanes had no dry equipment for a change between halves, and lime burns started to tell. As a consequence of lime burns, the Hurricanes went to Southwest Louisiana handicapped by the loss of several lineman and two backs.

The *Ibis* described Brett as a man who "is short of stature, heavy of muscle and likeable of nature. He works harder than the squad when in scrimmage and has been known to break benches between his fingers like matches during tight games."

By the end of the season, there must not have been any benches left to sit on because the Hurricanes scored only 26 points while winning three games, losing four, and tying one. Brett, like Rix, quit after just one season.

Next to join the Hurricane coaching merry-go-round was Tom McCann, who in 1931 also faced an ambitious schedule that consisted of 12 games. His teams went 4-8, 4-3-1, 5-1-2, and 5-3-1 in a four-year stint lowlighted by financial problems and highlighted by the birth of the Orange Bowl stadium and Orange Bowl Classic.

The biggest problem was that the athletic program, largely football, did not pay its way. According to the *Golden Anniversary History*, expenditures for the first five years were $151,609 but income was only $105,238.

"Whatever publicity and public support football generated

Coach Tom McCann.

did not produce offsetting revenues to pay for it," Tebeau wrote. "In fact, all segments of the university operation were producing deficits, and the administration could least justify them in athletics."

Thus the UM Athletic Association was formed in September 1931, and it assumed responsibility for management and finances. But that proved little more successful. Two years later the committee resigned and the university again took over the bills and the management of the athletic program. After the school's bankruptcy sale, the bills were paid off, to the surprise of the creditors.

In 1932, President Ashe, who had staunchly supported football, wondered if the sport should be dropped. But the board of trustees thought that would be unwise. Instead, boxing, tennis, swimming, basketball, and golf were temporarily dropped as varsity sports.

The Hurricanes were only 3-3-1 during the regular season, but they triumphantly entered the bowl business on January 1, 1933, when they upset favored Manhattan, 7-0, in the Festival of Palms game before a capacity crowd of 6,000 at Moore Park.

"This proved to Miamians and the sporting world that the Hurricanes can really play a snappy brand of football," said the *Ibis*.

A 5-0-2 season followed in 1933, but the Hurricanes lost to Duquesne, 33-7, before 7,500 at Moore Park in the second Festival of Palms game. Duquesne was rated among the nation's best and was coached by Elmer Layden, one of the Four Horsemen of Notre Dame.

Later in 1934, the American Legion met in Miami and built a 4,000-seat grandstand which Earnest Seiler, recreation director for the City of Miami, bought for $1,000. Aided by the Works in Progress Administration, seats were set up at the site of the present Orange Bowl, which was known then as the Wooden Bowl.

The Hurricanes played their first game there January 1, 1935, before 8,000 and lost to the Eastern champion of small colleges, Bucknell. At halftime, the UM band paraded around the field followed by a truck carrying several coeds in an orange-colored bowl. From that humble beginning grew the Orange Bowl Classic and famed halftime extravaganzas produced by Seiler and viewed by millions on national television.

In 1935, a few university supporters became interested in hir-

Wooden Bowl, with 4,000 seats, was forerunner of today's Orange Bowl Stadium, with a seating capacity of over 75,000.

ing Red Grange as coach and were ready to raise the required $75,000 salary, a hefty amount for then. But President Ashe nixed the attempt because the salary and the implied emphasis on football were too much. His own salary was about half that.

Nevertheless, the selection of Irl Tubbs as coach and athletic director signaled a new commitment to intercollegiate football. Tubbs' first squad went 5-3 with only 15 players—hailed as 60-minute iron men—seeing most of the action.

The season marked the tenth anniversary of the school and the football program. "Progress has been slow, but at last they are ready for a shot at the big time," wrote John B. Ott in the *Ibis*. "...In the past decade Miami teams have been good, bad and indifferent. This uncertain progress has been due to unhappy experiences in finances for athletics.... The fight has been a winning one, and the future looks bright. From here on, the Hurricanes are 'ready to go.'"

Coach Irl Tubbs.

Ott selected an All-Time Hurricane team for the first decade:
 left end, Robert Masterson, 1935
 left tackle, Edward Grazcyk, 1933
 left guard, Walter Dansky, 1933
 center, Bill Kimbrough, 1930
 right guard, Evan Lindstrom, 1930
 right tackle, Walter Buck, 1933
 right end, Rod Ashman, 1929
 quarterback, Cliff Courtney, 1929
 left halfback, Cecil Cook, 1935
 right halfback, Johnny Bates, 1932
 fullback, Ted Bleier, 1930

Tubbs guided the Hurricanes to a 6-2-2 record in 1936, the only losses coming against Mississippi and South Carolina. The crowds began to swell as 9,400 attended the Stetson game when the Hurricanes won the championship of Florida's Little Four (Miami, Stetson, Rollins, and Tampa); 10,000 showed up for Ole

42

Miss and 11,000 for South Carolina.

The regimen installed by Tubbs and his assistant, Pat Boland, was paying off. Reported the *Ibis*: "While off the gridiron, the football boys kept excellent training. They were kept on a special diet, went to bed at 10 p.m. of their own accord, and never gave Coaches Tubbs and Boland anything to contend with. It's no wonder then when all is said and done that the University of Miami did go forward, that we did attain greater football glory, when one considers the type of individual the university has on its football team: the healthy, rugged, sincere, and dependable gridster."

But Hurricane supporters were dismayed at the end of the season when Tubbs and Boland resigned and took over the coaching reins at the University of Iowa.

Harding And Legacies

Though Howard Schnellenberger accomplished more in his first two years than his predecessors did in the same span, there remained an underlying question as to whether he would exit as so many others had after a few seasons or whether he would stay long enough to leave something for posterity.

"Posterity's a big word," he told *Herald* columnist Edwin Pope as the 1980 Hurricanes prepared for the Peach Bowl. "But I would like to leave a legacy to posterity. A contribution. Like Jack Harding did."

Harding did more to establish stability and credibility in football and the total athletic program than anyone before him. When he replaced Tubbs after the 1936 season, enrollment was 1,000 and the athletic program was limited to football and tennis. When he ended the dual role of coach and athletic director to become fulltime athletic director in 1948, enrollment was 10,000 and the program consisted of basketball, baseball, swimming, track, golf, polo, and boxing.

In 1936, crowds of 5,000 were satisfactory at most football games. In 1948, basketball and boxing drew that much and football attracted a total of 250,000.

When Harding became coach, the Hurricanes usually played small schools. Before he finished, he had defeated Florida, Clemson, West Virginia, Michigan State, Texas Christian, and Texas Tech. And his 1945 team went 9-1-1 and beat Holy Cross in the Orange Bowl Classic.

In his nine years as coach, Harding won 54 games, lost 32, and tied three.

Dr. Ashe had known Harding at the University of Pittsburgh

Jack Harding.

and was instrumental in bringing him to the UM. Ashe was a member of Pitt's administrative staff when Harding was a running back in the early 1920s.

Nicknamed Spike, Harding was a deeply religious Catholic, and once he sprinkled holy water on himself before a tough game at Pitt. His teammate, Andy Gustafson, whom Harding later brought to the UM, said, "I'm not Catholic and I'm not superstitious, but I wasn't going to fight the thing. I told him to sprinkle a little on me, too."

Harding's hobby was golf and he sported a 12 handicap at the Riviera Country Club. His low-key demeanor was a sharp contrast to most college football coaches.

"Even on the days of our biggest games, he was never irritable," recalled his wife, Louise. "He had a fatherly closeness to his boys. The boys used to drop around at the house. We were all one big happy family.

"One day Jack and I took a ride past the old Cardboard College and then the magnificent new campus, and Jack said, 'We're the luckiest people in the world because we're privileged to see a dream come true.'"

Harding began to lay the groundwork in 1937 beginning with a 40-0 victory over Georgia State before 8,000 in the new Roddey Burdine Municipal Stadium, popularly known as the Orange Bowl or Burdine Orange Bowl because of the New Year's classic. The concrete and steel structure replaced the old wooden stadium and had 23,000 seats. It was built by a federal grant and funds loaned to the city by the government and cost about $250,000.

The new stadium was the site of the 1938 Orange Bowl Classic

The concrete and steel stands of the Orange Bowl replaced the Wooden Bowl in 1937.

but the Hurricanes did not play in the New Year's game until 1945. The Orange Bowl Committee felt the UM could not provide competition for the caliber of visiting teams that would attract crowds. Because the game was primarily for publicity purposes, the committee increasingly sought two teams from out of town that might also bring fans.

But Harding soon began to build a program that one day would be attractive to the Orange Bowl Committee. His 1938 squad was the best to date at the university, winning eight of 10 and beating Florida at Gainesville in the first meeting of the schools. The Hurricanes were Southern Intercollegiate Athletic Association champions for the first time and repeated as state champions of the small schools. The 23,367 who saw the Georgia game, a 13-7 victory, was the largest crowd to date in Florida.

Wearing long winter underwear on a bitter cold day, the Hurricanes lost, 18-6, to Drake at Des Moines, Iowa. Back home, they upset Duquesne, 21-7, as New York Mayor Fiorella La Guardia sat on the bench of the visitors, his adopted team. In that game, Touchdown Tommy fired seven times, once nailing an official in the pants. He spent the rest of the night picking buckshot out of his seat between plays.

The biggest explosion of the season, however, was the 19-7 surprise over the Gators in the third game. About 15,000 fans, including 3,500 from Miami who came by train, attended the contest. That initiated the biggest rivalry on the UM schedule.

"Flushed with the success garnered in their first two battles," reported the *Ibis*, "the Hurricanes breezed into Gainesville the morning of Oct. 14, behaved themselves that night, and the next evening, led by Captain Eddie Dunn and a fighting spirit, they promptly muzzled the surprised Gators."

Dunn scored all three touchdowns—a feat worthy of sainthood—after Florida took a 7-0 lead in the closing seconds of the first half. Walt Kichefski, one of the UM's greatest ends who later became a Hurricane coach and the world's leading Gator Hater, fondly recalls playing that day in Gainesville.

"Florida had refused to play us until then," Kichefski said. "We were the young upstarts with big ideas and dreams and they looked down their noses at us. They were an all-boys school then and were more obnoxious than they are now. They were meaner than rattlesnakes. But when we walked off the field at the end of

Varsity team of 1938 that upset Florida in the first game in the series, pictured in Washington, D. C., before game with Catholic University.

the game, their fans were as quiet as a graveyard at midnight.''

In 1938, backers of UM football organized a Quarterbacks Club ''to encourage united civic support for the University of Miami and its football team.'' The club was to supplement, but not take over, what the university itself could not do to strengthen the program. About 3,200 members joined at one dollar apiece.

Support from the Quarterbacks Club included $250 to improve the practice field, and four years later it raised $3,000 to rebuild the field. The club also bought a diathermy machine for the training room, plus equipment for filming games and some practices. It sponsored the annual spring game and a weekly luncheon during the season at which coaches and players discussed games. The club functioned until 1955 when it gave the leading role to the Eaton Foundation.

The leading role on the field during Harding's era was played by Dunn, who is generally considered the Hurricanes' first football hero. A native of Pittsburgh, he came to the UM on a football scholarship in 1935 and captained the team his freshman and senior years. He set numerous game, single-season, and career

records for rushing, scoring, and punt returns. Most of his rushing records stood until Ottis Anderson broke them between 1975-78. But Dunn still holds the career touchdown record of 25.

"He was a good leader," recalled Kichefski, "and he could fly. He ran the 100-yard dash in 10 seconds flat, and that was moving in those days. We used the old single wing formation. The Philadelphia Eagles drafted him but he chose to stay here and coach."

Dunn was UM backfield coach in 1939 and became interim head coach and athletic director when Harding was called to serve in World War II in 1943 and 1944. He continued as an assistant until 1953 and helped assemble the 1945 team that went 9-1-1 and won the Orange Bowl Classic. He also designed the first UM baseball field and was coach from 1947 to 1954.

"He was directly responsible for the great football teams we had in the early 1950s," said Dr. Harry Mallios, a running back on those teams who became athletic director in 1980. "He was a demanding coach, a perfectionist."

Kichefski, a native of Rhinelander, Wisconsin, was the other standout in the early years of Harding. He was co-captain of the 1939 team and earned All-American honorable mention. He played with the Pittsburgh Steelers from 1940-42, coached the UM

Eddie Dunn.

line for a year, then returned to the pros in 1944 before going back to the UM as an assistant in 1945. Later he was promoted to head offensive coach and assistant head coach. Among his pupils was three-time All-American defensive end Ted Hendricks. In 1970, Coach 'Ski was named acting head coach and athletic director when Charlie Tate resigned two games into the season. He later served as head of the UM Athletic Federation.

"In 1936, when Eddie Dunn and I started playing on the varsity as sophomores, our dressing room had old pegs with numbers on them," Kichefski remembered. "Practice was where the Riviera Country Club is now. We'd take an old log and run it over the field to knock down the sandspurs. It was a dust bowl. Then we'd sit in class and squeeze the sandspurs out of our legs.

"In '37, we practiced behind the Coral Gables Coliseum. We'd take a bus to get there. Then in '38 we practiced on the

Biltmore golf course, a nice place. Later we had a field on Blue Road; then they built one off LeJeune where we stayed until the present fields were built."

There were big expectations from the 1939 team because only five players were gone off the strong 1938 squad. But the Hurricanes went only 5-5, including a 13-0 loss in the Orange Bowl to Florida that ruined homecoming before 26,000 fans. Monday morning quarterbacks blamed the disappointing season on the fact that there were too many complacent seniors and Dunn had graduated.

The downfall started right after an event that was supposed to be uplifting. Harding took the entire team to Camp Pinnacle in North Carolina for a two-week training period that would avoid Miami's later summer heat and humidity. But Wake Forest, ironically a school from North Carolina, drubbed the Hurricanes, 33-0, in the opening game of the season in the Orange Bowl.

Harding faced a rebuilding job in 1940 with a small squad consisting of eight seniors, eight juniors, and 16 sophomores. The 3-7 record included a 61-14 loss to Texas Tech, which kept its starters in the game for all but three minutes. The Hurricanes rebounded with an 8-2 season in 1941, including a 6-0 revenge over Texas Tech, plus a 7-6 upset of South Carolina and a 14-0 triumph over Florida before a state record crowd of 30,000.

Hit heavily by losses to the armed forces, a sophomore-dominated team in 1942 compiled a surprising 7-2 record. The Associated Press said, "Little Miami must be considered with the other major football teams in the nation."

The favorite play of the season was "the Sally Rand naked reverse" that running back Walter Watt used for touchdowns against Furman and South Carolina. The Hurricanes stopped Florida, 12-0, to claim the state championship and win the Lou Chesna Memorial Trophy named after the former UM guard killed in an accident during his last football season (1937).

Harding left for active duty with the navy the next year, and Dunn took over the varsity. But chances of football continuing seemed dim. Many students had entered the armed services, and those in the army's specialized training programs could not play. And V-12 students, mostly freshmen, were ineligible. Moreover, many men could not be away from their stations for more than 48 hours, and there was a shortage of nearby opponents because most schools had abandoned intercollegiate sports.

Yet UM football continued. When President Ashe returned in September 1943, from 15 months with the War Manpower Commission in Atlanta, he said football would remain if five opponents could be scheduled. Six games were played in 1943 (the Hurricanes won five) and nine in 1944 (they went only 1-7-1) against service teams and a few colleges.

In 1943, home attendance averaged 15,000, one of the largest totals in the South. The quarterback was Arnold Tucker, who later played in the famed backfield at West Point with Doc Blanchard and Glenn Davis. And one of the ends was Al Rosen, who later starred in baseball with the Cleveland Indians but never played baseball at UM.

The following spring, basketball and boxing were reinstated but not baseball. Said the *Ibis:* "Baseball, the one sport at which Miami is never successful, was attempted again, but failed. There was no coach for the team; spring football interfered."

After the horrendous 1944 season in which the Hurricanes did not score until the fifth game, the *Ibis* wrote, "We were not so pretty good." The headline on the story said: "Wait 'Til Next Year. Squad Got Lots of Exercise, Little Satisfaction in 1944."

In general, the Hurricanes simply were outmanned. For instance, the armed forces team from Fort Pierce, which clobbered them, 38-0, featured players from the National Football League champion Chicago Bears.

Only a handful of lettermen returned in 1945 and the Hurricanes were expected to win only three or four games. But enrollment began to grow as hundreds returned from the service. Many men had played football at the university or on service teams and that made up for the lack of lettermen.

Harding returned from the war in September and took his old jobs as coach and athletic director. He did not know the names of all his players before the opener against Chattanooga, but soon many of the names were household words in the Miami area as the Hurricanes developed into one of the Cinderella teams of the nation and went 9-1-1, including a last-second victory over Holy Cross in the Orange Bowl Classic.

"Hans Christian Andersen could not have written a tale of make-believe to compete with the unbelievable saga of the 1945 Hurricanes—a little-known Miami eleven won the right to national acclaim as the 1946 Orange Bowl victor,'' the *Ibis* reported.

Senior lineman Edward (Red) Cameron and William Levitt were named to the Associated Press Little All-American team. Fullback Harry Ghaul, a freshman from Burlington, New Jersey, finished fourth in the nation in scoring with 100 points and led the nation in punting with an average of just under 42 yards. He was named honorable mention All-American.

"All we did that year was keep the hitters," recalled Kichefski, who returned from the Pittsburgh Steelers to be an assistant coach. "We fired all but 18 players. Then we recruited again and started practice in the middle of the summer. If they flunked, we sent them home. We had a bunch of orangutans."

Before leaving the Steelers, Kichefski recruited Ghaul from under the nose of club owner Art Rooney. Ghaul had gone into the service right out of high school but had been discharged for having high blood pressure.

"Ghaul was the best punter in the Steeler camp," Kichefski recalled. "I asked Rooney if he was going to make the club and he said he didn't think so. So I told Harry I'd get him a scholarship at Miami.

"After he left camp, Rooney said, 'It was a mistake not to keep that kid.' Ghaul could kick from one end of the field to the other. He kept us in games for four years. What a weapon! Talk

Harry Ghaul.

about hang time!''

Crowds for the Georgia game of 24,308 and the Florida game of 25,564 taxed the capacity of the Orange Bowl in 1945 and led to decisions to enlarge it by 11,000 in 1946.

The Hurricanes beat the Gators, 7-6, on a wild extra-point play. The Gators blocked Ghaul's kick, but Inky Mazejka grabbed the ball in mid-air and headed for the sideline. Just as he was being tackled, he lateralled to Ghaul, who carried it over.

After the Hurricanes whipped Auburn, 33-7, to finish the regular season, they received the Orange Bowl bid the following Monday morning. School was officially in session, but after 11:30 a.m., classrooms were deserted by professors and students. Many decorated cars with orange, green, and white streamers and joined a 200-car cavalcade down Flagler Street to the El Commodoro Hotel where the decision was to be announced.

It was the UM's first bowl invitation since 1934, and the Hurricanes made the most of it. In the first half, Joe Kurll scored for Miami on a reverse and Stan Koslowski threw a touchdown pass for Holy Cross, but both teams missed the extra point.

Holy Cross had the ball in the game's closing seconds and a 6-6 tie appeared certain. Crusader halfback Gene DeFilippo threw a final desperation pass toward end Frank Parker open downfield.

Al Hudson raced 89 yards for the winning touchdown on the final play of the 1946 Orange Bowl game against Holy Cross.

But the ball bounced off Parker's hands and into the hands of the Hurricanes' Al Hudson.

Hudson, a former Miami Edison High track star, juggled the ball momentarily before running 89 yards for a touchdown as time expired.

As Harding began his tenth season in 1946, his staff had grown from one assistant, Hart Morris, to seven. The size of the squad had ballooned from 30 to 110.

Fortified by several lettermen and prewar players returning, the Hurricanes went 8-2. The following February, Sir Winston Churchill accepted an honorary degree of doctor of laws from the university, prompting him to quip, "No one ever passed so few examinations and received so many degrees."

Harding passed most of his examinations as coach. But when the Hurricanes lost their last five games in 1947 for a 2-7-1 record, he decided he had coached long enough. On February 20, 1948, he retired as coach to become athletic director full time.

Gus And A Coming-Out Party

A man once stopped Andy Gustafson on the street after Gus had retired as coach and athletic director at the UM and asked if he had any money.

"No," said Gustafson, "but I've got memories that are worth millions, and they mean that much to me."

Gustafson, who died in 1979 at age 75, also left a million memories to Hurricane fans and alumni.

At a school which has hired 15 coaches in 54 seasons, Gus' 16-year endurance record is a marvel. He compiled a 93-65-3 record, produced four bowl teams, and appeared on national television nine times. Two other teams probably would have received bowl bids if the program had not been on NCAA probation for recruiting violations in the mid-1950s.

Gustafson was a running mate of Harding at Pittsburgh in the early 1920s under Coach Pop Warner. Upon graduation in 1926, Gus became head coach at VPI until 1929. He was an assistant at Pitt through 1933, then became Earl (Red) Blaik's first assistant and backfield coach at Dartmouth. He remained there until going to Army with Blaik in 1941, where he was there seven years through the golden age of West Point football. He coached the famous Army backfield of Arnold Tucker (the UM's quarterback in 1943), Doc Blanchard, Glenn Davis, and Rip Rowan.

The Hurricanes had been using variations of the old Pitt single wing and more recently an L formation, something of a cross between the single wing and the T. Gustafson installed the Army T formation with variations.

He developed several outstanding players and produced victories over many noted rivals to add luster to the growing UM pro-

Andy Gustafson.

gram in the 1950s and 1960s. On the basis of records, attendance and All-American players, these became the golden years of football in the first half-century of the university.

Gustafson was known for his sharp football mind, volatile temper, and frequent generosity. He was held in affection by players but not always by rival coaches and acquaintances.

A heavy drinker until late in his coaching career when he became an active member of Alcoholics Anonymous, he at least twice tried to punch sportswriters, one of whom had written of a 20-0 upset by Fordham in New York in 1953: "Miami's longest drive of the day was back to the hotel."

New York columnist Dick Young also panned the Hurricanes and Gus pinned the column on the bulletin board before Fordham visited the UM in 1954. The Hurricanes won the rematch, 75-7, and Fordham dropped football.

Gustafson helped revolutionize offenses in the college game, notably with the form of a belly series called the Miami Drive Series. It was an option series built around a power fullback and was a forerunner of the veer and wishbone.

Every play started with the quarterback putting the ball in the fullback's belly, then letting the fullback keep it, or pitching back to a halfback, or running it himself, or passing.

Three of Gus' quarterbacks have become college head coaches: Don James, who led Washington to the 1978 Rose Bowl victory; Fran Curci at Tampa, the UM, and Kentucky; and George MacIntyre at Vanderbilt.

"The biggest thing I learned from Coach Gustafson," said MacIntyre, "was that if you ever get beat, you go put on your best clothes, comb your hair, shine your shoes, and go face people. When you win, you dress and act the way you want to.

"After one game in the Orange Bowl, we were coming off the field and some guy spit in Coach Gustafson's face. He didn't even wipe it off. He wouldn't even show that he noticed. But assistant coach Walt Kichefski had the guy in two steps."

Dr. Mickey Demos, Gustafson's physician, suggested the bout with alcoholism was largely responsible for Gus' generosity.

"Many times, former players would call him and ask a favor," said Al Hudson. "He never said no."

Former UM president Dr. Henry King Stanford concurred. "I was impressed with his ability to win friends for the university. I was tremendously impressed with the courage and tenacity he showed in overcoming alcoholism."

Upon Gustafson's death, his wife, Mandy, said: "He had a wonderful life. He did all the things he wanted to and he did them in style."

The Gustafson Era began in 1948 when Whitey Campbell starred at fullback in a 25-0 victory over Rollins before 34,599 in the Orange Bowl. It was the largest opening crowd to date.

The Hurricanes drew a record 42,827 the next week in a 19-10 loss to Villanova, then 46,127 for a 42-21 loss to Georgia.

After the 4-6 season, Gustafson lamented, "We didn't have the depth to tackle the kind of schedule we played. You've got to have manpower for that."

He started to get that manpower in 1949, a 6-3 season that included a 28-13 victory over Florida in the Orange Bowl before a state-record 55,981. Campbell and tackle Leo Martin were named

Whitey Campbell, football, basketball, and baseball star, who was voted the best all-around athlete in the UM's first 25 years.

honorable mention All-American at the end of the season.

Then came the glorious 1950 season, the year the Hurricanes came of age. The highlight, of course, was a 20-14 victory at Purdue the week after the Boilermakers ended Notre Dame's unbeaten streak at 39 games. George Gallet, the UM's sports information director who had followed Hurricane football since the first season in 1926 until his death in 1981, rated the Purdue victory the biggest in the school's history and the one that put the program on the national map.

"The nation finally realized that there is a university down on the tip of Florida," the yearbook, the *Ibis*, said.

The Hurricanes finished 9-1-1, losing only to Clemson, 15-14, in the Orange Bowl Classic. In beating Purdue and Iowa, they became the only school to beat two Big Ten teams. They finished fifteenth in the final Associated Press poll and thirteenth in the United Press poll, the highest to date for the university.

Only five touchdowns rushing and five passing were allowed, and no team scored more than twice. The Hurricanes led the nation in interceptions with 31, but only five UM passes were intercepted.

Al Carapella, a converted fullback who played right tackle, became the school's first All-American (except for Little All-Americans) as he was named to the AP first team on defense. His tackle against Iowa stopped a drive at the one-yard line in the final

The 1950 team that put the Hurricanes on the map.

Al Carapella.

minute.

Other stars included Leo (the Lion) Martin at defensive end; linebackers Wilfred Stolk, Pete Mastellone, and Joe Lyden; receivers Tom Jelley and Ed Lutes; running backs Harry (the Scooter) Mallios, Frank (the Tuckahoe Terror) Smith, and Jim Dooley; guard Don Mariutto, and quarterbacks Jack (Mr. Short Pass) Hackett and Bob (Mr. Long Pass) Schneidenbach.

Hackett, better known as Mighty Mouse, was a touching success story. He had started four years in high school at McKeesport, Pennsylvania, then polio struck and left him paralyzed from head to foot.

But he overcame the disease in time to enter the UM and spark the freshman team and later lead the varsity as a sophomore. He barely weighed 140 pounds, and one foot was two inches shorter than the other from polio. He starred in the upset of Purdue and a romp over Pittsburgh, then was hurt and replaced by

The Scooter, Harry Mallios.

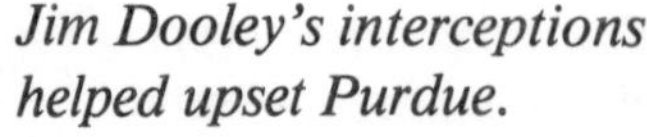

*Jim Dooley's interceptions
helped upset Purdue.*

Schneidenbach, who had started the season at fullback.

A week before the Purdue trip, the Hurricanes defeated Villanova, 18-12, in the Orange Bowl, and left Villanova coach Jim Leonard unimpressed. "We don't have much. We have students for tackles," he said. "Purdue will slaughter Miami, but you should do well with everyone else."

Meanwhile, Purdue was beating Notre Dame in the rain at South Bend, 28-14, behind the passing of Dale Samuels.

The next week at West Lafayette, Indiana, Purdue took a 7-0 lead. But the Hurricanes rallied for 20 points in the second half. Samuels was intercepted six times, twice by Dooley, twice by John Castagno, once by Jack Del Bello, and once by Joe Lyden, who returned the ball 53 yards for Miami's first touchdown. Smith scored the other touchdowns on runs of 50 and 18 yards.

No doubt Purdue was ripe for an upset after pulling off a victory at Notre Dame. "We were beaten by a more aggressive team," said Purdue Coach Stu Holcomb. "Our squad was in the doldrums."

The Hurricanes were in the clouds. "We were definitely up for the game," understated Gustafson. "They (the Hurricanes) were not tired at halftime, and they were still convinced they were the better football team. I believe our line whipped Purdue's line, and that probably is the real answer to the ball game."

The UPI account of the game began: "The heady wine of unexpected conquest produced a mammoth hangover Saturday for Purdue's conquerors of Notre Dame, who in turn were defeated, 20-14, by Miami's southern hurricane in a football upset that was equally as staggering as last week's downfall of the Irish."

The *Miami News* reached Notre Dame coach Frank Leahy in New Orleans, where his Irish had defeated Tulane, 13-9, and asked him to comment on the Hurricanes' upset.

"Coach Andy Gustafson must have done a wonderful job," said Leahy. "I have known for several years that Andy was one of football's better coaches. But I honestly did not believe he could possibly bring Miami to such great heights in such a short space of time.

"Saturday's convincing victory over Purdue definitely proves that the University of Miami is a big-league football team in every sense of the word. From this date on they must be reckoned with in consideration for national honors. My hat is off to Andy Gustaf-

Hurricanes celebrated 1950 victory over Purdue.

son and his fine football team."

Back in Miami, students, fans, and alumni celebrated for three days. And they gave the Hurricanes a homecoming that—if estimates are accurate—was greater than those the Dolphins received after winning Super Bowls in 1973 and 1974. An estimated 100,000 people turned out to cheer, whistle, honk horns, shoot off cannons, explode firecrackers, and wave flags—American, Confederate, and hurricane warning.

"In the Slop Shop a moment after that final whistle, pandemonium broke loose," reported the *Ibis*. "A blizzard of shredded napkins and newspapers buried the floor and tables, and garbage can lids were pressed into service to collect money to send telegrams of congratulations to team members. The rally at the airport Sunday added fuel to the fire and by Monday classes didn't have a chance.

"Students in the dorms, the Student Club and Hurricane rooters all over Miami crowded their radios waiting for the final gun that would sound the victory blast sealing the incomparable upset of Purdue.

"When the moment came...students deserted their dormitories and homes and swamped to the Student Club. Band members grabbed their instruments and played a medley of Miami

64

fight songs as they converged on the Club.

"The riotous turmoil went unabated in the Slop Shop as jitterbugs danced on the table tops. Cat-calls of 'Who Beat Purdue?' and answers of 'We did' were echoed through the halls."

Immediately after the game, a horn-blown motorcade of 150 cars started through Coral Gables' streets. That was just a warm-up for what was to come.

There's a saying that all roads lead to Rome. But in Miami on the day after the Hurricanes beat the team that beat THE team, all roads led to the airport. Of the estimated 100,000 who tried to get there, an estimated 30,000 surged through police barricades and lines set up hastily at the airport when the team's chartered plane, called the *Dreadnaught*, arrived.

The plane had to circle the field repeatedly while police begged the crowd to clear the runway. Outside the airport, thousands more sat in cars trapped in a massive traffic jam backed up two miles. Drivers who wanted to go the other way were unceremoniously pushed off the road.

A police motorcade brought the team out of the airport gate and down Flagler Street from LeJeune to Seventeenth Avenue. Bands and majorettes led the motorcade of players in convertibles to the Bayfront Park amphitheater for a rally, where 7,500 people —about 1,000 more than capacity—squeezed in to see the team.

The *Herald's* Page 1-A banner headline on Monday said: "100,000 Cheer Football Victors." And the lead story by Jack Thale began: "Blase Miami cheered its lungs out Sunday for a football team that fought its heart out." An accompanying story by Lawrence Thompson began: "Miami, that allegedly sophisticated resort city, took down her hair, threw off her corset and broke into a college cheer Sunday when her football team came home with Purdue's treasured scalp....The town was one big noise, a noise half way between a million automobile horns and a thousand cow bells, all going at the same time. Even the prisoners from the 16th to 25th floors of the courthouse were tossing out confetti, homemade out of toilet tissue."

All hurricanes have an eye, a period of calm in the center of the storm. The eye of the 1950 Hurricanes occurred when a supposedly so-so Louisville team came to the Orange Bowl and pulled off a 13-13 tie. The UM was lucky to get away with that.

With the game knotted at 13-all, Louisville made a successful

Fans raced onto runway at Miami airport when the team returned from Purdue.

Traffic jams were common as fans flocked to airport after Purdue game.

attempt for the extra point. But there were too many men on the Louisville line, and the next kick was wide.

Yet the storm gained strength again and the Hurricanes defeated Florida, Iowa, and Missouri to finish the regular season undefeated. Then came the only taint of the season, a 15-14 loss to Clemson in the Orange Bowl Classic. It is a game that ranks as perhaps the biggest hard-luck defeat in UM history.

Clemson dominated the first half, leading 9-1 in first downs, 153-39 in total offense, and 13-0 in score. But Miami grabbed a 14-13 lead in the third quarter. Mallios ran over from five yards on a pitchout from Schneidenbach for the first TD, and Smith scored the other on a 14-yard pass from Hackett. Watson kicked both extra points.

The Hurricanes seemed to be heading for another score when they drew three successive 15-yard penalties. The first nullified a score; the others ruined good runs. Still another penalty pushed the Hurricanes back to their one-yard line, where a safety cost the game when Sterling Smith tackled Frank Smith behind the goal line.

In 1951, the first hand-picked Gustafson team had reached its senior year. Grantland Rice, long-time dean of American sportswriters, predicted the Hurricanes would be ranked no worse than ninth nationally. Instead of the undefeated season fans dreamed of, the UM lost three games.

An invitation to the Gator Bowl eased the disappointment, however, especially when the Hurricanes gained revenge by whipping Clemson, 14-0.

The *Ibis* put the year in perspective when it said, "It seemed as if The Year had arrived in 1950, and '51 was anticlimactic. America's southermost college didn't electrify the sports world—but the notch in big-time sports reserved for Miami was filled competently.

"Win, lose or draw, in the sports arena Miami has made its climb, and now the grind begins. It is harder to whip up enthusiasm for a gangling adolescent than for a blooming baby and now that Miami has had its coming-out party, the real fight begins—the fight to gain the dignity and decorum of sports adulthood."

They had little trouble in fighting for fans in those days. A total of 339,963 attended the eight home games in 1951. That figure ranked fourth in the nation, and it has never been topped at the UM, though the average of 42,495 has been surpassed six times, the last in 1967.

The Hurricanes owned a 4-1 record and their pass defense was No. 3 in the nation when Babe Parilli of Kentucky riddled them in a 32-0 rout played in 15-degree temperatures at Lexington. The UM rebounded with a 21-7 victory over Florida before 61,000 homecoming fans in the Orange Bowl.

Then in the grudge fight with Clemson at the Gator Bowl, the Hurricanes were underdogs because Smith and several linemen were sidelined by injuries. But Gustafson's team controlled the game as Mallios scored both touchdowns and Elmer Tremont kicked both extra points and frustrated Clemson by punting nine times for a 44.5 average. And Dooley, who later became head coach of the Chicago Bears, intercepted four passes.

Nick Chickillo, 1952 All-American.

Gus faced a rebuilding year in 1952. Moreover, injuries and the call of the draft for the Korean War hurt his depth as the Hurricanes won only four of 11 games. Nick Chickillo, a 5-11, 220-pound guard and tackle, made the Paramount All-American first team at guard while linebacker Rex Shiver was AP honorable mention All-American. Attendance varied widely as 11,846 showed up for Stetson and 53,916 saw Alabama visit the Orange Bowl.

In 1953, a 14-10 upset of Florida saved an otherwise unsatisfactory 4-5 season. National champion Maryland drubbed the Hurricanes, 38-0. And in their first visit to New York, they bowed to Fordham, 20-0, and the Polo Grounds as fans belabored them with catcalls and suggested they bring a bigger band and leave the football team at home in the future.

Probation But Not Devastation

As fast as training rules were made, a hard-nosed, hard-headed Hurricane halfback named Gordon Malloy would break them.

"For three years, he had gone steady with trouble," wrote Luther Evans in the *Herald*. "His social life reached its peak as a junior when he helped make a garage out of a cocktail lounge as fists and bottles flew. He was shocked when Gus put the monkey on his back by appointing him captain his senior year in 1954."

Upon hearing the news, Malloy asked permission to talk to the squad in private. "No guy has broken more rules or caused the coaches more headaches than me," he said. "But now I'm captain. I'm gonna live by the rules. If I can do it, everybody else can. Any guy who doesn't toe the mark is going to have to answer to me."

The Hurricanes toed the mark and surprised even their most optimistic fans as they won eight of nine games and returned to national prominence. End Frank McDonald became the first UM player to make two All-American teams—AP and *Look*. And for the first time in school history, the Hurricanes were ranked among the top 10 at the end of the season—ninth in both the United Press and International News Service polls and eleventh in the AP. They were sixth before their only loss, 14-13, to Auburn in a game in which they squandered a 13-0 lead in the last seven minutes.

Malloy, fullback Don Bosseler, halfback Whitey Rouviere, and quarterbacks Carl Garrigus and Mario Bonofiglio spearheaded Gustafson's "drive series" as the Hurricanes finished sixth in the nation in rushing, averaging 284 yards per game, a school record which still stands. The "drive series" was a variation of the

Coach Andy Gustafson, end Frank McDonald, and assistant coach Walt Kichefski (from left to right).

split-T and the fullback ride. Every play looked alike but featured different ballcarriers hitting different holes or the quarterback passing.

Most plays would begin with a feint to Bosseler. The backfield deception was carried out so well that Bosseler had to be tackled every time. Even the quarterbacks sometimes kept their own halfbacks in suspense on a few option plays.

"If we were in doubt," said Rouviere, "think how the guys on the other team must have felt."

And Gus admitted that even he sometimes wondered who had the ball. "If they could fool me," he said, "they must have made the other team miserable."

Though the Hurricanes had toed the mark in 1954, the school had not. On October 24, after the fourth game, the NCAA put the

UM on probation for violating rules against paying the way of prospective players to campus. The penalty cost the Hurricanes a certain bowl bid.

Their creed then became: "If we can't go, nobody we play will." The next week, they jolted defending national champion Maryland, 9-7, to oust the Terps from the bowl picture.

In response to the probation, the university created the Julian S. Eaton Education Foundation under charter dated May 6, 1955. Funds from the foundation could be used to aid athletes, but only under the same rules that were available to other students. The Eaton Foundation also could raise money to support the athletic program as long as it was not directly related to aid for athletes. During the next 12 years, it loaned $155,000 to 1,367 students and contributed $153,000 to the athletic program.

The NCAA probation was not lifted until January 10, 1957. But the penalty did not hamper interest in the Hurricanes. Average attendance actually increased during a 6-3 season in 1955. Moreover, the seven home games were carried on nationwide radio by the Mutual Broadcasting Company. And though the team was banned from playing in bowls, it appeared on national television for the first time in the opening game at Georgia Tech, a 14-6 loss.

Attendance at home games totaled 321,347, fourth highest in the nation. And the average per game was 45,907, a record at that point and a figure surpassed only four times since then.

The Orange Bowl's capacity was increased from 68,000 to 75,000 that season, yet that was not large enough to seat the 75,685 who saw Notre Dame make its first visit to the state. The Irish won, 14-0, as Paul Hornung engineered both scores with his passing.

The Hurricanes finished fourteenth in the final AP poll after playing a rugged schedule that featured four teams ranked higher—TCU, Georgia Tech, Notre Dame, and Pitt.

The UM had received two one-year probations and had expected them to end October 24, 1956. But at its January meeting in 1956, the NCAA ruled the school still had not conformed to the rules and the probation was extended for a year. There was some question as to whether this meant until October or the following January.

The NCAA meant January. Thus an 8-1-1 Hurricane squad that ranked sixth in the AP, UP, and INS polls at the end of the season—highest ever in school history—could not play in a bowl.

Don Bosseler.

The community was outraged. On November 15, the *Herald* ran an editorial headlined: "The NCAA Is Unduly Cruel To Hurricanes." It noted the probations cost the school three trips to bowls at approximately $125,000 per bowl. "We say that's too much."

Naturally, Harding and Gustafson thought so, too. "It's difficult to believe that the NCAA council is not vindictive toward us," said Harding. "I feel that their action in keeping us on probation longer than two years is arbitrary to say the least."

Added Gus: "I'm shocked and terribly disappointed."

The Hurricanes were considered a "sleeper team" at the beginning of the 1956 season. Depth was a question and the squad of 46 players included 23 unproven sophomores. But Bosseler, who was named the AP's first-team All-American fullback and was drafted in the first round by the Washington Redskins, led them to within two minutes and 45 seconds of an undefeated season.

In a 7-7 tie in the fourth game, the Hurricanes played their worst and Georgia its best. But they rebounded to upset fourth-ranked TCU at Fort Worth, 14-0. Told they were still on probation, they took their frustrations out on Clemson, 21-0, and Florida, 21-7, at Gainesville. But at homecoming in the season finale, Pitt handed them their only loss, 14-7, in the first UM home game televised nationally.

The AP, in addition to putting Bosseler on the first team, gave All-American honorable mention to Sam Scarnecchia, Ed Oliver, Tom Pratt, and Jack Johnson. Attendance continued to remain solid as the Hurricanes averaged 41,084 for eight home games. They even had "subway alumni" in the form of 60 Canton, Ohio, business and professional men who bought tickets for the Maryland game in the Orange Bowl. The weekend jaunts started in 1955 when some of the men flew to Miami for the Notre Dame game and liked the trip and the team.

Meanwhile, talk of the UM joining a conference was increasing. The school was being considered along with Florida State, Southern Mississippi, and Houston as new members in the 12-team Southeastern Conference.

But a drawback was the reluctance of SEC members in some states to schedule intersectional games in which they might go against teams using black players. In 1955, a controversy developed when Georgia Gov. Marvin Griffin objected to Georgia Tech playing in the Sugar Bowl because its opponent, Pittsburgh, included a black in the lineup.

The SEC should not have worried about the UM, however, because it did not integrate its team until 1967.

Talk of another conference resurfaced two years later. Harding went to the NCAA meeting at Cincinnati and asked to have the UM considered in discussions about forming a super conference called the All-American Conference with 12 colleges, including Pitt, Army, Navy, Notre Dame, and Pacific Coast schools. But the conference never got off the ground.

When the NCAA finally lifted the UM's probation in January 1957, it also killed a proposed nationally televised game for late in the month between the Hurricanes and two-time defending national champion Oklahoma in the Orange Bowl to benefit Hungarian refugees.

The game was expected to raise at least a half-million dollars for the project. Henry Ford II, chairman of President Dwight D. Eisenhower's Committee on Hungarian Refugees' Relief, tried to drum up interest by writing the NCAA asking it to waive its rules.

But the NCAA executive secretary, Walt Byers, said the NCAA and the Big Seven Conference (now Big Eight) had rules against postseason play unless certified by the association's extra-events committee, "and there's no way to obtain certification at this time."

The next fall, with a 142-pound "Mighty Mite" named Fran Curci at quarterback, the Hurricanes bounced through a 5-4-1 season in which they lost to the Gators, 14-0, for the first time in five years but dumped Pittsburgh in the nationally televised final game, 28-13.

The Pitt game drew only 28,231, smallest crowd since 1952 and considerably below the season average of more than 40,000. But each team received $90,000 from NBC, so the UM did not squawk. In fact, the athletic program realized a profit in 1957 of $64,000 from income of $949,519. All but $24,000 came from football.

Gus declared that it was not a boastful year, "but not a losing year either." He could not say that in 1958, however, as the injury-riddled Hurricanes slumped to 2-8 for only their second losing season in a decade. They fumbled away a 20-0 opening loss to Wisconsin "and the whole season seemed to go with it," said the *Ibis*.

Some fans half-jokingly wondered if the problem stemmed from the horrendous locker-room facilities, or from the fact that Gus had relaxed his no-marriage rule.

As recently as 1950, recruits had been forbidden in the Hurricanes' locker room because it was crowded, antiquated, dismally dark, and usually chilly. Moreover, it was not unusual for the aged shower room floor to collapse, carrying athletes with it.

"Letting a boy see our dressing room would be the quickest way to lose him," Gus said of the facility located in the old Cardboard College on the North campus. In 1951, athletic offices and locker rooms were constructed on the South campus at the site of the present Hecht Athletic Center. The original building was constructed with the help of a $25,000 contribution from the Orange Bowl Committee. In 1958, a new dressing room and a second floor with offices and meeting rooms were built.

Fran Curci as quarterback.

As for the married players, there were 12 on the squad in 1958, a surprising figure considering that six years earlier Gus had decreed: "No more married players on the squad. Married boys just have too many personal problems to concentrate on football and their studies, too."

When Gus learned that Edison High's All-Southern tackle Jackie Simpson was planning to wed, he cut back his efforts to talk him into enrolling at the UM. Simpson went on to Florida and became a star halfback. Thus Gustafson said good-bye to the no-marriage rule at Miami.

Whatever the problems causing the 2-8 season, the fans had Gus on the firing block for the first time. Meanwhile, *Herald* sports editor Jimmy Burns discovered that Gus was not even under contract and did not need one. The myth that he had a long, protective contract came in 1950 when the Hurricanes went 9-1-1 and Gus was sought by many other schools. The story then was that the late president, Dr. Ashe, gave him a 10-year contract.

"When I came here in 1948," said Gustafson, "I told them it would take three years to build up a good football team. Dr. Ashe wrote me a letter when I was approached by Minnesota, stating that he hoped I would stay. I've even misplaced the letter, but I don't feel that I need it. Frankly, I don't think I should be fired.''

Neither did the university's current president, Jay F. W. Pearson, who said Gustafson was not alone in blame for the poor season.

As Gus plunged ahead, the Hurricanes rebounded somewhat for a pair of 6-4 records in 1959 and 1960. In spring practice in 1959, former Cleveland Browns star quarterback Otto Graham helped the coaching staff. And Hank Stram joined Gus' forces as a full-time assistant.

Stram had been at Notre Dame the two previous years, including 1957 when the Irish ended Oklahoma's 47-game winning streak. At his alma mater, Purdue, and at Notre Dame, he developed standout quarterbacks such as Dale Samuels and Len Dawson at Purdue and George Izo at Notre Dame. Though Stram stayed only one year at the UM before becoming head coach of the Dallas entry in the new American Football League, he coached Curci to All-American honors.

Curci was Miami's golden boy then. A business major who made the dean's list his last four semesters, he was president of Sigma Nu fraternity; was tapped by the leading men's honoraries on campus, Iron Arrow and Omicron Delta Kappa; played on several intramural teams; set most UM passing records; and was voted outstanding player in the state.

The Hurricanes had a shot in 1959 at a bid to the Orange Bowl Classic until they lost the season finale to Florida, 23-14, before 25,000 shivering fans in Jacksonville. The Hurricanes had held a 14-13 lead going into the fourth quarter.

Losing to the Gators and missing bowl chances were not the only concerns as the 1950s closed and the 1960s began. There was increasing discussion throughout the community over two issues the UM eventually would have to meet head-on: the arrival of professional football and integration.

When the university opened negotiations for a new rental contract on the Orange Bowl in 1958, it asked that the stadium not be available to professional or other college teams from September 1 through December 10. Harding wanted the contract for 10 years and made no secret of being alarmed by continued reports that a pro franchise would be established in Miami within a few years.

After eight months of talks, a five-year contract was signed. As in the previous contract, the UM would give the city 10 per cent of ticket sales for seats at one dollar each or less and 15 per cent of sales for higher priced tickets. The city agreed to give $17,000 for advertising purposes in promoting the UM's athletic events and the city of Miami. The school continued to have first priority on all dates, but the contract did not bar a pro team.

"Have no fear," said Pete Rozelle, the National Football League's new head, when he attended a September 1960 exhibition game between Pittsburgh and Baltimore in the Orange Bowl. The contest drew 33,265 in poor weather.

"The two could grow financially fat together," added Rozelle, who disputed the saturation-point theory. "The University of Miami has a terrific schedule this year. And from what I understand, they play good football. There is no reason why that should change. I don't see how 14 pro games would cut into their attendance. The fans only ask for good football; they don't set a limit to it. In baseball, they play 77 games at home and they don't feel that is too much."

Rozelle foresaw Miami as an NFL member in 1962. But the city did not get its pro franchise, the Dolphins, until 1966, and that was in the AFL, not NFL.

The feared "intrusion" by the pros also renewed talk of the importance of moving into a cozy stadium on campus.

"We agreed to play our games in the Orange Bowl when it was originally built," said Harding in 1960. "And we have a moral obligation to continue doing just this. However, I feel, and have always felt, that our games should be played in our own stadium on our own campus.

"We think the bowl is too big for our needs. I know we drew 60,000 for Florida and 55,000 for Syracuse this year. But I'll tell you this. I would rather have a 50,000-seat stadium on our own campus.

"Our season ticket sales have reached a plateau year after year. They stop when all the best seats go. People know they can sit back and watch the teams, see how they do, watch the weather, etc., before buying tickets. They don't have to worry about seats because they know there always will be plenty of seats in the bowl.

"But if we had a stadium with only a 50,000 capacity, then they couldn't hesitate. It would create more of a demand for season tickets."

Harding's comments have been echoing around the halls of

the university ever since. Schnellenberger made the same points when he proposed a stadium in 1979.

Harding carried his campaign a step more in 1961 when he wrote a column for the *Herald* saying: "History has proved that colleges which have attempted to play their games in downtown stadia whether in ball parks or in municipal stadia have not been successful in doing so. This policy has been tried in New York City, Philadelphia, Boston, Baltimore, Pittsburgh, Chicago, St. Louis, just to name a few without success. The colleges that have tried this have eventually given up intercollegiate football, or have built suitable stadia on their own campuses . . . .

"Our average attendance in the Orange Bowl is 40,000. Limited seating follows good business principles by creating a demand for seats. College football belongs on its own campus. There it can compete with professional competition because of the campus atmosphere if nothing else."

In 1962, there was a proposal to finance a stadium by building a men's dormitory (for students, not players) as part of the stadium complex. Rent for the dorm would in time pay for the building.

Concurrently, a fan named Dick Jones wrote to the *Herald* suggesting that at least one million dollars could be raised for a stadium by allowing anyone to buy a seat for $100. For the donation, the person's name would be placed on the seat. "I think this method would create more interest in the university and give all donors a feeling of belonging, and therefore create more sincere support for all university activities," said Jones.

Both ideas never got beyond the drawing boards. Nor did Miami city commissioner Joseph X. DuMond's proposal in 1962 to build a 70,000-seat stadium on 100 acres off the Palmetto Expressway between Tamiami Trail and Southwest Twentieth Street for $5 million.

When Hurricane fans were not talking about a stadium or the pending arrival of a pro team, they wondered what role integration would play on the football program. Should the UM seek black players and risk angering some backers? Wouldn't other schools in the South refuse to play Miami? Would a black athlete feel comfortable at the UM?

The university had been slow in its football program to change from the established policies of segregation in the South.

Nevertheless, it was a pioneer of integration.

In 1940, a game between the UM and UCLA was canceled because UCLA had two black players—Jackie Robinson and Kenny Washington. Robinson went on to become the principal in breaking down the color line in pro baseball, and Washington was a near unanimous All-American. In 1946, a game with Penn State also was canceled because Penn State had black players. But in 1950, Gustafson and his team broke a Southern tradition by playing against black players in a 14-6 defeat of Iowa.

Then in the late 1950s, UM athletic business manager Harry Wiener tried to secure permission from the city to open a reserved whites-only section in the Orange Bowl to blacks. At the UM-Wisconsin game in the Orange Bowl in 1958, there were complaints that "hundreds" of blacks were turned away at the game because the end zone section reserved for them was sold out. Miami police told Weiner that it was unlawful to sell tickets in white sections to blacks. Black leaders pointed out that federal courts had consistently ruled against segregated use of public facilities such as parks, golf courses, and stadiums as well as public buses.

On January 31, 1961, the UM trustees voted unanimously to open the doors to "all students," though six years passed before the Hurricanes signed their first black player, Ray Bellamy.

"We've already completed most of our freshman recruiting, and I can tell you we didn't contact any Negro player," Gustafson said upon the trustees' announcement. Though Gus was a product of the East, he had never coached a black player at Pitt, Army, Dartmouth, VPI, or Miami. And he did not envision rapid integration at the UM.

"Even if we entered upon an intensive recruiting program for Negroes, I doubt we would get many from Pennsylvania, Ohio, or up that way where the best players are produced. A Negro coming here from there probably would find too many conditions to which he is unaccustomed."

There was a definite bitterness to the new policy among parts of Coral Gables. But the barriers in South Florida were coming down one by one just as they eventually would throughout the South. At the Floyd Patterson-Ingemar Johansson heavyweight championship fight March 13, 1961, for instance, seating was not segregated at the Miami Beach Convention Hall. That was a significant breakthrough.

The Age Of MIRAcles

There is no truth to the legend that George Mira could throw a football over the press box and out of the stadium at the Orange Bowl. But do not try to tell that even today to the customers in Key West at George Mira's Pizza Huddle, where the walls are lined with trophies, plaques, and awards won by the cocky, temperamental, colorful, showboating, theatrical, fingernail-biting, good-looking, and amazing natural athlete named George Ignacio Mira.

In his native Key West, they talk of Mira as Alabamians do of Bear Bryant. They say George may not have known how to walk on water, but he sure knew where the stumps were.

At the University of Miami during the 1961 through 1963 seasons, Mira became the school's greatest quarterback and No. 1 hero. His passes broke fingers and ruined egos. He shattered virtually all the school's passing records in leading the Hurricanes to a pair of bowl games and earning All-American recognition twice.

The press called him The Matador. Of Spanish descent, he had dark skin, dark eyebrows, and ears that stuck straight out. And he had enormous hands that had developed from throwing beer cases on his Uncle Mario's truck since eighth grade.

"The light-footed Mira treats onrushing linemen as the famous Spanish matadors—side step and dance away from wild bulls," the UM's press guide gushed. The plaudits from opposing players and coaches were no less exaggerated.

Dennis Gaubatz, LSU center: "He's uncanny. And the way he runs away from a receiver and still sees him, that guy must have eyes not only in the back of his head, but in both ears."

Air Force coach Ben Martin: "Once I thought everybody except me had a hand on him, but he still completed the pass. Having

Mira is like having a coach on the field."

Bob Devaney, the Nebraska coach, after the Gotham Bowl: "He's the greatest passer I ever saw in college."

Maryland Coach Tom Nugent: "He's Willie Mays in a football uniform—electrifying. The most dangerous man in football when he's cornered."

Ara Parseghian, Northwestern's coach: "He is the quickest quarterback I have ever seen. He's incredible. He actually seems to be better with men hanging all over him."

And Bryant: "Mira is about as great a quarterback as I've ever seen. He's slippery and hard to hold. He fakes well. He does everything well. His accuracy on passing is amazing."

Gustafson simply said: "He's the greatest single contribution to a football team I've witnessed in all my years in the sport."

Minnesota Viking coach Norm Van Brocklin saw Mira throw four touchdown passes in the spring game before his senior season and tried to think of all the NFL quarterbacks who could throw better. "I gave up," he said. "There were none."

Mira could throw sidearm (when too sore to throw overarm), left-handed (for the winning touchdown against Florida in 1961), and even catch his own (which he did with a pass that rebounded off a TCU lineman in 1962). His only fault was that he thought he was six-feet tall. He was barely 5-11, though listed as 6-0.

In 1963, sports information director Gallet issued a 16-page booklet on *The Amazing George Mira* and said: "Alabama was after him all day in Tuscaloosa last year, chasing him out of the pocket and round and round every time he tried to pass. He always got the ball away. Finally in the fourth quarter they put him down. You should have heard the crowd. It was like a great war had ended."

Describing Mira's bullet-like passes, *True Magazine* wrote: "He throws a pass which in its low, flat trajectory almost resembles a tank shell that will surely enter the receiver's belly and come out the other side."

That was not so far-fetched a statement. As UM assistant Whitey Campbell recalls, "He broke Ben Rizzo's finger with a pass."

So, wondered the fans, why could not the receivers trap the ball in their chests? Assistant Jim Root explained why. "In his first spring intrasquad game, George hit a guy on the chest with a 15-yard pass, and it bounced all the way back to the line of scrimmage. It sounded like a cannon going off."

In another scrimmage, 230-pound tackle Jim Hetrick smashed through the line throwing up his hands to block a pass. Mira got the pass off, and on his follow-through the side of his hand came down between Hetrick's last two fingers. Almost like a butcher's cleaver, Mira's hand chopped through Hetrick's metacarpal bones, practically splitting his palm in half. Twelve stitches were needed to sew the hand together.

Mira's father, Jimmy Mira, Sr., who ran the equipment at the Key West ice plant, is a former pro boxer who never played football. Son George built a legend as a fighter at Key West High. His idol was Joe Louis, and he could recount round and time of knockouts in every championship fight he had.

Once in a high school game at Hollywood, Florida, a 290-pound tackle, a Seminole Indian named Jesse James Osceola, kept biting George in the leg on the bottom of a pileup. "If you keep doing that," said George, "I'm gonna have to rap you." Osceola played the rest of the game as a vegetarian.

The Mira household on Packer Street, which was renamed George Mira Street on George Mira Day in December 1962, was a constant parade of sons, daughters, nieces, nephews, aunts, uncles, and neighbors. The kitchen was the favorite meeting place and debates—usually on sports—would rage for hours.

But the Mira clan was known to act, rather than discuss, if it heard nasty comments about the Key West team.

"One night," recalled Papa, "we are getting beat, and the guy behind me calls one of my boys chicken. Well, boy, I turn around and say, 'How much time left?' He points to the clock and says, 'Five minutes.' I say, 'That's just what you got left till you go down.'"

George also was a baseball star in high school. He compiled a 31-2 record as a pitcher, firing two no-hitters and leading the Conchs (rhymes with honks) to the state Class A title two years. One of his teammates in baseball and football was John (Boog) Powell, who later played with the Baltimore Orioles.

The Orioles offered George $13,000 to sign. But Papa said he would not sign for less than $30,000 because he could get that back by earning a college degree.

Mira never played baseball at the UM, though Coach Ron Fraser tried to lure him to the team when he took over the baseball program in 1963. Fraser had been away from college sports for three years while directing the national baseball program in Holland and did not know Mira.

One day, Fraser heard a mitt popping behind the dugout and discovered it was Mira playing catch with a friend. Fraser asked Mira if he pitched baseball, and Mira said he did in high school.

"You throw harder than anybody I've got," said Fraser. "How would you like to come out for the team?"

A reporter standing nearby related the story in the newspaper, and the next day Gustafson called Fraser into his office and gave him a list of football players "free to play baseball, too." Mira's name was not on it.

Though George did not become a multisport star at Miami, he was a multifaceted personality. There was Mira the Raging Bull who would take no lip from teammates. Miller, his end, would come into the huddle and say, "I can beat the corner back a mile." Mira would retort: "Shut up or I'll run you off the field." Mira also would fume when place-kicker Bobby Wilson missed an extra point. "George can't kick a football from here to that wall," said UM trainer Dave Wike, "but he always was trying to coach Wilson."

There was Mira the Clown. On one plane trip for a game, he

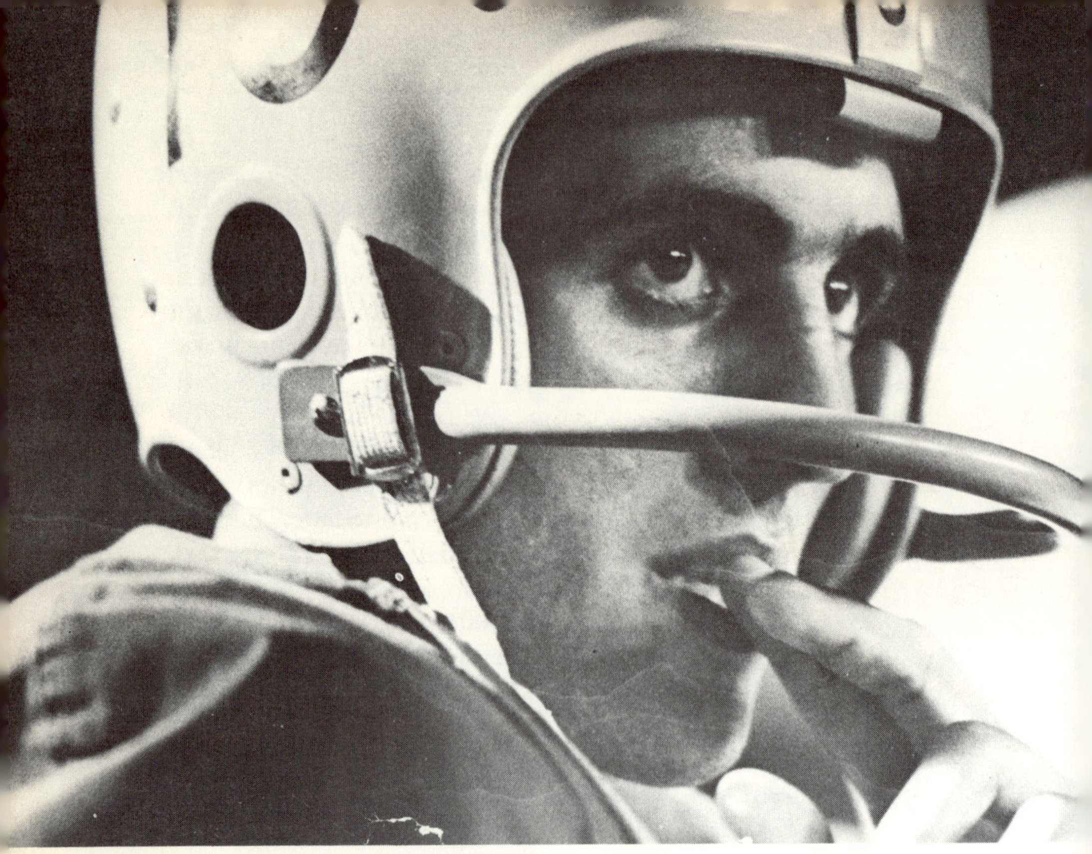

Mira in a rare pensive moment.

End Bill Miller, favorite target of Mira.

suddenly disappeared. Then the plane's public address system crackled and a loud voice with a thick Spanish accent said, "Thees ees Captain Mira. We are heading for Havana."

There was Mira the Showboat, who, when tackled, acted as though the cameras were rolling and he were taking a bullet in the chest. Against Penn State in 1961, sore ribs made it almost impossible to breathe, but he passed the Hurricanes to a 25-8 upset. After he collapsed for the third time when a lineman took a shot at his tender ribs, Penn State end Bob Mitinger yelled, "Give him an Oscar!" There were suspicions Mira would play the injury bit for all it was worth. Said assistant Root: "I ran out to him at halftime in the Penn State game and said, 'You all right, George?' He said, 'Yeh, I guess so. How's the crowd taking it?'"

There was Mira the Hypochondriac. Trainer Dave Wike had sugar pills that would cure him of everything from heartburn to heatstroke to cancer. Mira was afraid of planes, so he would take pills to put him to sleep when he flew; that is, except for times he commandeered the P.A. system. Mira constantly would complain of colds. "He blames the Miami climate," said Wike. "He tells me, 'It's not like Key West.' He talks like Miami is the North Pole. Everybody else comes south to play at Miami, but this guy says, 'I never had colds till I came north.'"

The week the Hurricanes played in the 1961 Liberty Bowl at Philadelphia, Mira came down with tonsillitis and was flown to Philadelphia at the last minute. Wike got a navy antarctic jacket for him. Mira was limp and his timing off in the 15-14 loss to Syracuse. When the season ended, Gustafson ordered him to have his tonsils removed. Mira refused. They bickered for five weeks before George finally went to the hospital. "He doesn't like the knife," said Gustafson.

And there was Mira the So-So Student. He was a physical education major with a C average and little interest in books. He made no bones about the fact that he was preparing to be a pro player. "I always have a little trouble in schoolwork," he once said. "We speak mostly Spanish at home, and I have trouble sometimes reading English. Here I am majoring in physical education, but what's messing me up bad is this humanities program. It's all about Greek gods and poets and mythology. Yeah, Shakespeare, too. I am not interested. Still, I wish I could learn in the classroom as fast as I learn football."

Though he may not have endeared himself to his professors, everyone else in the Miami area adored him. When he returned from a trip to New York to receive an award, he held his arms out as if to encompass the city and said: "This is my town!"

It was love at first sight for Gustafson and UM fans. On the day of his first varsity game—the 1961 opener his sophomore year against Pitt on national television—Gustafson put Mira in total charge.

"It's your club to run, George," Gus said. "You can throw the ball whenever you like. I don't care if you're on the goal line. And don't worry about a thing, George, because you're the greatest."

Though the Hurricanes lost to Pitt, 10-7, in the Orange Bowl, Mira and senior end Miller launched a spectacular season in which they became the greatest passing combination in school history to that point. Miller was named to seven All-American teams, including the AP first team. Mira completed 81 of 172 passes for 1,000 yards and eight touchdowns, though he missed the Colorado game and parts of Navy and Penn State because of rib injuries.

Injuries plagued several other players, and at one time the top four linebackers were out. There was a theory going around that what the Hurricanes needed was more orange juice to heal injuries faster. At least, that is what the Florida Citrus Commission tried to prove.

During the 1961 season, it conducted an experiment in which 18 players drank a quart of juice a day and another 18 drank none. Yet both groups took about the same number of knocks.

"It's an unsound experiment," said trainer Wike. "They gave us some orange juice and some questionnaires, but you just can't go about it that way. For a research project, you need more control. Some of these boys taking the orange juice were the ones getting hurt. After all, if somebody barrels in, clips you from behind, and breaks your leg, it doesn't make much difference if you drink orange juice or not."

Despite the injuries, the Hurricanes got off to a juicy 5-3 start that season, though there were rumbles that Gustafson still should be ousted. The lead story on the front page of the *Herald* on November 16 reported that a minority faction of the trustees wanted to make a change at the end of the season even though Gus had another year to go on a three-year contract. Their main complaint was that Miami should have more championship teams.

Gus was in his fourteenth season with an 81-65-4 record. There was speculation that Harding would retire as athletic director, Gus would replace Harding, and Stram would leave Dallas of the AFL to succeed Gus. But President Pearson said there was nothing to the report.

The critics were muffled the next week when the Hurricanes edged Northwestern, 10-6, and received a no-strings-attached bid to the Liberty Bowl in Philadelphia. They celebrated a week later with a 15-6 triumph over Florida in the season finale.

The bowl bid was Miami's first in 10 years and earned the school $100,000 plus national TV exposure on NBC. The UM seemed attractive to Philadelphia because there were 20 Pennsylvanians on the team.

They must have felt right at home because the Liberty Bowl was played in 20-degree weather. Miami took a 14-0 halftime lead on a 12-yard run by James Vollenweider and a 60-yard punt return by Nick Spinelli. But Syracuse rallied behind Heisman Trophy winner Ernie Davis to win in the final minute.

The following spring, Baltimore Colts superstar quarterback Johnny Unitas was invited to work with Mira during spring practice, and the project proved to be an instant success. Ten minutes after arriving, Unitas had straightened Mira's crouching stance behind center, moved him closer to the center, corrected a false step he unconsciously took after accepting the snap, lengthened his stride on the dropback, and increased his retreating speed.

"Having Unitas help coach me is the greatest thing that ever happened to me," said Mira.

Unitas was equally impressed with his pupil, saying, "He has got all the basic fundamentals, everything he needs to be a pro quarterback. He throws the ball real well."

When the school year ended, it had been the most successful in athletics in UM history as the eight varsity teams amassed a record of 83-30. Tennis was 17-0, soccer 8-0, golf 8-1, baseball 17-9, basketball 15-9, swimming 6-3, football 7-4, and track 5-4. But a tight budget forced cuts in the total number of scholarships for the upcoming 1962-63 school year from 172 to 140, though the quota of 100 remained in football.

Yet 100 was not enough, because the Hurricanes lacked depth in 1962. True, they went 7-3 again during the regular season and earned a bowl bid. But against top-ranked Alabama, they led, 3-0, at the half and lost, 36-3. And against No. 2 Northwestern, they trailed, 14-7, at the half and lost, 29-7.

Mira, nevertheless, had his finest season in 1962, running and passing for 2,059 yards and 12 touchdowns. He finished second in the nation in passing, was fifth in the Heisman Trophy voting, and was named outstanding amateur athlete in Florida. He was practically the concensus All-American quarterback, making the first team on AP, *Look*, CBS-TV, and the *New York Daily News* and second team on UPI, *Sporting News*, and Coaches' All-American.

By defeating Florida, 17-15, in the final game, the Hurricanes earned bids to the Gator Bowl and the second annual Gotham Bowl in New York. They chose New York with its flashing lights, Broadway theaters, and Yankee Stadium. But what they got was a newspaper strike, a poorly promoted game, and lousy weather.

Both Miami and Nebraska threatened not to show up for the game. When Robert Curran, director of the game, failed to forward contracts to the universities, UM and Nebraska officials demanded the Gotham Bowl put $60,000 immediately in escrow to cover expenses or they would not leave for the game. In fact, the Nebraska squad was at the airport waiting until partial payment was placed in escrow.

"We accepted a Gotham Bowl invitation without signing a contract," UM president Dr. Henry King Stanford recalled later. "Meanwhile, we began hearing stories out of New York about the impecunious position of the Gotham Bowl. We were supposed to leave Miami on a Thursday and play Nebraska in New York at 11:00 a.m. Saturday. By Wednesday noon, when we still had not received a contract, I became increasingly worried that we might have to stand the cost of our expenses.

"I made a series of calls to New York. Finally, I had to demand assurance from Mayor Wagner that the $30,000 in expenses would be in escrow or we would not play the game. I had set a final deadline of 10:00 p.m. About 15 minutes before that, the mayor called and said the money was in the bank."

It is too bad the game was played in 17-degree weather in ice-plagued and snow-banked Yankee Stadium before 6,166 fans and no national television audience. The nation missed a wild affair in which the lead changed hands six times before Nebraska won, 36-34.

Dr. Henry King Stanford, UM president 1962-1981.

Mira had his finest hour, throwing 24 completions for 321 yards and two touchdowns as the Hurricanes rolled up 502 yards total offense to Nebraska's 296 and took a 34-12 lead in first downs. Mira was named Most Valuable Player by the press, which hailed him as the greatest passer to appear at Yankee Stadium since Johnny Lujack of Notre Dame in the middle 1940s.

Two months after the Gotham Bowl, Harding died, and Stanford announced that Gustafson would succeed Harding as athletic director and that his coaching responsibilities would end December 31.

In a tribute to Harding's career, *Herald* sports editor Jimmy Burns wrote: "The University of Miami's rise in the intercollegiate football world was started by Harding as coach in 1937. It continued when he became athletic director in 1948.

"It was Harding's idea that a cosmopolitan city like Miami demanded a strong national schedule. He adhered to the philosophy that an athletic director should not worry how hard a schedule his team plays.

"Harding's persistence and sincerity led to some of the nation's top colleges sending their teams here to play. Notre Dame,

Purdue, Wisconsin, Northwestern and others came with misgivings and returned with confidence.

"The influence of Harding as a gentleman, schedule maker and sportsman will continue. Harding did his work well. When he died, he left the Hurricanes with complete football schedules through 1967."

Gustafson felt it was important that the university remain independent rather than join a conference. "Through the national recognition the university has gained, we have managed to make up attractive football schedules," he said. There has been little talk of joining a conference since then.

Gus was asked why he did not retire before the 1963 season despite his critics. "I've got the best quarterback I've ever had, the best passer I've ever seen," he replied. "Retirement can wait."

As interest began to build for the final season of Gustafson and Mira, 7,200 fans jammed Hialeah Stadium for the spring game. Mira's passing and sophomore halfback Russ Smith's running led the Green squad to a 28-6 victory over the White.

Then Burns, saying he wanted to see "small-town spirit," launched a campaign to fill the Orange Bowl's 70,200 seats for the opener against Florida State. Civic leaders, politicians, and the Orange Bowl Committee backed the project, and even ministers and churches were asked to join in. The *Herald* frequently ran "Let's Fill the Bowl" sigs with lists of places to buy tickets. And the *Miami News* gave away a free trip for two fans to London.

A rally drawing 2,000 fans was held on the Wednesday night before the opening game at the Bayfront Park bandshell. Miami Mayor Robert King High, whose administration had just spent one million dollars putting in new lights, end zones, and other improvements, predicted the Orange Bowl would be filled. And President Stanford, in jest, ordered Gustafson to win all his games.

Mira did not believe that the latter was an impossible feat. "My view is we'll go undefeated this season and play in the Orange Bowl game," he said. "We enjoyed playing in the little bowls but now we want to make the big one and it would be a great farewell gift for Coach Gustafson. The feeling of most of us is we'll be undefeated and No. 1 in the country."

That statement must go down with those in history which claimed the Titanic was unsinkable and Dewey would beat

Truman. The Hurricanes lost the ballyhooed opener to FSU, 24-0, drawing a less-than-filled Orange Bowl crowd of 57,596. The offense did not score a touchdown until the fifth game; and though Mira equaled Don Klosterman's national record of 368 completions for the season, the Hurricanes went only 3-7.

After the 31-14 loss to Georgia in the fifth game, senior flanker Nick Spinelli said in a television interview, "We're trying to win, but we don't know what's wrong with us. If any of you people know what's wrong, or think you do, please write us."

Later he admitted the response was more than he expected. "Man, I got scads of letters," he said. "But not one of them really had anything constructive. All they did was cut up Coach Gus and cut up a lot of the guys. There were some dillies."

But what went wrong with a team that on paper showed so much promise? *Herald* assistant sports editor Edwin Pope saw three reasons:

1. Miami coaches and followers overestimated the latent talent available. Talk of an Orange Bowl bid was grievously premature.

2. Injuries in key positions whittled away 20 percent of Miami's original strength, including halfback Russ Smith and fullback Pete Banaszak, thus there was no balanced running and passing attack.

3. The offensive line was lethargic and unpredictable. Miami just was not a hungry team.

Though the football program had a gross income of $1.2 million in 1963, it lost $65,000 and the total athletic program had a deficit of $269,000, which was made up from the university's general fund.

Before stepping down as coach at the end of the season, Gus picked the following for his all-time team for 16 years at Miami:

Offense—ends Bill Miller and Larry Wilson, tackles Dan Conners and Norman French, guards Ray Arcangeletti and Bob Eggert, center Jim Otto, quarterback George Mira, halfbacks Frank Smith and Gordon Malloy, fullback Don Bosseler.

Defense—ends Leo Martin and Frank McDonald, tackles Al Carapella and Sam David, guards Jim O'Mahony and Tom Pratt, linebacker Pete Mastellone, backs Jim Vollenweider, Carl Garrigus, Whitey Campbell, and Jim Dooley.

At the annual football awards dinner, Gustafson preferred to

Dan Conners, All-American tackle.

reflect on the highlights of his career rather than the lowlights of his final season. ''The bigger schedules and national recognition of our teams by sportswriters and football authorities have been gratifying,'' he said. ''I think the university has helped make the country more aware of Miami, and our teams have been instruments in that endeavor.''

The Name Game

While meeting, of all places, in a Sunday school room, the UM board of trustees selected Charlie Tate as Gustafson's replacement in December 1963. But Tate was not its first choice.

The university had been shopping for a name head coach, and there had been considerable support for Walt Kichefski to be elevated to the head job after 20 years on the staff.

When Dr. Stanford announced in August before the 1963 season that nominations were welcomed, Gustafson said he wanted Kichefski to succeed him. Even Pittsburgh Steeler owner Art Rooney wrote a letter boosting Kichefski's nomination, and the UM Alumni Association came out strongly for him.

"Kichefski fills every qualification a head coach should have," said Gus. "He knows how to get along with people in newspapers, radio, and television work. And Walt is dedicated to the game of football. He thinks football from morning to night, and when he goes home he greets his wife as 'Gator Hater.' It's sort of a joke with them."

Prominently mentioned as prospects were Bob Devaney of Nebraska; Stram, who had left the UM for the head job at the new Dallas team in the American Football League in 1960; Ara Parseghian of Northwestern; Jerry Claiborne of Virginia Tech; and Bill Peterson of Florida State. Devaney, whose team played Auburn in the Orange Bowl Classic, was first to be interviewed.

"Devaney met with the athletic committee of the board of trustees for breakfast at my home," Dr. Stanford recalled. "We got the impression he wanted to come. But when he went back to Nebraska, they mustered funds for a house and insurance policy for him and he stayed.

Charlie Tate and the ever-present cigar.

"Later, I spent two and a half hours with Stram in a hotel in Kansas City. He said he was too obligated to Lamar Hunt (owner of the Dallas team that later became the Kansas City Chiefs). A few years later, Hunt fired him.

"I wrote to Ara and called him," continued Stanford, who has uncanny recall. "He was in New York City and I extolled the weather in South Florida. We agreed to meet in Memphis on the Monday after Thanksgiving for breakfast. I was there for an accredition meeting. He called the Sunday before the meeting to indicate something had come up he felt obligated to look into. I came away with the hollow feeling I may have forced Notre Dame's hand in hiring Mr. Parseghian."

Stanford and UM officials then huddled to come up with more names. Tate was mentioned most often. He already was a "name" coach in South Florida, having led Miami High to four state titles in five years (1951-55). An All-Southeastern Conference fullback for Florida, Tate coached the freshman at his alma mater

94

in 1956 and moved on to Bobby Dodd's staff at Georgia Tech the following year.

"Tate was considered enthusiastically when we couldn't get a name," said Stanford. "From all accounts, he got along well with his students. They wanted to play for him.

"One of our trustees, Daniel H. Redfearn, had died, and the funeral was to be in the United First Methodist Church of Coral Gables. It occurred to me that if all the athletic committee members of the board were going to be at the funeral, we would save everybody another trip by meeting after the funeral. We met in a Sunday school room and Tate was elected coach.

"The most difficult job I ever had to do as president was to call Walt Kichefski and tell him we decided to bring Tate in," Stanford continued. "Never has there been anyone as loyal as Coach 'Ski, not only to football but to the total University of Miami. He and his wife are sincere members of the university, and this didn't affect his devotion at all."

Kichefski remained on the staff. Ironically, nearly seven years later Stanford called him into his office again, this time to elevate him to the head coaching job that Tate had surprisingly left after the second game of the 1970 season.

Tate was a cigar-chomping man who had a hearty, all-out way of laughing. They called him Jolly Cholly. He was jolly in a golf cart or at a cocktail party but was gruff and hard-nosed as a coach. Sometimes he'd close the door to his wood-paneled office and just sit for hours thinking football.

Tate, who confounded fans by occasionally punting on third down, also was involved in several controversies during his roller-coaster UM career. In fact, the problems began before he ever coached a game.

In June 1964, six players including two starters were suspended until at least February 1965, for allegedly cheating on final examinations. Two days later there was a report that Tate and Gustafson had a rift, but both emphatically denied it.

Tate had been quoted as saying he was critical of the laxity of discipline among Miami players under Gus' tenure. Tate denied it and said, "I said there had been a discipline problem with some freshmen not having known last fall who they'd have to answer to this season since the new head coach hadn't been picked."

That 1963 freshman class was considered the biggest and

fastest at the university to date. It also was the largest numerically with 49, of which 21 were from Pennsylvania and only one was from Florida, end Don Musick of Tampa. The entire squad, including upperclassmen, represented 17 states.

During spring practice, Tate lamented the fact that "we've only got six or seven players." So he signed 11 junior-college transfers, but only two eventually helped—cornerback Andy Sixkiller and linebacker LeRoy Lewis. Tate knew it would be a rebuilding season because he faced a tough schedule and had only 16 lettermen.

"We're fighting a long war with a short stick," he said.

Tate decided he and his staff could fight the war better by literally living with the players 24 hours a day the first two weeks of practice in September. "We're going to eat, sleep, and drink (milk) with the players," he said. "Living right in the dorms with the athletes will enable us to get better acquainted with them."

Tate also broke a 30-year tradition of team and student solidarity by moving the bench to the south side of the Orange Bowl while the band and student seating remained on the north side. Tate sought the move because he had hitched up two television sets at the bench to cables from the press box. One gave him a chance to watch the action from above as well as on the field. The other showed replays of key opponent plays. Tate also wanted to make more use of the elevator on the south side to bring Polaroid pictures made from the press box to the bench.

But none of this translated into a victory until the sixth game of the season. The Hurricanes started 0-4-1 before finishing 4-1. The heir to Mira on the erratic offense was sophomore Bob Biletnikoff, brother of Florida State star receiver Fred Biletnikoff. The defense allowed an average of only 13 points a game and held California's Craig Morton, who was second nationally in total offense, to his worst game of the season.

Meanwhile, problems continued to mount. Running backs Pete Banaszak and Russell Smith often were hurt, four key players either left the squad or flunked out before the season began, and two starters were kicked off at midseason for breaking curfew. In all, 17 players since spring had flunked out or been booted off.

Again in 1965, the Hurricanes proved to be unpredictable. They were upset by Southern Methodist, 7-3, in the opener, then they jolted ninth-ranked Syracuse on the road, 24-0. Biletnikoff was hurt early in the 34-27 loss to LSU and replaced by sophomore Bill Miller, who is not to be confused with the 1960-61 UM All-American end of the same name. But the season was salvaged by a 16-13 upset of the tenth-ranked and Sugar Bowl-bound Florida. And the Hurricanes finished by fighting the Fighting Irish of Notre Dame to a scoreless tie.

Defense again was superb most of the season and linebacker Ed Weisacosky, dubbed ''The Baby-Faced Assassin,'' was named All-American.

The team was even more cosmopolitan than the previous year as 20 states and two foreign countries were represented. Place-kicker Ramon Poo was born in Spain and wingback Speedy Gonzalez was born in Mexico. And there were two Indians in the defensive backfield—Sixkiller and Jim Wahnee. Even the Hurricane Football Network reflected the cosmopolitan nature of the team as it reached a whopping 200 stations in 11 states.

That would soon shrink—as the UM had feared—because of the arrival of pro football in South Florida. On August 16, 1965,

Ed Weisacosky.

an AFL franchise was awarded to Miami with play to begin in 1966.

"Competing against a professional team may force us to play more games away from home," said Gustafson. "However, we wish the Danny Thomas group (which bought the Dolphins) good luck in their effort."

Two of the leading high school coaches in the area feared the worst from the birth of the Dolphins. "Pro ball here is going to affect attendance at our college games," said Nick Kotys of Coral Gables. "High schools have their own core of fans. I don't think there will be enough money to go to three football games on a weekend." Added Miami High's Bob Carlton: "I doubt that most people in Dade County can afford to go to so many games, and someone is going to be left out, either high school or college."

Tate took the view that the most interesting team would get the biggest crowds. "I am hopeful that we can expand the football dollar and that there will be no loss for anyone," he said.

According to the Dolphin lease signed with the city, the UM was to get scheduling priority for its games in the Orange Bowl, and the Orange Bowl Committee was to have guaranteed safe guarding for its games. Joe Robbie, co-owner with Thomas, said: "We wish the Orange Bowl Committee every success with their various promotions, and we hope the University of Miami has a 10-0 season and a full house at every home game in the Orange Bowl."

Dolphinmania did not sweep South Florida overnight, however. The first weekend the Hurricanes and Dolphins both played at home, the UM drew 41,756 on Friday night for Georgia and the Dolphins drew 23,393 for Denver on Sunday. On the Thursday before that, Miami High and Norland, the state's No. 1 and No. 2-ranked teams, drew 20,532.

Overall, however, Hurricane home attendance dropped from an average of 49,163 in 1965 to 39,471 in 1966, the Dolphins' first year, though the UM's record improved from 5-4-1 to 8-2-1. Dolphin attendance averaged 26,061 in 1966 and did not pass the 35,000 average until 1970 when Don Shula became coach and the AFL merged with the NFL.

A Breakthrough In Integration

Before integrating its football program, the University of Miami made it clear it would not be in the business of recruiting black athletes simply to be pioneers in the South.

"If and when we find a Negro athlete who is qualified to come to the University of Miami, there will be no trouble on that score," said Gustafson when he became full-time athletic director after the 1963 season. "We are not going to recruit a Negro player just to be the first in the South to do that."

Miami football had been more a case of involuntary segregation than any outright policy against integration. "Andy Gustafson's recruiters have scanned the crop of Negro athletes for several years," *Herald* columnists Edwin Pope wrote. "They just haven't been able to find one they thought would be right for the breakthrough. Or, having found one, they were unable to land him."

There was one sitting practically on their doorstep in 1963. Cyril Pinder of Attucks High in neighboring Broward County said he was interested in becoming the first black player at the UM. And he possessed the two credentials long considered mandatory by UM officials in seeking an athlete to break the color line: a good football player and a good student.

Pinder was rated the best black halfback in Florida; he was a B-plus student and a member of the National Honor Society.

"I think it might make me play a little harder," Pinder said when asked of the prospect of breaking the color barrier at the UM. "I think I'd consider it an honor to be the first at Miami."

But the university appeared to have jumped the gun in revealing its interest in Pinder. He eventually signed with Illinois while the UM fretted over losing its contracts with certain opponents who might oppose integration.

In May 1964, Tate and Gustafson claimed that contractual involvements with several opponents were the only obstacles to recruiting blacks. There was no problem on games in the Orange Bowl. But two games were scheduled at LSU and two at Tulane, and athletic segregation was strictly enforced in Louisiana. There also was a fear of problems involving games at Vanderbilt, VPI, Auburn, and Alabama.

"There is no point in trying to recruit a Negro if he will not be able to compete in every game," said Tate. "We are not about to go into this thing without first obtaining the agreement of all the opponents we already have scheduled."

The UM did not sign its first black player until two-and-a-half years later. Breaking the color line was Ray Bellamy, a 6-5, 210-pound split end from Lincoln High in Palmetto, Florida. Assistant Coach George MacIntyre won the recruiting battle over Nebraska, Indiana, Illinois, Florida, Florida State, and Florida A&M for Bellamy, who starred on a 9-1 team and was a B-plus student and president of the student council.

"Bellamy's not the only colored player we're after," said Tate. A few months earlier, Tate had brought Maceo Coleman, a

Ray Bellamy became the first black football player at the UM. Looking on as he signed the grant-in-aid were (from left to right) Hurricane assistant George MacIntyre, Ray Bellamy's brother Sylvester, and Lincoln High School coach Eddie Shannon.

black tackle from Nashville, to campus for a visit. But Coleman enrolled at Purdue. Miami did not sign its second black player, Tom Sullivan, until 1968.

If you do not count Maryland and Texas, Bellamy was the first black player at a major college in the Deep South. But when he signed in December 1966, he downplayed the significance of the event. "I expect people to accept me as just another ballplayer, not as the first Negro to play with Miami," he said.

But Bellamy was not always accepted as just another ballplayer. He got hate mail ("We're going to round up all you niggers and ship you off some place," said one), and a player from Georgia Tech took a couple of punches at him in a freshman game.

Bellamy, who was shy and careful in what he said, shrugged it off. "I figure if they kept busy fighting me, they wouldn't have time to win the game, too," he said. "They (Georgia Tech) thought they could make me mad and get me thrown out of the game, but they were wrong." He caught five passes for 57 yards and Miami won, 21-0.

As for the hate mail, Bellamy said, "I just turn them over to the coaches. I don't let it bother me."

Bellamy lived up to the UM's hopes that he would become a standout player. He earned a starting job as a receiver for three years. During his sophomore season, he caught 37 passes, a school record for a sophomore.

Ironically, that turned out to be his best season. A near-fatal automobile accident in 1970 limited his playing time and he saw brief action as a senior. Bellamy also developed into a leader off the field. In 1971, he became the school's first black student body government president.

"I'm glad I came to the University of Miami," Bellamy said. "I didn't have any problems, at least no more than I would have if I'd gone to some other school.

"You have to realize that when a guy kicks you when you're down or smacks you after the whistle, he's not doing it because you're black. He's doing it in the heat of a game."

Sullivan, a touted tailback from Jacksonville, spurned offers from Florida, Florida State, Georgia, and Tennessee to sign with Miami after Bellamy's sophomore season. He developed into one of the greatest backs in UM history and he still holds the school record for yardage on kickoff returns.

"The problem of being the second colored player at Miami didn't enter my mind," said Sullivan. "I just wanted to play for Miami and to get an education. I was treated fairly, just like any other player on the squad."

The UM's attempts to land another touted black, Coral Gables High quarterback Craig Curry, backfired. The day after he said he would attend the UM, a phone call to his house brought the following message: "Tell Craig Curry that if he goes to Miami, I'm going to kill him."

Then in mid-July, word spread that Curry was discontented with the UM. Another caller said, "If Craig Curry doesn't go to Miami, I'm going to kill him."

Curry, who quarterbacked Coral Gables to a 13-0 record and mythical national title, eventually reconsidered signing the UM grant-in-aid and enrolled at Minnesota.

He said there were three things which made him change his mind about the UM: "They told me I didn't have to take an entrance exam. Then a week after school is out they tell me I do. I don't think they want me, and I don't think they'd let me play quarterback."

Tate countered that he had told Curry several times his grant would not be official until he took the college boards and that he intended to use him at quarterback. Once he took the exam, his score did not project a 1.6 grade average in college, the NCAA minimum, which meant he had to sit out his freshman season at Minnesota.

In 1969, the UM signed its third and fourth black players, running back Chuck Foreman and defensive back-receiver Burgess Owens. By the fall of 1971, Fran Curci's first year as head coach, there were 14 blacks on the squad including the first black quarterback, Kary Baker of state champion Miami Edison High. Curci also hired the school's first part-time black assistant coach, Carroll Williams, who had starred at Miami's Archbishop Curley High and Xavier University and had been an assistant principal at Edison.

By 1976, there were 32 blacks and 54 whites on the squad, and each season since then the ratio has been similar.

Looking back on his six years (plus two games) as coach, Tate now wishes the UM had acted faster on integration. Asked to reflect on the decline of the program and his quitting during the

1970 season, Tate said, "The lack of a top-notch quarterback was about as big as anything. And we probably should have gone to (black athletes) a little quicker than we did. But you were damned if you did and damned if you didn't. You needed 'em to win, but a lot of people hadn't gotten used to the idea yet."

The Stork Delivers

To develop greatness in football, according to Charlie Tate, a team needs three bones.

"First, you've got to have a funnybone," he said before the 1967 season. "Football is not fun. It's sweat and bruises and tears. And you've got to learn to laugh at adversity to keep going.

"Your team also must have a wishbone. You must wish big—to have a dream—and make it come true.

"But most important of all is backbone. No matter how slow we've started since I came to the university, all my teams have played well as the season went along. And I believe this squad has a good, solid backbone."

The real backbone of Hurricane football during the 1966, 1967, and 1968 seasons was a 6-8, 220-pound defensive end called "The Mad Stork" by the public, "All-American" by the press and coaches, and "sir" by the opposition. His real name: Ted Hendricks.

George Gallet, the UM's sports publicist for more than four decades, rated Hendricks the greatest player in the university's history. He is the only Hurricane named All-American three years. He was concensus in 1967 and 1968 and made one All-American team his sophomore year in 1966, a year in which most of the selectors picked a couple of ends named Alan Page of Notre Dame and Bubba Smith of Michigan State.

In 1968, Hendricks finished fifth in Heisman Trophy voting and was named Outstanding Lineman of the Year by UPI and the Washington Touchdown Club. He made nearly 350 career tackles and was the Most Valuable Player in the 1966 Liberty Bowl and 1967 Bluebonnet Bowl.

Ted Hendricks, leaping for an interception against Northwestern.

Born in Guatemala but raised in South Florida, Hendricks was an outstanding student as well as an athlete. He ranked seventy-fourth in a class of 1,190 at Hialeah High and won a *Miami Herald* Silver Knight Award for talent, achievement, and leadership. One of the reasons he enrolled at the UM, he said, was for the opportunity to take an honors curriculum in math with a minor in psychology.

"I sometimes wish I was just a student," he once said. His courses included electromagnetic theory, statistics, differential equations, topology, and mathematic analysis. His chief hobby was dismantling cars, not ballcarriers.

Hendricks surprised his own mother, Angela, when he first put on pads and a helmet. "He never was an aggressive person," she said. "He avoided fights as a child. I can remember telling him to hit back, but he wouldn't."

At Hialeah High, Hendricks initially played quarterback but was turned into a pass receiver. He was named to the prep All-American first team and was groomed as a pass receiver on the Hurricane freshman squad.

But Miami coaches realized his talents could be channeled into better use on defense. Kichefski, the ends coach, took charge and molded a player who has become one of the greatest defensive ends in college and pro history. To get maximum use of that potential, though, Kichefski had to bench Hendricks for the fourth game of the season his junior year.

"He was right," Hendricks recalled later. "I was approaching a stage of development where I knew more than the coaches did. I was playing my own game. Good old coach 'Ski taught me something right there, as he did throughout my college career. I discovered that he is a man of principle who does what he says he'll do. I give him a lot of credit for my development.

"Anyway, after he demoted me, I started looking within myself. I told myself I'd better get back to basics. By the time I got in the LSU game, I was ready to play, all right."

LSU wished he had not. The slogan all week for Tiger practices had been: "We're going to knock Hendricks out of there for quarterback Nelson Stokley." But Hendricks loomed over Stokley all night in the game at Baton Rouge. Twice he forced him to fumble at critical moments, and in the fourth quarter he threw Stokley for a 14-yard loss when LSU had moved into field goal range and was two points behind. Miami won, 17-15.

After his second knockdown, Stokley returned to the bench gesturing in anger. "Never mind what I was saying," he said later. "I don't normally use that kind of language. But you can guess, can't you? I'll give you a hint. Hendricks."

In Hendricks' sophomore season, 1966, the Hurricanes compiled their best record since 1956, 8-2-1, and beat Virginia Tech in the Liberty Bowl. Called The Calamity Kids, The Upsetters, and The Spoilers, they beat four teams ranked nationally in the top 10—Rose Bowl-bound Southern California, Orange Bowl-bound Florida, Cotton Bowl-bound Georgia, and Colorado. Hendricks hounded Florida's Heisman-Trophy-winning quarterback Steve Spurrier all day as Miami knocked the Gators out of the top 10.

The Hurricanes finished ninth in the final AP poll and tenth in UPI, and only eight points kept them from having an undefeated and untied season.

Defensive back Tom Beier was a consensus All-American, while end Larry LaPointe was named to the National Blocking Team's first team, and center Bill Chambless was picked for the second team. Beier, a 5-11, 200-pound senior, made 17 tackles in the

Tom Beier.

"The Mad Stork" Ted Hendricks hovered over Florida Heisman Trophy winner Steve Spurrier in 1966 upset.

10-7 upset of fifth-ranked USC.

Even Mira fans had something to cheer about—George's younger brother, Joe. After two years of bouncing from quarterback to cornerback to safety, Joe Mira settled in as the No. 2 running back. Every time he came off the bench the fans roared, partly out of habit from yelling for George.

Though Joe did not pan out as a college quarterback, he had a slightly better passing record than George at Key West High. Another brother, James, had better records than both but did not go to college and became a barber.

Before the 1966 season, President Stanford said the UM must play in a bowl game or appear on regional or national television to break even financially. He said the school loses $200,000 a year on football and another $100,000 on other sports.

But football reaped a $100,000 bonanza when the Hurricanes received a bid to the Liberty Bowl in Memphis and that enabled the football program to finish in the black.

They could have used some of the money to buy heaters at the Liberty Bowl. It was so cold for the game that the palm trees the Coral Gables Chamber of Commerce had planted on the field died. Light rain mixed with snow fell as the Hurricanes' frozen offense was held to minus-17 yards in the first half against Virginia Tech.

But Tech managed only one first down after the first quarter and the Hurricanes rallied from a 7-0 deficit to a 14-7 victory. Bill Miller's seven-yard pass to Mira scored the first touchdown, and Miller's completions of 12, 11, and 38 yards to Jimmy Cox set up Doug McGee's winning touchdown run from the one.

After Hendricks was named the bowl's Most Valuable Player, Tate said: "He could be anything he wants to be. That's the kind of potential he has. Why, he could even be governor."

Tate was not doing so badly, either. On December 20, 1966, he received a new four-year contract calling for a substantial increase in pay. It replaced his present contract that was to expire December 31, 1967.

The following February, Tate turned down a chance to succeed his former boss, Bobby Dodd, at Georgia Tech. Tate's wife and two daughters had grown up in Atlanta, and Tate weighed the offer carefully.

"My insides didn't tingle with the idea of going," he said. "I

Coach Charlie Tate (center), on a victory ride after 1966 victory over the University of Georgia, received congratulations from Georgia coach Vince Dooley (far right).

tried to look where you're going to be happiest. I guess for every 10 people we know in Georgia, we know 50 in Miami.''

He said other factors included the national recognition the UM had received as a football power, the effective recruiting program he had established locally and nationally, and Tech's high academic standard.

"I didn't think I could better myself by going to Tech," he added. "If you make a parallel move, it has to be a sure thing. I feel we've built something at Miami and I want to continue the job."

On his desk was a gold bowl, a gift from the Fort Lauderdale Touchdown Club. A piece of cotton, an orange, a gold bell, and a velvet rose were inside the bowl, representing the four bowl teams the Hurricanes beat in 1966.

Jolly Cholly was smiling, and for good reasons. At the start of the 1967 season, his Hurricanes received their loftiest preseason rankings in history. *Playboy* magazine's Anson Mount, a former theology student and the magazine's public affairs manager, picked the UM No. 1 and Tate as Coach of the Year. Hendricks was named to *Playboy's* first team, senior end Jim Cox was named to the All-American squad, and quarterback David Teal was named

Sophomore Back of the Year.

Football News tabbed the Hurricanes No. 2; *Sports Illustrated* and *Street And Smith* magazine had them No. 3, the AP No. 4, and *Look* magazine No. 5.

"This is the busiest I've ever seen it since I came here in 1935," said Wilbert Bach, Gallet's co-publicist. "Boy, we had two people cover our game with Southeastern Louisiana that year. One reporter from each Miami paper. And they beat us, 2-0."

Perhaps the Hurricanes spent too much time reading press clippings in 1967. They lost their first two games, 12-7, at Northwestern, and, 17-0, in the Orange Bowl to Penn State. It marked the fourth time in five years that Miami had lost its first game.

"The only way we'll ever go unbeaten is to start with five open dates," one veteran observer said.

The play that doomed the Hurricanes at Northwestern was a reverse pass on which Wildcat quarterback Bill Melzer pitched to left halfback Chico Kurzawski and then caught Kurzawski's pass for nine yards and the decisive fourth-quarter touchdown. Hank Collins had fumbled on a punt attempt on his nine with five minutes left to set up the score.

The Hurricanes, switching to a pro-type offense, had no continuity at quarterback with Miller, Teal, and converted fullback David Olivo all playing at Northwestern. An interception of Miller set up Northwestern's first score. The quarterbacks also had trouble passing in the Penn State shutout.

"Too bad I can't trade for a quarterback or buy one," said Tate.

If press clippings and quarterbacks were not the problem, Tate wondered if the fact that 24 players—a school record—were married was a problem. A decade earlier at Miami and many other schools, marriage meant forfeiting scholarship.

"I don't encourage marriages by players, but I don't discourage it either," said Tate. "If their parents want to go along with it, who am I to stop them?"

Tate also wondered if spies weren't lurking around the practice field. When an unfamiliar face peered over the curtained fence one day, Tate yelled: "What business have you got watching us?! Get away from that fence!"

He remembered the time in 1956 when Gustafson and his staff caught a spy the night before their opener with South

Carolina. A coed living in a Coral Gables apartment reported to them for several nights she had heard a husky young man calling Columbia, South Carolina, from a pay phone in the building, passing on information on Hurricane practices. Gus and Kichefski cornered the guy, a former South Carolina player, and he tearfully confessed he had been spying with field glasses. The favored UM barely won, 14-6.

So Tate took no chances. He had campus police stationed daily at both gates.

Eventually the Hurricanes began to win in 1967, though that had little to do with spies or married players and had more to do with the fact that Hendricks was playing spectacularly and that the offense had been switched to a run-oriented attack with Olivo and Miller alternating at quarterback.

Against Pitt, Hendricks blocked a quickkick and ran it back to Pitt's 16, setting up a touchdown in a 58-0 rout. Against Virginia Tech, he enabled Miami to get its winning score by slamming the ball out of the quarterback's hand and then recovering it 20 yards farther downfield. And against Tulane, he twice stole the ball from the quarterback in a 34-14 triumph.

The Hurricanes won six straight after the embarrassing start and vaulted into bowl contention heading into the Notre Dame game, which was dubbed the Disappointment Bowl for both clubs. The Irish had been favored to repeat as national champions, but they lost two early season games to Purdue and Southern California.

The Disappointment Bowl did not disappoint the throng of 77,265—largest ever to see a UM game in the Orange Bowl before or since. Miami jumped to a 13-3 lead, but the extra point after the second touchdown was missed and that probably cost a tie. Notre Dame opened a 24-16 lead in the fourth quarter, then Miami cut it to 24-22 but missed the two-point conversion.

Notre Dame quarterback Terry Hanratty found Miami's defense the best he had faced and he threw only 12 times. "I read all about that Hendricks," he said. "I knew what his number was, 89; how much he weighed, 220; how tall he was, 6-8. I did not believe he was as good as people said. I was right. He was better."

The defense led the Hurricanes to a 20-13 victory in the regular-season finale against Florida as it made five interceptions and recovered two fumbles. Then in a seesaw Bluebonnet Bowl game, Colorado scored two fourth-quarter touchdowns to win,

31-21. The bowl bid plus two regular-season television appearances brought in $348,000 and enabled the football program to produce a $114,000 profit on a $1.4 million budget.

The following June, Gustafson retired as athletic director and announced that the schedules for the next 10 years were nearly completed, leaving Tate only six dates to fill.

"Charlie and I have worked just like Jack Harding did when I was coach," Gus said. "He'd ask me if I wanted to play football's very best teams and I'd say, 'If we make money, I'll play anybody.' And Tate feels exactly the same way."

Additions included Texas for 1972, Oklahoma for 1973, Colorado for 1975, Duke and Texas Christian for 1976, Penn State for 1977, and Kansas for 1977 and 1978.

When spring practice began in 1968, Kichefski estimated that a leaping Hendricks presented a 14-foot obstacle for a quarterback to throw over. He also presented a 14-foot target to throw to. So guess who worked out at offensive end for the first time since his freshman year?

"We're going to try to help Hendricks get the Heisman Trophy by using him at offensive end in certain situations," said Tate.

Thus Tate created the Jump Ball Offense on the goal line with 6-8 Hendricks, 6-4 Bellamy, and 6-3 Dave Kalima in the lineup. The quarterback would use a shot-put motion to fire the ball high in the end zone and the receivers would try to win the jump ball.

But Hendricks suffered a chest injury and missed the spring game. The Jump Ball Offense was used only once—late in the fourth quarter of a 28-7 victory over Northwestern in the opener.

"If we had to beat teams by 28 points to get in our Jump Ball Offense, I saw no future in that," said Hendricks.

It is just as well it was scrapped because Hurricane quarterbacks probably would have had trouble finding even those tall targets. *Sports Illustrated*, which ranked Miami seventeenth before the season, said, "The Hurricanes have everything except a way to deliver a blow by air." Added Tate: "Having a pro offense like ours with great receivers but no first-rate quarterback is like having a new limousine with a chimpanzee at the wheel."

The man most often at the wheel was Olivo, a 6-2, 215-pound senior who did not attract rave notices from pro scouts. But the main reason the Hurricanes were only 5-5 in 1968, Hendrick's

Walt Kichefski with his pride and joy, Ted Hendricks.

senior season, was a poor offensive line.

"We got caught short," Tate said after losing the last three games. "It was a rebuilding year. We got caught short up front on the offensive bunch. We were worried to death before we ever started."

After defeating Northwestern and Georgia Tech in the first two games, the Hurricanes headed for Los Angeles for a much-heralded battle between The Mad Stork and The Orange Juice, USC's vaunted running back O. J. Simpson. Simpson gained 163 yards and scored two touchdowns before 71,189 in the Los Angeles Coliseum and sat out the last 10 minutes as the Trojans handed Tate his worst loss to date, 28-3. Miami had drives to the 5, 20, 33, and 17 but stalled in the first half.

Hendricks never really had a chance to battle Simpson one-on-one. "I'd remembered what Vince Lombardi always said," USC Coach John McKay said afterward. "'Run at the other team's strength.' Well, we ran one of our first plays at Ted Hendricks and we found out he was there all right, so we didn't try to test him much more.''

Said Simpson: ''He shucks off most blockers, or pushes them away and gets around them. He's real strong in the hands and arms. He likes to play cat-and-mouse with the quarterback, too. Force him to pitch, then get the ballcarrier.''

USC ran only 14 of 61 plays toward his left side; Hendricks made 10 tackles. Only twice was he in position to grab Simpson and stop him for no gain.

Rebounding with victories over LSU and Virginia Tech, the Hurricanes moved up to ninth in the AP and UPI rankings. Florida and Florida State also were in the top 20 at midseason, a phenomenon that would not happen again until 1980.

But Miami disappeared from the top 20 after a 31-6 blasting by Auburn, a game in which Olivo was nailed by blitzes for 99 yards in losses. Orange Bowl-bound Penn State then whipped the Hurricanes, 22-7, and Alabama prevailed, 14-6, in the first regular-season game ever televised at night nationally. Florida finished the Hurricanes' swoon by beating them, 14-10, in the season finale.

Hendricks had made 247 tackles in the 1966 and 1967 seasons combined; but he had only 103 his senior season, as more than 75 percent of the plays were run away from his end. That diminished his outside hopes of winning the Heisman Trophy.

''That doesn't bother me,'' he said after finishing fifth in the voting. ''I never really thought I had a chance to beat out backs like O. J. Simpson and Leroy Keyes. But I do feel I've been cheated out of the chance to prove what I could do this season. I knew it was all over for me, as far as getting much chance to be in the thick of the action, when even Simpson ran the other way.''

Nevertheless, Hendricks made everybody's All-American team for the second straight year. ''He's the only player I know who could make All-American at four positions,'' said Florida coach Ray Graves.

When the UM retired his No. 89 uniform after the season Kichefski proudly said: ''There ain't never been one like him ever...ever.''

Now You See Him,
Now You Don't

Optimism abounded before the 1969 season, but the cynics wondered if the UM was not crying wolf again. Remember 1963 when George Mira predicted a 10-0 season and the Hurricanes went 3-7? Remember 1968 when the preseason polls picked them among the top five teams and they lost the first two games?

"We're liable to have a helluva football team," Tate said. "Not just an average team, but a team that might be really excellent. I'm really excited about it."

A headline in the *Herald* said: "Quarterback Depth Sends UM Grid Hopes Sky-High." But Tate obviously oversold himself on his team, and though there may have been depth at quarterback, no one rose to the top to take command.

The Hurricanes scored only five touchdowns in their first four games, and the quarterback spot remained unsettled. Tate finally decided on redshirt sophomore Kelly Cochrane over Lew Pytel, the preseason No. 1, and David Teal. Pytel later transferred to Tampa.

Complicating the quarterback picture was the saga of Dean Stone, whom the UM had won in a recruiting battle with Notre Dame in 1967. Stone had set a New Mexico state high school record with 27 touchdown passes in 10 games his senior year, and Ara Parseghian had considered him one of the two best quarterbacks his scouts had looked at in 1966.

Stone said he picked Miami because he wanted a career in oceanography. But two years later, he had neither a career as a quarterback nor as an oceanographer. The UM had moved him to defensive back because there was no place for a rollout quarterback in Tate's dropback passing offense. And in class Stone found there was no place for a football player majoring in marine biology, because the sport made it impossible to keep up with the three and four-hour labs. Stone thus became a starting safety during his sophomore season in 1968.

"You've got at least four times as many chances of making it in pro football as a defensive back than as a quarterback," he said, accepting his plight.

Regarding classes, Stone said, "My professor put it to me straight last year. He told me, 'You can do one of two things. You can play football or you can major in biology, but you can't do both.' So I got out. Now I'm trying to catch up as a business major.

"It's not because I believe that football is more important than getting a good education and a degree. Actually, I think football is secondary. But in my case, football comes first because football made it possible for me to go to school. I probably put more into football than my studies. I don't know whether that's right or wrong. But you gotta do it."

When the Hurricanes started 1-3, giving them a 1-7 record over a two-year span, Tate was told to his face that a lot of "downtown businessmen" no longer thought he deserved to be Miami's coach.

"I'm sensitive, I'm a human being," Tate said. "But I believe I'm a better coach now than when I came here."

Tate responded by demoting Bobby Best to third-string running back and Ray Bellamy to No. 2 split end. But the Hurricanes went only 3-3 in the remaining games and criticism mounted. Rumors spread in late November that downtown businessmen attempted to raise money to buy up the last year of Tate's contract. Stanford was asked if he contemplated any change in Tate's status, and he diplomatically responded by saying, "No, not at this time."

Meanwhile, the Miami Touchdown Club sent a "vote of confidence" telegram for Tate to Stanford.

In January 1969, Tate knew he faced a must-win situation so he signed nine junior college players whom he hoped would provide immediate help.

"We're attempting to plug the dike in places where plugs are most needed," he said. One place was quarterback, a problem ever since George Mira had ended his UM career in 1963. Sixth-year performer David Teal—he had been redshirted twice, once by the UM and once by Uncle Sam—emerged as the top quarterback at spring practice.

There were several other places to plug, because six players had quit the team since the end of the season. "The guys here play as individuals, not as a team," said junior guard Steve Henson when he quit. "They don't care about winning. It's not just in football, it's their whole attitude on life. They don't even want to go to school."

Though Tate earnestly sought to recruit more players from Florida than he had before (there were 18 Floridians on the 1968 roster), he did not endear himself to the state's coaches and athletes with the comments he made about the current high school crop. He called it the leanest he had seen.

"I just don't believe that year in, year out, there are enough blue-chippers in Florida, or any state where there are three schools the size of Florida State, Florida, and ourselves, for us to survive just taking Florida boys. I don't care where the players come from, I'm not going through that again (a 5-5 season, seven games with one touchdown).

He was right. The Hurricanes went 4-6 in 1969, losing to Florida State and Houston by only two points but being bombed by Alabama, 42-6, and Florida, 35-16. In the freshman class that fall, there were only six players from the state, three of them from South Florida.

Tate's insistence on recruiting out of state proved costly. A survey that year indicated the UM spent $55,000 on recruiting, while Florida spent $37,000, and FSU spent $30,000. The UM also had a $30,000 deficit in football for the year, and the total athletic program deficit was $451,000.

Meanwhile, as football, basketball, and the entire UM athletic program became under attack, President Stanford appointed an ad hoc committee on athletics in 1970 to evaluate the situation and make recommendations.

James S. Billings, Jr., an alumnus and a trustee, served as chairman of the committee which met for six months and considered options from all aspects of the athletic program. No one questioned that there was a useful purpose to intercollegiate athletics, but the committee found that the program, like the entire university, was overextended and underfinanced.

The committee's report squelched talk that football would be de-emphasized, and it concluded that the athletic program represents "one of the few remaining centripetal forces that serve to remind the university that it is a common community existing for certain purposes and serving honorably to those ends."

Committee members felt it was important to keep athletics in proper perspective and to maintain the program within the resources of the university. The committee also concluded that basketball must be discontinued "temporarily" until an adequate facility for practice and games be built on campus. That "temporary" status has continued into the 1980s as President Stanford had reaffirmed that a campus facility was needed before the program be reinstated.

The ad hoc committee strongly urged the support of club sports which would serve more students with a greater variety of interests. The committee further recommended that the university hire an athletic director who was not a coach of a major sport, and that led to hiring Penn State's longtime and highly respected but now retired athletic director, Ernie McCoy, for a few years.

Out of the committee's recommendations also came the UM Athletic Federation, which was formed to raise support and money for athletic activities. Kichefski became director in December 1970, and Walter Etling, Eddie Dunn, Judge John Gale, and Jerry Wright were formed as a steering committee.

The Athletic Federation received McCoy's strong support, and it soon produced tangible results. In 1971, businessman George Light gave $100,000 to light the baseball field, which was named after his son Mark, who died of muscular dystrophy at age 16. Another gift of $95,000 in 1974 started the funds to build a concrete baseball stadium.

While athletics in general appeared under attack, the football program in particular felt under seige as Dolphin hysteria began to grip South Florida in 1970. Don Shula arrived as head coach of the Dolphins that year and the AFL merged with the NFL. Immediately the Dolphins, who went 4-2 in exhibition games, surpassed the UM in season-ticket sales for the first time, topping 23,000 while the UM was pressed to reach 18,500, a drop from 27,500 three years earlier.

Tate admitted the pros had an edge unless the college competition could win big. "They start receiving publicity and attention in July and our boys don't get rolling until September," he said in July. "They're all over the papers and TV screens already.

Nobody's hearing many peeps out of the college troops."

Tate entered the 1970 season with a 33-26-3 record at Miami and only one year left on his contract. "You can't bank on anything in this business," he said. "You win a few, go to two bowls, you think all is rosy. Then the well dries up just a little and you're supposed to be cliff-hanging." But Tate had one thing going for himself: Miami had not pushed any coach over the cliff by firing him—yet.

In August Tate said off the record to a reporter: "If I live to be 95, I'll never understand the fans down here. They want you to pass with fourth down and seven yards to go from your own 10. Can you imagine the people at Tennessee or Alabama or Auburn or Georgia or Georgia Tech ever feeling that way? I know football. I've always been a winner. I know what it takes to win. I've even tried to change to please these fans, but some of the things they want are unreal."

The ads promoting season-ticket sales turned out to be unreal, too. They billed 1970 as "The Year of the Big Score." There were big scores, all right, but it was the opposition doing most of the scoring.

Miami's only big-scoring day came in the opening game against lackluster William and Mary, a 36-14 romp. The game drew 27,286, the smallest opening crowd since 1953. The Dolphins' home opener attracted 57,140.

In their second game, the Hurricanes were upset at Georgia Tech, 31-21. On the following Tuesday, Tate dropped a bombshell: he resigned immediately as coach and athletic director.

"Actually, he resigned three times in 24 hours," Stanford recalled. "He did it first on the phone on Tuesday. I said, 'You can't do that,' and I canceled all my appointments and went to his office. I found him very depressed and said I wanted him to sleep on it.

"That night, I called Walt Kichefski and asked him to come over at 10 that night. I said, 'I want you to do something for me and the university and I won't entertain "no" for an answer. I think I'm going to announce your appointment tomorrow at 3:00 p.m. as head coach. I don't know for sure. I'm meeting with Charlie Tate at nine-thirty in the morning.'

"Walt heaved a big sigh and said, 'I thought you were calling me in regards to handling the responsibility of United Way on campus.' I said, 'No, I want you to take the team and go all the way.'

"The next morning, Charlie was composed, rational, and said he would go ahead and resign," Stanford continued. "I accepted. We wrote the press release of his announcement together at my desk. We mentioned how he had defeated USC and LSU for the first time and in one year we beat four bowl-bound teams and tied Notre Dame.

"We held the press conference and I certainly put one on the press. They thought I was going to report on the ad hoc committee. When I made the announcement, the silence almost blew the roof off."

Tate did not attend the press conference and was unavailable for comment. But he left a statement which said in part: "I trust that much has been accomplished on and off the field in the development of young men with whom it has been my great pleasure to work . . . with the thought only of what would be in the best interest of the university and its athletic program it was my decision to resign."

Players were stunned. "It's like hearing your father died suddenly," said quarterback David Teal.

Stanford said there was no pressure from him or from the trustees for Tate to resign. So why would he abruptly disappear in the midst of a young season and a 1-1 record?

"This was a marriage that simply had seen too much bitterness to survive," wrote the *Herald's* Pope, who thought the decision was right. "He knew he had to win seven or eight to keep his head off the block in December . . . . He made few attempts to conceal his dislike for an Orange Bowl Committee he believed deliberately ignored his teams. He was not Miami's kind of football coach."

Part of Tate's problem, according to a highly placed UM official who asked not to be named, was his wife. "She was very emotional, high strung, and had to be carried out by stretcher from the press box one night," the official said. "Our quarterback was being intercepted a lot and she hyperventilated and fainted in the press box. In 1969, following our 42-6 loss at Alabama, Charlie was down in the dumps because we were really inept. But she yelled at the players on the plane for hurting her husband's career."

Upon resigning, Tate literally vanished from the public for five days, then was interviewed in Jacksonville at his brother Buddy's home. "I haven't been hiding from anyone," Tate said. "I'm just trying to collect my thoughts. I just got tired of the job. I thought I might be better off somewhere else."

He cited growing pressure as the underlying reason. "It wasn't fair to the kids. It wasn't fair for them to be trying to save a man's contract. It hurt their playing."

Not until November 7 did Tate grant an in-depth interview. Reached at his home in Leesburg, Florida, Tate revealed that his wife, Anna Lee, and his three sons had been harassed by obscene phone calls, defilement of his yard with a "load of manure," and vandalism of his car. He cited the lack of communication between the administration and the athletic department. And he said he was disenchanted with the spiritual climate of college campuses and was concerned over the increased use of drugs by students.

"When they'd call my house and anybody would answer the phone, they'd say, '---- you, Mrs. Tate.' And I said to myself, 'Now wait a minute, this ain't right. I mean, the hell with it.'"

Tate reiterated his frustration with pro football. "They get such a substantial head start each season and so much publicity because of it, and they get a star who stays in the area a long time, they can hang a hat on it. Now if we could keep Ted Hendricks forever, fine. But by the time we get one identified as being real good, he's gone. Then your college student doesn't play as big a role as he used to in your attendance. Also, if your attendance isn't going so good in the pros, you can always move the franchise. But you can't move a college campus."

Since leaving the UM, Tate has lived a checkered career in and out of coaching—from backfield coach of the New Orleans Saints to high school coach in Sebring and Live Oak, Florida, to head coach of the Jacksonville Sharks of the short-lived World Football League.

Several years after leaving Miami, Tate said he should have resigned at the start of the 1970 season, not two games into it. "You shouldn't go into the last year of your contract needing to win to save your job. That's not fair to your players. But I made the mistake of thinking I could pull it out."

He conceded that his pride prompted the sudden act and that he was too thin-skinned to accept a lot of criticism. "I got down on myself. It didn't look like anybody was coming to my rescue...and everybody seemed eager to get my tail out of there. If I had waited a week, I probably wouldn't have done it. But I got so sick of it, I couldn't stand it. I made a mistake, I guess. I should have sweated it out and taken my lumps.''

Kichefski, 55 and passed over for the head job before, wound up taking the lumps for the rest of the season when he accepted Stanford's offer to be interim coach. The Hurricanes won their first game under him, 18-11, over Maryland. But the lack of a good offensive line ruined the running game, and they lost six straight before scoring a stunning, 14-13, upset at Gainesville over Kichefski's hated Florida Gators, whom he simply called "The Gator." The season ended on a sour note, though, when Houston rolled to a 36-3 record that pinned a 3-8 record on Miami.

As the season dragged on, dissension grew. Second-string quarterback John Hornibrook made statements in the press critical of both the coaches and the entire football atmosphere at the UM. On November 4, Kichefski dismissed him from the team.

After the final game, Kichefski said that he was not interested in the head coaching job following his interim reign and that he would end his 27-year career at the university if he was passed up for the vacant athletic director job.

Kichefski, in fact, was passed over as McCoy was hired. But again he swallowed his pride and stayed at the university, accepting the job of heading the newly created Athletic Federation.

He retired from that job in 1978 but has remained a consultant to the federation, as well as a loyal booster of the university, and the World's No. 1 Gator Hater.

"Everything that has happened to me along the way has worked out for the best." he said. "I've been able to stay here. Hank Stram tried to hire me nine years in a row. And when Gus was offered the Minnesota job in 1950, he wanted me to go, but I said, 'No, I'm staying right here.' He said, 'So am I.'"

The same could not be said for Tate.

Gator Flop
And Fifth Down

The "Little General," Fran Curci, was hired December 19, 1970, to march the Hurricanes out of the trenches and toward the front line of college football. But he never had envisioned that the field would be littered with mines in the form of player defections, the controversial Gator Flop and Fifth Down plays, increasing Dolphinmania, and decreasing Hurricane attendance.

After two years on the job, Curci would surrender and move on to the University of Kentucky.

Curci's hiring by Miami was a "Johnny Comes Marching Home" story. He was the popular, energetic, and youthful looking former Hurricane All-American quarterback who was believed to be just what the program needed.

"Coach Curci will bring a vitality and vision to our football program," President Stanford said. "He is one of the nation's most imaginative and exciting young coaches."

Curci, 32, had built the University of Tampa into a small-college power while compiling a 25-6 record in three years. In 1970 he had gone 10-1, including a 31-14 victory over embarrassed Miami.

"This is the greatest challenge of my life," said Curci upon signing a four-year contract at Miami for an estimated $25,000 to $30,000 a year. "It's a long road back. I'm ready to get started."

One of the first things he did was place signs in the coaches' offices and the weight-lifting area that said: "WHAT DID I DO TODAY THAT WILL PUT THE UNIVERSITY OF MIAMI CLOSER TO THE NATIONAL CHAMPIONSHIP?"

It took gall to put the sign up considering the fact that the Hurricanes had won only 12 of their last 31 games. As the *Herald*'s

Fran Curci as coach.

Pope wrote: "It sounds like a flea challenging an elephant to a ground-shaking contest."

Said Curci: "We can't fool around. We don't have four or five years to build a winner. We have tremendous competition from the Dolphins but we have always been South Florida's football team and we plan to continue to be. Everything in our program is positive. We have everything right here to become a University of Southern California. Our South Florida recruiting area has more people than the whole state of Arkansas."

Curci set his first goal as recruiting Coral Gables High School's All-State linebacker Ralph Ortega. But he lost him to Florida. Curci did sign Coral Gables' other star, Neal Colzie, to a regional letter of intent but later lost him to Ohio State.

Colzie said he signed early with Miami to get recruiters off his back, and he thought Ohio State had more to offer. "If I stay at Miami," he said, "I have to wait and see if he (Curci) will become a winner."

The Little General installed a strict regimen. He did not want hair sticking out of players' helmets so he would personally clip violators in the training room. And he made it mandatory for players to make two visits a week to the "Pride Room" for wrestling matches against teammates during the five-week, off-season conditioning program.

Ten players quit during spring practice, though none was a starter. Several said the program under Curci had become "too intense," and the coaches "seem like computers.... They don't seem to be able to communicate as human beings."

The Pride Room could have been called Punishment Room. Yet no word of the brutality going on there reached the press until the spring of 1973, shortly after Florida State received considerable attention from the media about its "chicken wire room," in which players had to wrestle in a crouched position beneath a low chicken-wire ceiling. Twenty-eight FSU players quit or had their scholarships terminated that spring, and exiles charged a "survival of the fittest" approach.

UM running back Silvio Cardoso said in 1973 that if FSU players "had done what we had to do, there would have been a lot more quitting than they had. People would just walk out with no teeth, their eyes beat up from that Pride Room. They talk about wrestling. Ours was fighting, not wrestling. It was biting and kicking and pulling hair, anything you could do in there. Our first day of spring practice (in 1971) we had a three-hour practice with no water break, and it was really hot."

Running back Johnny Williams suffered a broken jaw and said he saw two other players get badly twisted ankles in the Pride Room.

The regimentation continued with the first practice in the fall of 1971. It began at six-thirty in the morning before breakfast. Though 120 showed up, that still was not enough in terms of quality depth. And once again the Hurricanes lacked a good passing quarterback.

Before the first game, Curci dismissed perhaps his best guard, Wiley Matthews, for disciplinary reasons. Assistant Coach Jon Mirilovich had been riding him hard in practice and Matthews yelled back.

The Hurricanes lost their first game under Curci, 20-17, to Florida State before about 20,000 in the Orange Bowl. But they won their next four, highlighted by Chuck Foreman's twisting, 50-yard run late in the first half of a 41-17 rout of Baylor. Old-

Chuck Foreman in 1971 action.

timers agreed the run was the finest by a UM back since Frank Smith's 50-yarder in the 1950 upset of Purdue.

But the Hurricanes went into a skid when the undersized offensive line could not protect quarterbacks John Hornibrook and Kelly Cochrane. They lost their last five games for a 4-7 record. The crowning blow was the infamous Gator Flop, one of the rare occasions in sports in which one team purposely allowed another to score.

It happened when a 3-7 Florida team defeated a 4-5 Miami team, 45-16, in the Orange Bowl before 37,710. Leading 45-8, and with Gator fans screaming "Let them score! Let them score!" the Gators staged a massive sitdown on the Poly-Turf and permitted the Hurricanes' Hornibrook to score a touchdown from eight yards out so that the senior quarterback John Reaves would have a last-minute shot at Jim Plunkett's career major-college passing record.

After the kickoff, Reaves was nearly intercepted, then he

Gator Flop:
a) Play action began.

b) Gators flopped down
on field.

c) Flop device allowed
Florida quarterback
John Reaves to break
major-college passing
record.

fired a 15-yard pass to Carlos Alvarez, which ran his career yard-age total to 7,546, two yards more than Plunkett. He later hit on a three-yard toss to run his completions to 33 in 55 attempts for 348 yards and four touchdowns against Miami and 7,549 total yards. Everything went right for Reaves; he even caught a 17-yard touchdown pass from Tommy Durance.

On the play in which Reaves broke Plunkett's record, the Gators drew a 15-yard unsportsmanlike penalty because they raced on the field to bury Reaves under an avalanche of happy humanity. And in a wild postgame celebration, they ran to the east end zone pond and jumped into the water, heaving Reaves with them.

Curci refused to congratulate Florida Coach Doug Dickey and headed straight for the dressing room where he assailed his rival coach.

"It was the worst thing I have ever seen in football," Curci said. "I used to admire Doug Dickey as a coach—his record speaks

for itself. But tonight I lost all respect for him as a coach and as a man. What he did shows absolutely no class.

"There was enough time left (1:10) for Florida to get the ball back legitimately and give him another chance.... I know I would never do a disgraceful thing like that to anybody. College football is fighting for its life (against the pros) and can't stand acts like this. Actually, I feel sorry for Doug Dickey. I think he made a fool of himself. If he thinks that's the spirit of the game, he's got a long way to go."

In preparation for the game, the Hurricanes switched to the wishbone offense because Florida had been vulnerable to the run; but the Gators adjusted quickly. Meanwhile, the Hurricanes were clearly vulnerable to the pass.

"He was passing against a crippled team, and Dickey knew this," moaned Curci. "The only healthy man in our defensive backfield was Burgess Owens. No, Dickey knew he had us down,

Gators celebrated in Orange Bowl end zone pool after Gator Flop game victory.

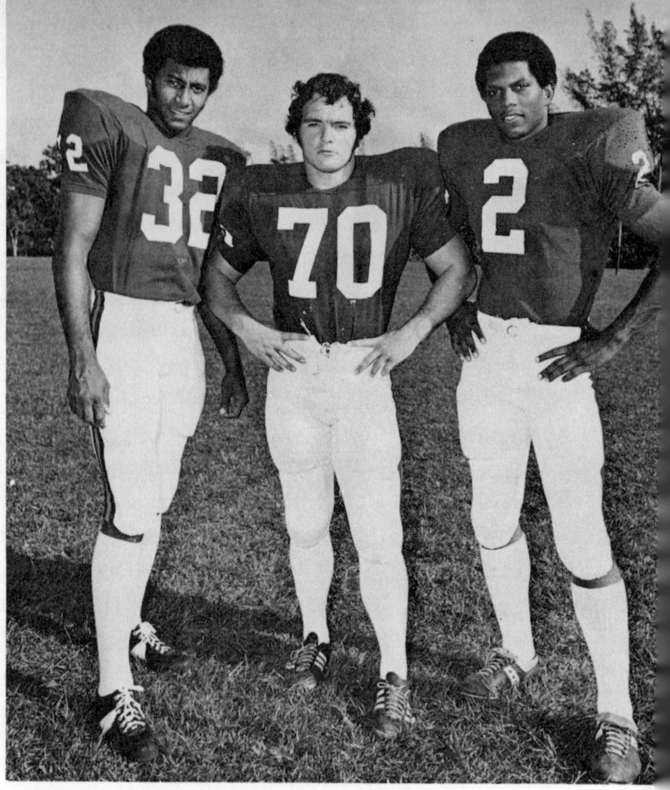

Chuck Foreman, Tony Cristiani, and Burgess Owens.

and he took advantage of it to kick the hell out of a crippled team."

What prompted the apparently impromptu flop by the Gators? A Florida assistant coach reportedly had asked Dickey if the Gators could allow Miami to score after Gary Altheide intercepted a Reaves pass with just over two minutes left. Dickey said no. Four plays later, with 90 seconds left, Florida called a time out and senior cornerback Harvin Clark went to the sideline to plead with Dickey. With a sheepish grin, the coach conceded.

"I just told 'em, 'Everybody lay down,'" Clark said.

After the game, Dickey grimaced and said to reporters, "I would rather not have had to do it that way. But certain records are worth going after, I guess. I did not mean to embarrass the Miami football team in any way. I certainly did not give our kids instructions to fall down like that. I was a little disappointed they did."

In the aftermath, Florida's University Athletic Association passed a resolution praising Dickey's decision. And Dickey would not second-guess himself.

"It didn't look to me like we were going to get the ball back any other way," he said. "And I felt in the best interest of our players I should try to help John Reaves.... Whether our guys stand around and play grab on the play or whether they lie down is immaterial, in my opinion. Besides, it was a split-second decision. We've never coached them on what to do to let another team score.''

Reaves, naturally, backed Dickey. ''Curci called us crybabies two years ago (in a speech in Daytona Beach while coaching at Tampa). This year it's his turn.''

The Hurricanes lost the season finale, after the Gator Flop, to Syracuse, 14-0, though there was one consolation. Foreman became the UM's all-time rushing leader for one season with 951 yards.

Attendance for the 1971 season averaged 29,799 for eight home games. Student attendance was particularly poor. Only 36 percent of the students went to the Homecoming game against Army. That compared with 86 percent of the students at Nebraska going to Homecoming, 54 percent at Texas, and 53 percent at Oklahoma. One UM game attracted fewer than 900 students.

Perhaps part of the problem was the fact that McCoy had required students to buy a $16 season ticket. That was because the school had dropped the $6 intercollegiate athletics portion of the student activities fee.

After the 1971 season, the UM launched a campaign to sell 45,000 season tickets. Julian Cole and Associates was hired to handle the advertising campaign. Cole displayed new posters and bumper stickers and came up with a new logo: the letter ''U'' was the key, as in ''U is on The Move,'' ''U is Great,'' ''U is Your Future,'' and in the late 1970s, ''U Gotta Believe.''

Also, the university decided to move all home games from the traditional Friday night to Saturday night, a move that was wise from the standpoint of recruiting and preparation for games but was unpopular with many longtime fans.

Curci cited other reasons for the switch. ''I think we'll get bigger crowds playing Saturday nights. That's because a lot of stores, even banks, stay open until nine or later on Friday nights. These people haven't been able to make our games. It's not like a long time ago when everything closed at 5:00 p.m. on Friday. Playing Saturday may help us work out some form of a package deal with the Dolphins which would enable people from other parts of the state to come into town and see our game Saturday night and the Dolphins play Saturday afternoon.''

The switch to Saturday nights lasted just one season, however. Attendance for five home games in 1972 tumbled to an average of 22,113. In 1973, home games returned to Friday nights except for late-season games with Florida and Notre Dame. The UM remained on Friday nights until the 1976 seasons, when again it was thought that a switch back to Saturday nights would increase attendance.

· Curci's second season not only saw crowds continue to slump but it saw controversies continue to increase. Silvio Cardoso, a Cuban nicknamed Quick Silvio, quit the team when left off the travel squad for the third game of the season, at Baylor. He said he was not given a chance.

The week before the Notre Dame game, Curci stunned players and raised eyebrows among fans by moving Foreman to wide receiver in an attempt to open the passing attack and shake up the Irish defense. Foreman, who was not happy with the move, had no carries from scrimmage and caught two passes for 16 yards in the 20-17 loss to Notre Dame.

Adding to Curci's woes, starting sophomore quarterback Kary Baker, the first black quarterback in the state other than at an all-black school, fractured and dislocated an ankle in the 37-14 season-opening loss to Florida State. Then backup quarterback John Hornibrook severed an artery and ligaments in his passing arm and ended his career late in September when he was horse-playing with teammates at the dormitory. That left only two quarterbacks, Ed Carney and Coy Hall.

On top of that, sophomore defensive tackle Rubin Carter and tight end Phil Corrigan were declared ineligible for the Florida game because they had previously signed letters of intent with Southeastern Conference schools. The UM, SEC schools, Florida State, and others in the South had a working agreement that they would not sign players who already were committed to another school.

The seesaw season ended with a 5-6 record. The Hurricanes did not win until the fourth game, 24-21, over Tulane, and they won that one thanks to an obvious fifth-down play that ignited a controversy as infamous as the Gator Flop.

With 54 seconds remaining in the game and fourth down being shown on the official NCAA play-by-play for the second time, Carney threw a 32-yard pass to Witt Beckman for the winning

Miami quarterback Ed Carney threw an incomplete pass on an apparent fourth down late in 1972 Tulane game.

touchdown in the Orange Bowl. The victory, before 18,956, snapped the longest losing streak in UM history to date, eight straight over two seasons.

As officials hurried off the field, they denied having made the mistake of giving the Hurricanes an extra down. But that was not what actually happened in the final series after Miami earned a first down at Tulane's 18 with 2:37 to go.

On first down, Foreman was stopped after a two-yard gain. On second down, Carney was almost trapped and he threw a sidearm incompletion in Foreman's direction. On third down, Foreman's spectacular one-handed catch of Carney's 11-yard pass was nullified by an illegal procedure penalty against Miami, and the Hurricanes were penalized five yards to the Tulane 21.

Thus it was third down and 13. Carney was spilled by Randy Lee for an 11-yard loss on a pass attempt at the Tulane 32 on the next play. Now it was fourth and 24. Then Carney overshot tight end Corrigan with a pass inside the Tulane five.

Their final chance apparently gone, the UM offensive players started off the field. But officials called them back. They said it was fourth and 24, when in fact it was fifth and 24.

Carney then dropped back and fired a post pattern line drive to split end Beckman, who made the catch at the goal a step in front of a defender and went into the end zone. Mike Burke kicked the extra point and the defense held Tulane in six plays.

In the Tulane dressing room after the game, assistant coaches kicked benches and lockers, screamed at newsmen, and sobbed openly. Players cried as they showered. But Coach Bennie Ellender was amazingly restrained.

He said he tried to get the attention of referee James Harper before the touchdown play but Harper "shook us off with his head. Certainly I'm disappointed and understandably shaken. Please don't talk to my boys. They've been through a bitter experience."

Curci claimed he did not really know what happened. "Our offense was coming off the field after Carney threw an incomplete pass. Then I heard somebody yell, 'You got another down.' Naturally, I sent the offense back in there."

"It was like God had answered my prayers," said offensive guard Golden (Pat) Ruel.

Witt Beckman (86) (far left) caught a 32-yard pass for a touchdown on a fifth down to beat Tulane.

Added Carney: "I thought we had used up our downs, so I ran off with the others. But somebody told me to go back in. I'm not going to argue with them when they tell me that. Actually, we planned a different play. But I felt that the primary receiver didn't hear the call in the huddle, so I checked off at the line of scrimmage and changed it to throw to Beckman."

In New Orleans, Tulane president Dr. Herbert E. Longenecker said he strongly suggested that Miami forfeit the game when he talked to UM vice-president Dr. Eugene Cohen and other school officials Saturday night and Sunday morning. He noted that since both schools were independent teams, there was no authority to which the matter could be appealed "except to the authority of good sportsmanship and institutional integrity."

Longenecker continued: "Had Tulane won a game under these conditions—a provable error of fact as distinct from a judgment situation—the alleged victory would have been rescinded by our own actions. And the game's outcome would have been reversed with the score reverting to that existing at the time of the illegal play. This is Tulane's policy."

UM president Stanford did not see the game because he was in Turkey. But athletic director McCoy put together a committee of university officials and board of trustees members on Sunday to review the facts and take action.

Research showed that this was not the first fifth down in college history. In 1940, Cornell received five downs against Dartmouth as the result of an oversight by official Red Friesell. Cornell scored the winning touchdown on the extra down with three seconds left in the Ivy League championship game. When game films revealed the referee had given an extra down to Cornell, the school forfeited.

Who was to blame in the Miami-Tulane game? According to news accounts, both Harper and John S. Duval, who was pressed into service during the game.

D. L. Claborn started the game as head linesman, but early in the second quarter he suffered a badly bruised left leg when several players ran into him. He could not continue, so the electric clock operator, Duval, was moved into action as head linesman. From a bench, Claborn worked the clock until halftime, then his injury became so painful he had to leave the stadium.

He was replaced by local high school official Ed Prime while

Duval continued as head linesman. Prime's presence made the scoreboard clock unofficial because it must be operated by an SEC official. Thus it was Duval who eventually awarded Miami a gift touchdown, although overall responsibility for the game belonged to Harper.

On Monday after the game, the UM announced it refused to forfeit. It got strong backing from the NCAA Rules Committee. McCoy said a "soul-searching" all-day review resulted in a decision that forfeiture would be inappropriate because Tulane still had a minute to score and change the outcome.

The UM contacted several national authorities for opinions, including University of Delaware athletic director Dave Nelson, secretary and historian of the National Football Rules Committee.

"Dave Nelson was violently opposed to our forfeiting," said McCoy. "He pointed out to us that a rule had been written after Cornell's fifth-down victory over Dartmouth in 1940 to preclude such future forfeit claims by any college team."

McCoy said he and UM officials had been worried about the image of the university. He said there was a considerable amount of early sentiment toward forfeiting.

"We're damned if we do and damned if we don't," said McCoy. "After delving into all the facts, we feel very strongly that our kids won the game within all the rules as the rules are written."

At Tulane, Longenecker had little comment. "I stated my position yesterday," he said. "There is nothing more for us to say."

Thus, twice in a year's time Curci was at the center of a major hassle, though he actually was innocent in both cases.

"How do I get into these things?" he asked facetiously. "I'm not a controversial guy."

When the season ended, Curci decided he had faced enough hassles. He quit and took the job at Kentucky, where John Ray had been fired after a 3-8 season. Kentucky was known then as "the coaching graveyard of college football." Ironically, he was leaving a school that was driving coaches to an early grave.

Curci was particularly intrigued that Kentucky was building a 58,000-seat stadium, was the only major school in the state, and was in the SEC. He also had been shocked by the fact that only 17,342 showed up at the Orange Bowl the week after Miami almost won at Notre Dame.

"The lack of support was eating me up," Curci said a few years later. "I had talked to John McKay when I was down there and he was at Southern California. I thought we faced similar situations. He said you have to go through a time until Dolphin-mania subsides. I came there at the lowest point. And there was no money. We had $50,000 to recruit, which was practically nothing. Maybe it was good that I left the University of Miami, because they got shocked about the program."

Some of his Miami players, however, said it was good riddance when Curci left. Senior defensive tackle Mike Barnes said, "I don't think the players looked up to him like they should a head coach." Ruel added: "I think he was a little inconsistent in his policies. Sometimes he'd say one thing and not quite follow through."

And running back Woody Thompson said he and about a third of the team would have transferred if Curci had remained.

"I'll tell you what used to happen on the practice field," Thompson said. "Jon Mirilovich (who went with Curci to Kentucky) would yell at me and berate me. He told me he didn't care if I ever played a minute. Mirilovich ruined a lot of good talent last year. He had bad rapport with the team. Actually, he was worse than Curci because he was making the decisions on who would play. I went to Curci to complain and he said he was sorry but he couldn't do anything about my situation because Mirilovich was running the offense and he (Curci) had no say-so about personnel."

Curci created yet another stir when UM coaches discovered he tried to talk 11 of the 30 players he already had signed at Miami into joining him at Kentucky. He told recruits Miami's athletic program was in danger of collapsing.

Curci eventually talked three into switching—Edison's Warren Bryant, who earned first-team All-American honors at Kentucky; Washington Gay of Edison; and Wendell LaPradd of South Dade.

"This is a strong ethical violation, but there's nothing we can do about it legally," said UM's recruiting chief Billy Proulx.

Daniels Facing
Unmuted Lions

Rubin Carter laughed mischievously as he recalled a scene in his neighbor's living room a few hours before a 1970 high school game between Fort Lauderdale's Stranahan and Nova.

"My next-door neighbor, Cathy Boykins, went to Nova," said Carter, a middle guard at Stranahan. "And she was telling me, 'Yeah, yeah, I'm from Nova.' It's supposed to be a real classy school. And so I said, 'Yeah, so what?' And she says, 'We going to beat y'all tonight.' And I said, 'Hey, y'all ain't going to beat us.'

"So she says, 'Yes we are,' and I say, 'Hey, I'm going to show you what I'm going to do to y'all football team.'"

Whereupon the 230-pound Carter moved into a four-point stance on his hands and knees next to the sofa. Bending his right arm, he flexed his muscles and made a fist. And with a thrust of his forearm, he knocked a leg off the sofa.

"And," Carter chuckled, "that was it."

Not quite. That night, Carter tackled two of Nova's quarterbacks so hard they had to be taken out of the game.

Carter also knocked the legs out from under dozens of ballcarriers during a stellar four-year career as a defensive lineman with Miami in the early 1970s. Concurrent with his career, offensive tackle Dennis Harrah was knocking down would-be tacklers in steamroller fashion. Both earned first-team All-American honors their senior year in 1974.

But to win against the Oklahomas, Nebraskas, and Notre Dames on the schedule, the Hurricanes needed many more Carters and Harrahs. They didn't have them, though, and the football program continued to spin wheels after Curci left.

Ernie McCoy hired Pete Elliott in November 1972, as assist-

Rubin Carter.

ant athletic director with one purpose in mind—for Elliott to succeed him as athletic director. McCoy also told Elliott that "if we get into an emergency, we have a damn good coach we can call on—you."

When Curci quit, Lee Corso of Louisville, who was a Miami Jackson High and Florida State quarterback, reportedly was considered to replace him. Both McCoy and Elliott made up lists of candidates, but McCoy's had only one name, Elliott's.

Less than 22 hours after Curci's departure, Elliott was persuaded to become coach. Elliott, 46, had been an All-American quarterback on Michigan's national champions in 1948. Though he only had a 45-60-1 career record at Nebraska, California, and Illinois, his California and Illinois teams played in the Rose Bowl.

At Illinois in the late 1960s, Elliott could have taken the easy way out during a slush fund scandal that led to his resignation. But he accepted responsibility for something that reportedly was going on without his knowledge. Since then, he had turned down several coaching opportunities and the athletic director's job at Illinois.

McCoy, 68, was persuaded to postpone retirement and remain as athletic director for another year. Meanwhile, Elliott put together a staff that included Nebraska's Carl Selmer as offensive coordinator, Oregon State's Bob Herndon as defensive coordinator, and Lambert Reed (the first black hired on a full-time

Dennis Harrah (71).

basis) as linebacker coach.

Selmer had been passed over as successor to Bob Devaney at Nebraska, which hired Tom Osborne. Herndon had worked under Elliott before, and Reed, who had rejected an offer from Curci two years earlier, had been coach at Miami's Killian High.

"I'm not here just to solve black problems," said Reed, whose trademark on the field was a striped Santa Fe railroad cap. "I'm here to make Miami a better football program."

Selmer was there to install the slot-I offense that Nebraska had used to win a pair of national championships. Coy Hall emerged as the No. 1 quarterback in spring practice, but he also emerged with a 30-day jail sentence on misdemeanor charges involving damage to a coed's car and a scuffle with campus police. He was ordered in Coral Gables Municipal Court to serve the first 15 days on weekends. Two days after his hearing, he starred in the spring game.

Elliott abandoned Curci's Pride Room and installed agility

Pete Elliott.

drills emphasizing running. The conditioning was needed because the 1973 schedule included Texas, ranked No. 1 preseason by *Sports Illustrated*; Oklahoma; Alabama; Notre Dame; Florida; and Florida State.

"We know it's not all going to be blue sky, but we expect to peek through the clouds a few times," said assistant coach Jim Walden. That was the first of many colorful statements the press quoted from Walden the next four years. They sought him out because Elliott and Selmer were so bland.

The first peek through the clouds came in Elliott's opening game, a 20-15 victory over fumble-prone Texas before about 30,000 in the Orange Bowl. That earned the Hurricanes a ranking for the first time since 1968—eighteenth in AP and nineteenth in UPI. After beating Florida State, 14-10, and losing at Oklahoma, 24-20, they advanced to sixteenth.

Yet a promising season quickly turned into a disappointing one starting with the Homecoming game in the Orange Bowl

Carl Selmer.

against West Virginia. The Hurricanes owned a 14-13 lead, had a first down and goal at the one, and were on the threshold of a 5-2 record that would earn them a television appearance two weeks later against Alabama.

But Kary Baker, who alternated at quarterback with Coy Hall, stood up an instant too long and lost a yard and a half. Silvio Cardosa could not score, and soon West Virginia had the ball with 1:43 to play and drove 95 yards to win, 20-14. Though the Hurricanes won the next week against a so-so Army team, 19-7, they staggered to the end of the season by losing to Alabama, 43-13, in a game that was not televised regionally or nationally; to Florida, 14-7; and to national champion Notre Dame, 44-0, in their worst loss since World War II. Elvis Peacock, Miami Central High's heralded running back, was a guest of the Hurricanes the night the Irish visited. It was no surprise when he signed with Oklahoma.

The 1974 season looked like an instant replay of 1973. Miami surprised Houston in the Astrodome, 20-3, and beat Tampa, 28-26, for a 2-0 start that earned a No. 16 ranking by AP and No. 12 by UPI. After a 3-0 loss to sixth-ranked Auburn, the Hurricanes won three of the next four for a 5-2 record and attracted interest from the Tangerine Bowl.

But again they stumbled in the stretch, the downfall beginning with an ankle injury to middle guard Carter and an embarrassing, 21-14, Homecoming loss to Florida State, which had dropped 19 straight.

That was just the start of problems. I-back Johnny Williams, disgruntled at being benched, charged in the press that the UM lacked leadership among players, that the coaches too easily forgave errors, and that the "old, grind-it-out plays" created a very predictable attack. Two days later, Baker was charged with grand larceny in an alleged theft of $249 from a federally funded summer job program. He had received two checks from the program but reportedly never had worked. He was placed in a pretrial intervention program because he had no previous record, and he attended meetings twice a week for three months and was ordered to organize a football clinic at Edison Park.

The next week, in a 28-7 loss to Alabama, fans booed Baker. But the Hurricanes held a postgame meeting and gave him a vote of confidence.

Miami closed out the season with a 14-7 victory over Syracuse and a 31-7 loss to Florida for a 6-5 record. A lack of depth, the UM's problem for years, was the main reason for another late-season swoon.

"Depth in college is not just a matter of back-up players," said Elliott. "It is having people who can play and who know they are going to play."

Miami did not have those people because it lost them in recruiting. Remember Coral Gables High's Neal Colzie and Ralph Ortega, linebackers who went to Ohio State and Florida, respectively? Both earned All-American honors in 1974. Remember Elvis Peacock of Central? He starred at Oklahoma.

From the high school senior class of 1974-75, the UM also lost such blue chippers as Herman Jones of South Dade and Leonard Mills of Killian to Ohio State, Elliott Walker of Jackson to Pittsburgh, and Reggie Kinlaw of Miami Springs to Oklahoma.

The Hurricanes did sign a blue-chip quarterback after the 1974 season, Clint Hurdle of Merritt Island, Florida, who was an all-state baseball player and honor student. But he never enrolled because he signed a pro baseball contract with the Kansas City Royals.

"Recruiting is the answer to winning," said Kichefski as he looked back in 1981 on his association with UM football since the 1930s. "Basically, all your coaching staffs are good everywhere, they have capable people. Through the years, we have been a long way from having the talent we needed. For 16 years, I did 80 percent of the recruiting."

Compounding the depth problem was the fact that the UM had trouble keeping the players it had. Of the 40 freshmen in the fall of 1970, only nine were still on the squad four years later.

The irony was that Miami continued to develop more than its share of pro prospects. Off the 1974 squad, All-American offensive tackle Harrah was drafted in the first round, running back Woody Thompson in the third, Carter in the fifth, offensive guard Joe Wysock in the fifth, and offensive tackle Bill Capraun in the seventh.

Late in the 1973 season, Elliott had said he intended to remain as coach "at least until my five-year contract runs out." But he said that before taking on the duties of athletic director when McCoy retired. On February 27, 1975, he resigned as coach to devote full time to his athletic director position. That reaffirmed the policy set five years earlier by the ad hoc committee on intercollegiate athletics, which stressed that the athletic director should not be a coach of a major sport.

Offensive coordinator Selmer, 49, was immediately named head coach and signed to a five-year contract at $30,000 a year. He was Miami's fifth head coach in six years.

Elliott denied there had been a tacit agreement made with Selmer two years earlier that he would be Elliott's successor. But the time of the coaching change—late February after most recruiting was completed—was the biggest surprise.

"I suspect that Carl Selmer will be the best of the five," Pope wrote in the *Herald*. "There were times when I felt that Pete was just too nice a guy to be head coach. He dreaded making decisions that would hurt anyone.... The time for a coaching switch was December, not the end of February. I don't infer deliberate deceit or misrepresentation. Only a certain tangle-footedness. And that old UM devil, indecision."

Most players said they did not see a problem in the transition since the UM did not bring in an outsider. And recruits said they had been forewarned.

The UM signed 30 players, 27 of them from Florida and only one—Hurdle—a quarterback. Most of the signees, though, were "leftovers" after the Reggie Kinlaws and Elliott Walkers went elsewhere. The exception was Ottis Jerome Anderson, a 6-1, 195-pound running back from Forest Hill High in West Palm Beach, where he averaged seven yards per carry as a senior.

Once again, Miami entered the 1975 season overscheduled but underdeveloped in depth. Selmer noted that there were 126 major-college football teams "and we may be better than at least 100 of them. But unfortunately we usually have to play the other 26 teams."

Added Stanford: "We're a bunch of Daniels venturing into the dens of unmuted lions."

Yet the coaches thought they had enough ammunition to platoon their entire offense. "We feel we have the depth all over to platoon the line and the backs," said offensive coordinator Herndon. In reality, there was not enough first-team material to cope with all the lions on the schedule.

Ottis Anderson shattered career rushing record.

Facing Georgia Tech and Big Eight powers Oklahoma, Nebraska, and Colorado, the Hurricanes lost their first four games to teams with a combined record of 18-2. It was little consolation when Selmer became the first losing coach to win the UPI Coach of the Week honor, which came after a 20-17 loss to top-ranked Oklahoma.

They beat Houston with 30 seconds left, 24-23, and beat Florida State with 13 seconds left, 24-22, on a Chris Dennis field goal for their only victories in a 2-8 season. (An eleventh game with Tampa had to be canceled when Tampa dropped football; no replacement could be found on the schedule.)

The Hurricanes should have been quitting while they were ahead. Since 1967, their early season record was 23-17 while their late-season record was 9-26 for an overall 32-43. They led Nebraska, 9-7, at the half before bowing, 31-16. They led Navy, 16-3, at Homecoming but lost, 17-16. That prompted Selmer to say, "Maybe by the third quarter we're too stereotyped."

The season ended on a frustrating, bitter note in the Orange Bowl as Florida posted a controversial, 15-11, victory. The Hurricanes dominated the game but failed to score on drives to the Gator 5, 22, 8, and 4. Late in the game, Miami players thought Henry Davis' knee touched the turf when he fielded a punt. They backed off and he ran 63 yards for the winning touchdown. Films showed a clip and an illegal block on the run.

Amidst the gloom, there was one bright hope for the future—Anderson, Miami's version of O. J. At the end of the season, he boasted: "I wanted to break every record here and to be the best they've ever had. I doubt I can break Archie Griffin's or Tony Dorsett's records, but if I get a line like they have I'll come close."

Anderson's older brother Marvin (Smokey) Anderson had been a star running back at West Palm Beach Roosevelt High, but he died in a accident when Ottis was nine. The goals he left unfulfilled were assumed by Ottis.

Anderson never got the line he dreamed of at Miami, though the blocking improved. But he did realize his dream of shattering the school rushing records. He led the Hurricanes in rushing his sophomore, junior, and senior seasons and became the school's all-time rushing leader with 3,331 yards, burying Eddie Dunn's record of 1,778 set from 1936-38.

"I run by instinct," said Anderson. "When I get the ball, I

just do it. I don't understand how I do it. My body just reacts. Sometimes I fake myself off my feet. I say, 'Hey, body, you want to push me? OK, do it.'"

Despite a classy home schedule that featured Oklahoma, Colorado, Houston, Navy, Notre Dame, and Florida, the UM averaged 21,000 fans. The day Miami and Notre Dame drew 24,944 (smallest crowd to see the Irish since World War II), Florida A&M and Bethune-Cookman drew 27,000 in Tallahassee.

Only two radio stations carried UM games—WINZ in English and WOCN in Spanish. There was no television highlights show and Channel 10 in Miami scrapped plans to carry the opening game from Georgia Tech live.

It is no wonder talk of the UM dropping football increased, but Stanford said there was no truth to it. "There are two reasons why the football program continues to be questioned," he said. "Neither generates from inside the university. First is the myth exploited by competitive talent recruiters; second is the inquisition from commentators and reporters asking about it."

Nevertheless, the questions continued as attendance dropped further and the record failed to improve. In 1976, only 1,500 showed up for the spring game at Miami-Dade Community College North, and attendance for five home games played on Saturday nights—Florida State, Duke, Texas Christian, Boston College, and Penn State—averaged only 16,290. That was the lowest since the 13,150 average in 1944. Only 6,866 season tickets were sold.

Meanwhile, Selmer did not endear himself with the media during his speech at the annual preseason press luncheon. Referring to the 21-14 loss to Florida State in 1974 which ended the Seminoles' 21-game losing streak, he said: "Nobody mentioned that our first four I-backs were out of the game (they were not). If it had been the Dolphins, it would have been all over the papers." He compounded the negative by suggesting that reporters mention UM attendance in the last paragraph instead of the first.

The season started with false hope and dancing in the end zone in a 47-0 rout of Florida State in the Orange Bowl. It was Bobby Bowden's second game as coach of the Seminoles. Anderson and wingback Larry Cain punctuated their touchdowns by doing the Funky Chicken in the end zone.

"We get together before bed check the night before the game and go over our choreography," said Cain. One dance was called

The Muscle. "All you do is flex your arms," said Cain. On another routine, called Rolling Six, Cain would kneel and roll the ball like dice. He also considered doing the splits but feared he would pull a hamstring.

Selmer did not disapprove of these actions which some thought were bush league. "I'm not going to stop anybody from doing it," he said. "I just ask that they don't spike the ball."

The *Herald* ran a page-one feature with a picture of Anderson dancing and slapping hands with quarterback E. J. Baker under the headline: "UM Campaign Promise: Chicken in Every End Zone."

Colorado coach Bill Mallory got a hold of a copy before the Hurricanes visited Boulder the next week and stuck it on the bulletin board in the Buffaloes' dressing room. "They ain't jigging in my damn end zone," he growled.

He was right. The Hurricanes were wallflowers at the dance. They never got close to the end zone in a 33-3 loss.

The next week, they returned to Big Eight country and played Nebraska, and for the second straight year they led the Cornhuskers at the half, this time 6-0, before tumbling. They held a 9-7 lead with 11 minutes left and had forced Nebraska to punt at the Miami 48 when the game turned around. UM coaches ordered a rush and defensive back Willie Jenkins flattened punter Randy Leesman, while officials ruled he did not touch the ball. Thus the Cornhuskers regained possession at the Miami 33, and they soon drove to a field goal. Vince Ferragamo later threw a 23-yard touchdown pass to seal a 17-9 victory.

After a 20-7 loss at home to lackluster Duke, the Hurricanes visited second-ranked Pittsburgh and its eventual Heisman Trophy winner Tony Dorsett. The defense contained Dorsett for a half, but the offense could not take the pressure off and fumbled five times. The Panthers romped, 36-19.

Selmer was so enraged that he made Anderson, running back Ken Johnson, and Baker carry a football with them at all times—including classes—the next week. Fumbles were not Miami's only offensive woes, though. Quarterback again was unsettled as Baker (no relation to Kary Baker), Frank Glover, and George Mason alternated and none assumed command. There were numerous delay-of-game penalties caused by snafus on the sideline and the huddle, and critics said the offense was too predictable and failed to utilize the receiving talents of Cain and Phil August.

And the dancing in the end zone stopped. "They had said they'd dance if we were ahead," said Selmer. "We haven't found ourselves ahead much."

The Hurricanes rebounded from the dead to thrash lowly Texas Christian, 49-0, and Boston College, 13-6, for a 3-4 record. Those were Selmer's last victories. With no letup on the schedule and no depth to meet it, the Hurricanes lost to Penn State, 21-7; Notre Dame, 40-27; Florida, 19-10; and Houston, 21-16.

Meanwhile, widespread discontent was growing among alumni and some players over what they considered to be Selmer's lack of positive leadership. The week before the Houston game, UM executive vice-president Dr. John L. Green, who was head of finance and oversaw the athletic program, decided that a coaching change was needed. He did it with the "advice and consent" of Stanford but without consulting Elliott. Green planned to inform the board of trustees of his decision on Monday after the game at Houston, then inform Selmer.

But the news leaked out and television stations reported early Friday evening that Selmer might be fired after the game. Thus Green decided he should call Selmer in Houston to tell him he "had been terminated" before he heard the news elsewhere. Selmer had gone with the team to watch a pro hockey game at The Summit, so Green paged him there to the phone and gave him the news.

"Everyone thought it was a crude way to handle things and I think John took a bad rap," said Stanford. "That's not the way John intended."

It marked the only time the UM has fired a football coach.

"What can I say?" said Selmer. "When you've been coaching as long as I have, nothing shocks you. But I'm surprised because I had no advance warning. I'd like to have had an opportunity to at least talk to the powers that be. Frankly, I don't think I had a super-fair chance. Most of the coaches I have I inherited. We played 'the world' and I never had a chance to choose a staff of my own. I would have made some changes in the staff at the end of this season, as much as I hated to, and without casting any aspersions on particular individuals."

As when Curci left for Kentucky, some players said "good

riddance'' to the coach. ''It's the best thing that could ever happen to the University of Miami,'' said Jenkins. ''He's not the man for this job. He's not head coaching material. He couldn't look the players in the face one to one. We have all this talent, but we didn't do anything.''

Several players promoted Walden as the next head coach. ''The concensus on this team is that everybody loves the man because he pulls for us,'' said linebacker Gregg Wallick. ''He gets us so psyched up on defense.''

When Selmer read Jenkins' and Wallick's comments the day after the Houston game, he went into a rage and charged Walden with being disloyal and promoting himself at Selmer's expense. The conflict between Selmer and Walden may have been inevitable because of the ineptitude of the offense contrasted to the competency of the defense headed by Walden, and because Walden's outspokenness filled a void left by Selmer's reserved manner.

''I'm not a showman,'' said Selmer. ''I didn't come here as a showman. Why should a head coach be put in a position where he has to outshine and show more magnetism than one of his assistants?

''I would go into a defensive meeting after a game to point out their mistakes as a slap on the wrist. It's like a father slaps a kid and the kid goes running to his mother. Jim Walden would tell the player, 'Don't listen to what he tells you. He thinks like an offensive coach.'''

Selmer later acknowledged he had a free hand to change assistants. But he said, ''I've learned a lot about human nature in two years. I've learned there are people in the world who'll step over you to help themselves and others who'll smile to your face, then go and talk behind your back.

''It hasn't been a rewarding experience, because in the process of it all, I feel I've lost a friend (Walden).''

Said Walden: ''I've tried to be the best defensive coach I could, and if I am guilty of anything, it was trying to provide this program with the best possible defense I could. If my personality offended anyone, I'm sorry. But that's the way I am and I'm too old to change it.''

Except for the one outburst, Selmer displayed restraint over the whole affair. He showed up for his final television highlights show (the program had been reinstated in 1976) and attended the annual Miami Touchdown Club banquet. Emcee Bill Bruce called Selmer a "realist" and added, "Carl has a card in his wallet that says, 'In case of accident, I'm not surprised.'"

Selmer, who later became an assistant at North Texas State and Kansas State, seemed to be the wrong man at the wrong time. "The football program is in need of new leadership," said Green. "We are committed to building a winning and appealing football team. We will go after a man that we think can accomplish that."

But who would want to become Miami's sixth head coach in the 1970s? Who would want to take over a program that had seen attendance dwindle to its lowest point in 30 years, that had seen recruiting fail to keep the blue-chip prospects in South Florida, that had suffered through eight losing seasons the previous nine years, that was being dwarfed by interest in the Dolphins, that was facing annual deficits of a million dollars?

Walden said he wanted it. So did longtime assistant Harold Allen, the ungrowly bear whose products included Bob Tatarek, Gene Trosch, Rubin Carter, Don Latimer, Mike Barnes, Gary Dunn, and current All-American Eddie Edwards. So did Dade County high school coaches Joe Brodsky, who had just directed Hialeah-Miami Lakes to the state title; Chris Vagotis of Killian;

Harold Allen, producer of numerous All-American linemen.

and Jim Thomas of Ransom-Everglades. The UM said thanks but no thanks.

It approached Ara Parseghian, who had retired as Notre Dame coach; Steve Sloan of Texas Tech; Pat Dye of East Carolina; Earl Bruce of Iowa State; Jim Stanley of Oklahoma State; Bud Moore of Kansas; Jackie Sherrill of Washington State, who removed himself by going to Pitt; Pitt assistant Joe Avenzzano; Vanderbilt's Fred Pancoast; and North Carolina's Bill Dooley, who nearly accepted.

Dooley drove to the Chapel Hill airport en route to accept the job, but minutes before boarding a plane to Miami he returned home to stay. The job then was offered to Brigham Young's LaVell Edwards, who also said no.

On December 27, Green found someone who would tackle the job, a man who had taken on so many recycling jobs he had the nickname The Garbage Man. He was Lou Saban, 55 years old, whose checkered career included coaching stints in college at Washington, Northwestern, Western Illinois, and Maryland and in the pros with Boston, Buffalo twice, and Denver. This was the

Don Latimer.

Eddie Edwards.

man who coached such standout running backs as O. J. Simpson, Floyd Little, and Cookie Gilchrist. Before they had played under Saban, none had gained 1,000 yards in a season as pros.

But this was also the man who stayed at the University of Cincinnati in 1976 as athletic director only 19 days.

Saban signed a six-year contract with Miami in the $50,000-a-year range and said, "Every job I've taken was not with a winner that worked its way down. This was the kind of challenge I wanted, although sometimes you can take on too much of a challenge."

Saban Builds A Foundation

Lou Saban became an expert in Mandarin Chinese during World War II. Cynics said that was appropriate for his job at the University of Miami because he would be taking over a program run like a Chinese fire drill.

The biggest gripe on the coaching staff had been money, or the lack thereof. One assistant said, "We never could get the money to film practices." Another said, "And just once I'd like to be able to take off on an emergency recruting trip without having to wait a week for a purchase order for my plane ticket."

As Walden departed for an assistant's job at Washington State (where two years later he became head coach), he said: "I feel like a man with his legs tied together when graded in the 100-yard dash. Too many people at Miami wanted to be Southern Cal without paying Southern Cal prices. Too many people here had delusions of grandeur. We were handicapped by a cheap-run program."

Ironically, in the early 1970s an unidentified middle-aged widow set aside $1 million in her will to help the UM football program—but she still is living. The money is to go into the school's general endowment fund with annual earnings of approximately $55,000 going each year to provide football scholarships. According to President Stanford, it is by far the biggest gift ever to UM football.

When Saban arrived, Green promised "total commitment," and mostly that meant money. Jim White was hired as promotions director, all practices were filmed, the weight room was remodeled and upgraded, the old dark green jerseys were shelved in favor of flashy orange jerseys with green trim and white numbers and white

Lou Saban.

pants. And more money was available for recruiting trips.

At spring practice, players respected Saban's knowledge of football and were impressed by his organization, efficiency, and authoritativeness. Saban said there would be no dancing in the end zone. "This shouldn't be a discotheque."

Saban also jolted his players and UM alumni and fans by his frankness. At halftime of the spring game, which drew 2,409 in the Orange Bowl, he grabbed the public address microphone and said, "We were a little sloppy in the first half, but you don't have to tell me about it. We know we have a lot of work to do, but somehow we're going to get it done. When we play Ohio State, we'll be ready to play."

At practice one day, as a receiver zigged when he should have zagged, Saban hollered: "Run straight like an arrow and not like a bow! Did you ever hear of Robin Hood? If he shot like that, we'd all be dead!"

At the annual Eaton Foundation dinner, Saban said: "There's no sense kidding you. I'm not going to tell you we've got a great future this fall, because I don't know. There are no miracles we can promise you."

A killer schedule did not frighten Saban. "I didn't know we open with Ohio State until after I talked a long time to Elliott and Green," he said. "But it's there and we're going to play it."

Saban had only 58 players on scholarship that spring. And an indication of how poorly recruiting had gone before Selmer's last year was the fact that only four players from that class were listed among the top 48 players on the depth chart.

On March 15, Saban dropped another bombshell. He announced that 12 scholarships, most belonging to sophomores, would not be renewed. It was like a pro coach announcing the cuts before the opening game of the season, but college coaches never did such things. If they did drop a scholarship, they did it quietly. Yet Saban called a press conference.

"These are not runoffs," he said. "This has nothing to do with numbers. There are people here who absolutely can't play. Why tell a kid he'll have a chance to make the club when I know he can't. There's no way we'll pull the wool over a kid. We'll tell it like it is."

Shortly after spring practice ended, sophomore tight end Mike McNichols died of injuries from an automobile accident at a party at Virginia Beach near Key Biscayne.

That was the first of three incidents to jolt the team before the Ohio State game. In early July, Saban underwent double coronary bypass surgery in Cleveland to correct two blockages in the arteries leading to his heart. He said the problem had existed for a few years.

He returned to work August 8. Three weeks later, his wife, Lorraine, committed suicide by hanging herself in the basement of their suburban Buffalo, New York, home. Mrs. Saban, who had diabetes and had been despondent over recent health problems, had been packing household goods in preparation for joining Lou in Miami.

"I'm going to have to stand tall," said Saban as he returned in time for the final week of preseason practice. He did stand tall, and so did his team in the opening game before 86,287 at Ohio State, the largest crowd ever to see a game involving the UM.

Woody Hayes' Buckeyes were expected to win, 40-0, but they escaped with a 10-0 triumph.

Saban was pleased with the effort, but he did not want the players to know it. He asked freshman split end Pat Walker why he dropped passes on Miami's first three possessions. "He said it was a lack of concentration," Saban said. "But 18-year-old guys go to war. That's what this is, miniature war…. I don't want them to play well and come in second."

The next two games also were on the road, a 10-6 loss against Georgia Tech and a 23-17 upset victory over Florida State as the defense badgered standout quarterbacks Jimmy Jordan and Wally Woodham and forced several mistakes.

Anderson gained only 48 yards in 18 carries against the Seminoles and invoked the wrath of Saban. "O. J., if you ever in your life perform the way you did against this team, you will never put on a University of Miami uniform again as long as I'm coaching."

Anderson recalled: "He told me I could be one of the best he has ever had. He said, 'I stayed on all the others, so don't expect me to lighten up on you.' He said I wasn't running the way I was capable of running. I didn't run to break anything. I just ran to get yardage. I'd get six yards and fall down."

For the home opener against a nondrawing card, Pacific, the university sent 30,000 free passes to alumni. An estimated 12,000 to 15,000 took advantage of the offer and the game drew about 30,000. Miami won, 24-3.

The Hurricanes dumped Kansas, 14-7, the next week for a 3-2 record. But when they were upset by Texas Christian, 21-17, the following week at Fort Worth, they never recovered to win another game. Saban also decided it was time to go with younger players and to tighten his discipline.

Freshmen Ken McMillian and Chris Hobbs moved into the starting spots at quarterback and halfback with Anderson, a junior, at fullback. But Saban benched McMillian just before the Homecoming game with Tulane because he missed the team bus. And the week of a visit to highly ranked Alabama, he suspended All-American middle guard Don Latimer for talking back to assistant coach Harold Allen in practice.

By midseason, five players had quit the team to either spend more time on studies or to drop out of school. That brought to 26 the number of players who had quit or been dropped from the squad since Saban had become coach.

The TCU setback started a losing streak of eight straight that continued until the third game of the 1978 season. With freshmen getting more and more playing time, the Hurricanes closed out 1977 by losing to Penn State, 49-9; Tulane, 13-10; Alabama, 36-0; Florida, 31-14; and Notre Dame, 48-10.

Saban knew the two most important ways to turn the program around were recruiting and putting fans in the Orange Bowl. After the 1977 season, he and his staff went on an unprecedented—for the UM—recruiting blitz of the entire East Coast and Midwest. Opposition recruiters invoked Saban's wrath by telling players he would not stay at Miami.

"Anybody who says that is out of his head," countered Saban. "I came here because I felt the University of Miami deserved more than it had gotten from its football program, and because it is a great place in a hundred ways, including all the people so anxious to help us. I am going to stay, of course, and we are going to get the job done."

Saban and his staff investigated more than 800 prospects, about 100 per coach, and they visited or talked to nearly 300. They all became veritable Henry Kissingers in all their travels.

"I don't know how many cities I've been to," said Saban. "Some I didn't want to go to. Like Toronto." A blizzard forced the Pittsburgh airport closed, so he had to fly to Toronto and Buffalo and rent a car to get to his destination.

The most traveled assistant was jovial and personable Bill Trout, a former UM lineman from Key West. "I felt like a Fuller Brush salesman," he said. "Lou had had the heart operation, and he had left a few other teams, so the questions I'd get from kids' parents were just brutal. 'Is Miami going to continue football? Is Saban going to stay around a while? Is Saban going to LIVE?'"

On the first day recruits could sign the national letter of intent, UM coaches landed 27 of the 28 they had signed to the state letter of intent binding only among Miami, Florida, and Florida State. That was a school record, and the bonanza included six Class AAAA first-team All-State players, also a record: Lester Williams, the nation's most highly sought lineman; Larry Brodsky; David Jefferson; Mark Richt; Chris Duffy; and Mike Rodrigue. Eventually, Miami signed the maximum 30 players, 19 of them from Florida.

That class, perhaps the best ever recruited at UM, included quarterback Jim Kelly of Pennsylvania, offensive tackle John Canei of West Virginia, defensive end Tim Flanagan of Virginia, defensive back Fred Marion from under the Gators' noses at Gainesville, defensive tackle Bob Nelson of Maryland, running back Mark Rush of Fort Lauderdale Stranahan, offensive tackle David Stewart of New York, tight end Mark Cooper of Miami Killian, offensive lineman Bob Hays of Ohio, and offensive lineman Frank Frazier of Tampa. All of them would play significant roles in the program's improvement.

Meanwhile, Elliott resigned as athletic director to join Bud Wilkinson's new staff with the St. Louis Cardinals. But before he left, Woody Hayes came to town as a favor for Elliott and was roasted at a fund-raising dinner that netted the scholarship program $50,000. Saban took on the added duties of athletic director, a move he later regretted because of the demands for raising funds, and the administrating detracted from recruiting and coaching. He was the university's fifth athletic director in 15 years.

Saban also regretted the remarks he made in the spring of 1978 over an incident that had anti-Semitic overtones. In fact, he almost resigned after the remarks produced a flurry of protest to his and other university offices.

The incident involved three football players—quarterback Jody Myers, linebacker Jim Pokorney, and walkon linebacker Mark Wittorf—and a 22-year-old man dressed in prayer garb, on his way to Passover services. The players threw him into a lake on campus, claiming he verbally provoked them.

Saban had not read the security police report of the incident when a reporter called for his reaction. "The whole thing sounds like a nice fiasco to me," said Saban. "Getting thrown in the lake? Sounds like fun to me."

As protests mounted, Saban amended his comments. "I wish to make it clear that I was totally unaware of any religious issues involved. I thought the incident to be simply a case of college men in a scuffle. Had I been aware of any religious implication or known of the seriousness of the matter, I would never have taken the attitude as quoted."

According to President Stanford, Saban told Green he was seriously considering leaving because of the incident. "We met in my office and talked him into staying," Stanford said.

At an appeals hearing, Myers and Pokorney won a reprieve to remain on the squad. Wittorf, already on strict disciplinary probation for a previous assault, was suspended for a year.

That spring, the Hecht Athletic Center's offices and facilities were being expanded thanks to a $1 million gift from the family of the late Isadore Hecht, owner of Flagler Dog Track. Actually, the whole football program should have been signboarded: Construction Under Way.

An 11-station radio network was set up, marking the first time since 1972 that games would be carried outside South Florida. WCIX, Channel 6, agreed to telecast all five road games, and ABC said it would televise the Florida State game from the Orange Bowl on a regional basis. And Saban reconstructed the offense by switching from the pro set to the veer.

But once again, a lack of depth was crucial. Only six players were left from the 19 signed by Selmer and his staff in 1976.

"It's going to be a tough year," Saban said. "But we're on the right course. Of 55 players who were on the field this spring, perhaps 25 can get the job done."

And once again, quarterback was an unsettled position. At the UM, there were usually three quarterbacks at any time after the George Mira era—one departing, one coming, and one playing. Myers quit school during the summer and E. J. Baker was moved to wide receiver. When McMillian hurt ribs before the opening game at Colorado, Saban went with freshman Rodrigue, who had earned All-State honors as a defensive back.

Miami lost, 17-7, then dropped its home opener to Florida State, 31-21. But Anderson gave Saban the sign he was looking for in his first run against the Seminoles. He broke a tackle and went 80 yards for a touchdown, almost twice as far as he had run in one play in three years at Miami.

The youth movement continued as Saban took 18 freshmen to Kansas and the Hurricanes put their running game together in a 38-6 rout.

Then came a trip to nineteenth-ranked Auburn. Veteran UM observers may point to the 22-21 victory at the end of the season over Florida as the game that "turned the program around," or the 26-10 upset at Penn State in 1979. But it was the Auburn game that set the stage for those triumphs.

Not only did the Hurricanes defeat a ranked team for the first time since the 1973 opener against Texas, but they did it in an uncharacteristic manner—driving the length of the field to win, 17-15, on Danny Miller's field goal of 24 yards with six seconds left after allowing Auburn to go ahead with less than two minutes left.

"What you're talking about is character," said Saban. But the character sought by Saban would fluctuate in 1978. Every time the Hurricanes took three steps forward, they took two backwards.

The week after beating Auburn, they fell behind, 24-0, in the first half at Georgia Tech. They dominated the second half but lost, 24-19.

"We are constantly fighting for respectability—on the road, at home, and in the community," said Saban. "This is something that engulfs us. After we beat Auburn, we were something and somebody. People were starting to talk about us. Then, bingo, within a period of 30 minutes, it reverses itself."

The next week, Saban dismissed starting offensive guard Larry Pfohl because of damage he caused to his apartment and to an Atlanta hotel room.

Miami bounced back from the Georgia Tech loss with a 17-16 victory at home against Utah State, then bowed, 20-0, at Notre Dame. At Tulane, the UM had a first down at the nine with 38 seconds left, but three incompletions and a sack of Rodrigue thwarted the drive and the Hurricanes lost, 20-16.

After the game, McMillian said the team might benefit from a new quarterback and questioned his ability to motivate the offense. Saban stuck with Rodrigue, an option quarterback.

Six freshmen started the next week against San Diego State and the Hurricanes launched a three-game winning streak, 16-14. They finished by beating Syracuse, 21-9, and Florida, 22-21, for a 6-5 record that was only their second winning season in a decade.

The victory over the Gators was the first since 1970, and the three-game winning streak was the first since 1966. Anderson gained 149 yards in the game for a season total of 1,266 yards, marking the first time a UM back surpassed 1,000 in a year.

Meanwhile, defensive tackle Don Smith, a 6-5, 252-pound senior from Palm Harbor, Florida, was named to two All-American first teams, giving the UM five All-American defensive linemen in six years. Smith also was a first-round pick of the Atlanta Falcons.

Though the season ended upbeat on the field, it was still downbeat at the gate. The Hurricanes drew an average of only 20,978 for four home games. That ranked seventy-sixth among 139 Division 1A schools. And it was a decline of nearly 9,000 per game from the previous year, when Notre Dame and Florida visited.

Saban was no tunnel-vision jock. He read political history and was asked to run for Congress while coaching the Buffalo Bills. But he wondered if he would ever see light at the end of the tunnel for UM football. In frustration over the failure of attendance to increase and over the huge athletic department deficit, he stunned even his own staff by quitting on January 4, 1979, to become head coach at the United States Military Academy in West Point, New York.

Saban had called West Point a few days earlier on behalf of one of his Miami assistants who was interested in the head job at Army. West Point officials said they were not interested in hiring an assistant, so Saban asked them if they might be interested in him. Saban also was known to have applied for the vacant job with the New York Giants.

On a Wednesday night, Saban told Green he was serious about the West Point job and would go there for an interview. Green met in emergency session with the board of trustees that night and the trustees reaffirmed a strong commitment to the football program, noting that the deficit for men's athletics had dropped from $1 million to $600,000. (That figure later proved to be inaccurate as the deficit surpassed $1 million.)

Saban accepted the Army job the next morning without notifying UM officials. Green learned of the decision only when Miami's sports information director, George Gallet, phoned West Point publicist Bob Kinney to find out whether Saban's negotiations had been completed. West Point officials did not seek permission to talk to Saban, but Green orally released him from the four years remaining on a $50,000-a-year contract.

"The General called me, but only after Saban had gone to Army," Stanford recalled later. "I don't think it would have been good to keep him because his morale would have been down, but if I had to do it over, I would have asked West Point to pay for his unfinished contract."

Why would Saban suddenly jump ship when it seemed to be rising from the depths of despair?

"Some people like to rebuild cars, I like to rebuild football programs," he said. "I thought I had done all I could do at Miami. I know it casts me in a suspicious light. I hate sounding like a hypocrite. But times change. Things change. I can't explain. It's personal. I wouldn't say it's my health."

Paul Massey, assistant athletic director who was named acting athletic director when Saban quit, said Saban showed no signs of dissatisfaction. "He ran his own ship here. Whatever he wanted, John Green gave to him."

But Green would be leaving the UM to go into the real estate business in California in a few months, though that was not known publicly at the time of Saban's resignation.

Reaction varied, some players saying they felt betrayed, *Herald* columnist Edwin Pope calling Saban a quitter and deserter, and Green praising Saban for moving the program forward.

"He said he'd be with us all four years," said running back Mark Rush, a member of the heralded 1978 recruiting class. "He said we're the guys Miami is looking for. He was looking for us to take them to the national championship. Then he turns around and leaves. Yes, I feel betrayed."

But Rush and other players did not think it was the end of the world. "He made the program what it is," said defensive end Barry Gonzalez. "It's not going to change that much. It'll hurt, but not tremendously." Added Rush: "We still have a good team. If everyone keeps together we'll be OK. He got us together and got us believing in him. If we can't do it without him, we couldn't have done it with him."

Pope's reaction was similar to that of many fans. In a column headlined "Make Coach Contracts Go BOTH Ways," he wrote: "Let the NCAA mandate clauses in all head-coaching contracts holding those coaches liable for the part of the contract they forfeit by quitting to take another job. Colleges have to pay off coaches they fire before contracts end, don't they?" He said blame must be shared by West Point, which "is supposed to be in the business of developing responsibility rather than encouraging flight from it."

Green, who had handpicked Saban for the job two years earlier, was not bitter. "We all know what Lou Saban has done for the university in two years and I am in no way resentful of Lou's decision.... I don't think this calls for re-evaluation. We've turned a corner. We're in a situation where Lou has done the most difficult task, and the person coming in will be able to build on this foundation. We're in this thing for keeps. This is not a fly-by-night operation. I and the board of trustees are committed to this on a longtime basis.''

As Green and others at the university believed, few people could have accomplished for the UM what Saban did. He made it possible for Miami to develop a program which Howard Schnellenberger would have an interest in heading.

Saban stayed at Army one year, then went to work for George Steinbrenner, first to oversee refurbishing of his horse race track near Tampa, then, in 1981, to be president of the New York Yankees.

In the midst of his year at Army, Saban admitted he missed the UM but declined to elaborate on his reasons for departing. ''It would only hurt Howard,'' he said. ''I want Miami to succeed. I realize the difficulty they still have in the process. It will just take a lot of work and time.''

In his office at West Point, there was a ragged, deflated football on a table. A friend had given it to him as a memento of their Third Regimen pickup team in the Army in 1944. Saban, who has a wry sense of humor, picked it up and said, ''I'm going to leave it like this, because it's a comparison to the guy holding it.''

Schnellenberger Builds A Champion

When Howard Schnellenberger moved into his office at the UM early in January 1979, he probably found curtains put up by Fran Curci, rugs laid by Pete Elliott, pictures hung by Carl Selmer, and furniture put in by Lou Saban. It seemed there was always a moving van out in front of the Hecht Athletic Center.

But Schnellenberger vowed to stick around a long time after the paint dried.

"I would be very happy if this were the last stop for me, because if it were, that would mean I'd be successful," he said. "A lot of people retire down here. Why not me?"

He also made it clear he intended to clean house. "I want to put my personal stamp on everything, because over the next five, six, seven, or eight years it's going to be Howard Schnellenberger's football program. I certainly don't want it to reflect anyone else after a period of time."

Green had approached Schnellenberger, who was recommended by intermediaries, a few hours after Saban's resignation was announced. Though the names of Arkansas' Lou Holtz and Washington's Don James were mentioned prominently in a meeting with the executive committee of the board of trustees, the only candidates interviewed were Schnellenberger and former Saban assistants. Three days after Saban left, Schnellenberger, 44, signed a five-year contract with a salary comparable to the package given Saban ($50,000 a year plus an estimated $30,000 in benefits including a television highlights show).

"Deep inside, I had an ambition to be a college coach all the time," said Schnellenberger, who pronounces his name "Snellenberger" with the "ch" silent.

Howard Schnellenberger interviewed at the Peach Bowl.

After playing one year ahead of Paul Hornung at Louisville's Flaget High, Schnellenberger wanted to go to Notre Dame but the Irish did not want him. He intended to sign with the UM in 1952 but Paul (Bear) Bryant offered a scholarship and he chose Kentucky, where he made the AP All-American first team as an end in 1955.

Following two years of pro football in Canada and a year in the United States Army, he began his coaching career on the staff of Blanton Collier at Kentucky in 1959. Don Shula also was on the staff. Schnellenberger moved on to Alabama in 1961 and helped Bryant produce national champions in 1961, 1964, and 1965. He recruited and coached Joe Namath and Ken Stabler and recruited Steve Sloan before going back to work under George Allen with the Los Angeles Rams from 1966-69. He joined Shula's Dolphin staff in 1970 and was top offensive coach on the 1972 Super Bowl champions.

Schnellenberger was head coach of the rebuilding Baltimore Colts in 1973 and went 4-10. After an 0-3 start the next season, owner Robert Irsay stormed the sideline during a game and demanded Schnellenberger play young Bert Jones ahead of Marty Domres. Schnellenberger told him to clear out and was fired because of it. He returned to the Dolphins and remained there until Green called from the UM.

"He's has a great football mind," said Bryant. "He has guts. He's real class." Added Shula: "He's a fine organizer, he has good knowledge of the game and he does a good job in preparation and presentation. He's an excellent coach and an excellent person."

Pope called the selection of Schnellenberger "an inspired choice. They needed a coach with winning literally built into him.... Coming off the Dolphin staff, Schnellenberger will not be traumatized by the eminence of South Florida's pro club. The problem is basic. The University of Miami must co-exist with the Dolphins because the Dolphins are not going to leave. The UM can co-exist by winning. End of problem."

Even Super Fan Al Minter, the controversial former South Florida radio and television sports commentator, hailed Schnellenberger's hiring. "He's a godsend to the program," said Minter, a UM alumnus who played freshman football. "The board of trustees couldn't have found him if he wasn't sitting on their doorstep."

A workhorse by nature, Schnellenberger arose at 5:30 a.m., was at his desk before seven and, if he didn't spend the night on his office couch, seldom got home before 9:00 p.m. the first few months at UM. He immediately began to fulfill his vow to put his personal stamp on everything.

He hired Earl Morrall, the All-Pro from the Dolphins and Colts, to be quarterbacks coach. He helped talk Charley Thornton, assistant athletic director at Alabama, into filling the athletic director position that had been vacant since Saban left. He named longtime UM recruiting chief Billy Proulx administrative assistant. He hired a new bilingual secretary (Maria Fernandez), who spoke English and Spanish, all the better to communicate in Dade County where there are more than a half-million Latins. He made 200 speaking engagements before the opening game. He helped convince UM officials to allocate $200,000 of the $708,000 in funds to upgrade campus residences toward refurbishing a three-story dormitory to house football players. (The players had been moved out of the building and scattered around campus in 1973 because of noise, rowdy parties, and damage to the building.) With the efforts of promotions man Jim White, he arranged for his television show to be carried via satellite on 250 cable stations from Juneau, Alaska, to Tucumcari, New Mexico.

Schnellenberger also replaced Walt Pomerko, who had been a UM trainer for 25 years, and Jimmy Hodges, who had been equipment manager for 20 years. The newcomers were Mike O'Shea, who had been with the Colts six years, and Terry Knight, a member of the National Equipment Managers Association. Pomerko became trainer for UM minor sports, and Hodges found a job in the UM cafeteria. There was even a new team physician, Dr. Joseph Kalbac, in place of Dr. Charles Burbacher, who had served the Hurricanes since 1937.

Then Schnellenberger unveiled the piece de resistance: a $4.8 million, 42,000-seat on-campus stadium which he said would be the answer to the financial problems and would be ready for the 1980 season.

"I'm not just optimistic; I know it's going to happen," said Schnellenberger. "I think we can find a donor for the entire amount and I expect that to happen pretty soon."

When the spring game drew 5,096 at Tropical Park, which is less than two miles from campus, Schnellenberger knew the UM needed its own stadium "with its own emotion. We can't sell enough season tickets in the Orange Bowl because people know they can buy on the moment. We could build a strong ticket-sale base in our own stadium, including preferential seating for donors. Every successful program has this."

Suddenly, the Hurricane football program was on the upbeat again. But what would UM football be without controversy and resignations? The resignation came May 14 from Thornton, who had been athletic director for only 10 weeks. Thornton returned to his job at Alabama, citing the physical problems of his wife, Doris. Shortly after he was hired, she fell off the roof of their home in Tuscaloosa and was hospitalized and physical complications developed.

"I really hate it because Miami has had so much turnover already," said Thornton, the fifth athletic director since 1970. "I am embarrassed by it, but this has nothing to do with the University of Miami.'' Thornton's main accomplishment—and an important one—was to arrange for ABC regional television coverage of the opening game in the Orange Bowl against Louisville, a $200,000 windfall for the program.

Thornton was quickly replaced by associate athletic director Dr. Harry Mallios, whose association with the UM went back three decades. Known as ''The Scooter,'' he had starred at fullback on two bowl teams in the early 1950s. He had been a professor in the school of education and had been the athletic department's academic advisor for several years.

The controversy? On June 22, Schnellenberger announced that McMillian's scholarship would not be renewed because he had become a disciplinary problem. He had slipped from No. 1 to 5 on the quarterback depth chart in spring practice.

Schnellenberger said McMillian had been late for meetings, had refused to attend a meeting, did not perform 100 percent, and had been involved with a problem with the dean of students, in which a woman student made charges of a verbal assault.

''Just tell the people I'm not guilty of anything,'' said McMillian, who had been suspended from one game his freshman year by Saban for missing the team bus. Regarding criticism of his playing, McMillian said: ''It's real tough being a black quarterback at Miami. They play racial games here.''

In the aftermath, McMillian transferred to Bethune-Cookman, and UM alumnus Chuck Foreman, an All-Pro with the Minnesota Vikings, cut his ties with his alma mater because he thought the McMillian affair had racial overtones.

But Foreman patched up his differences with the school in 1980 after a meeting with assistant coach Hubbard Alexander, who asked him to help recruit. Then he met with Schnellenberger and ''he satisfied my curiosity,'' said Foreman. ''The University of Miami has a lot of potential. Their success story has been a long time coming. Miami could be a big college football town. It's possible they could bring a national championship here if they get some support.''

Schnellenberger's first team needed moral support just to survive a demanding schedule. The Hurricanes became known as the Jet Lag Kids as they traveled more miles—a total of 28,000—than any team in the history of college football. In comparison,

Florida traveled 6,850 and Florida State 5,564 miles in 1979. The previous unofficial record was about 21,000 miles logged by Grambling in 1976.

Playing seven of its 11 games on the road, the UM visited Tallahassee twice to face FSU and Florida A&M, San Diego State, Buffalo to play Syracuse, Penn State, Alabama, and Tokyo to play Notre Dame in the Mirage Bowl.

"Join the Hurricanes and See the World," was the season's theme.

Schnellenberger installed a pro-veer offense that featured the running attack of the veer and the passing attack of the pros. Rodrigue was named the top quarterback at the start of the season ahead of Jim Kelly and Mark Richt, the latter ending up being redshirted. The offense sputtered for a half before uncranking for a 24-12 victory over Louisville in the season opener in the Orange Bowl. The game drew 41,129, the largest crowd in six years, despite a threat of rain and no local blackout of ABC's regional telecast.

In 1980 Jim Kelly became the best UM quarterback since George Mira.

But it was a papered figure because 30,000 attended for free on coupons distributed by Burger King. Nevertheless, it was a spirited start for the era of Schnellenberger.

The honeymoon ended quickly, however, as Orange Bowl-bound Florida State swamped the Hurricanes, 40-23. They returned home to win a 6-0 yawner over Louisiana Tech in the rain before 20,069, many of whom had showed up to see the school honor former UM student Sylvester Stallone, the Hollywood star of the movie *Rocky*.

Then came the ballyhooed meeting with Florida A&M, a game FAMU had sought for many years and one which the UM wished it had not agreed to play. It was scheduled as a two-game, home-and-home series, with FAMU the host for the first game. The series marked the first meetings ever between FAMU, a predominantly black school run by the state, and one of Florida's major football schools.

The idea for the series originated from FAMU coach Rudy Hubbard and Elliott in letters written in 1976. The first game was initially set for the Tangerine Bowl in Orlando. But FAMU decided it wanted the game in Tallahassee at FSU's Doak Campbell Stadium, a move the UM strongly opposed because it thought the game would draw better in Orlando. President Stanford intervened and said the UM would honor the original agreement allowing FAMU to pick its home site.

The Rattlers, the defending NCAA Division 1AA champions, looked at the game as a crusade in which they could prove they could play with the big boys. The UM, on the other hand, figured it had everything to lose.

The Hurricanes dominated the early moments with two long drives, but both stalled, and they managed only a 3-0 lead. Instead of being down by two touchdowns, the Rattlers had confidence they could stay on the field. As their running game ripped off 297 yards against a defense that had been stingy against the run, the Rattlers scored a surprising, 16-13 victory before 34,743.

It was a bitter loss for Miami, which had a first down at the three late in the game and failed to score. With 27 seconds left on fourth down, Schnellenberger elected to go for a tie but Danny Miller's 20-yard field goal missed.

UM players, particularly blacks, took the loss hard as many sobbed openly in the locker room. Several observers believed the setback affected morale enough to cost the Hurricanes a 31-20 defeat the next week at San Diego State, a team they should have beaten.

Yet the lack of a balanced attack also was a factor in Miami's 2-3 start for the season. The running game was virtually non-existent, as it produced only 69 yards against Louisville, 101 against FSU, 98 against Louisiana Tech, 115 against FAMU, and 117 against San Diego State. Facing Boston College the next week, Miami rushed for only 82 yards but Pat Walker caught a 58-yard touchdown pass from Rodrigue and Miller kicked two field goals in a 19-8 victory before only 15,013 at the Orange Bowl.

Against Syracuse, the running game netted 88 yards in a 25-15 loss. But Schnellenberger found a ray of sunshine late in the cold, dreary afternoon at Buffalo when redshirted freshman Kelly swiftly drove the Hurricanes for a touchdown, scoring on a 39-yard pass to Walker in the fourth quarter. That gave UM coaches an idea: Why not start Kelly the following week at Penn State, a school which had recruited the Pennsylvania native as a linebacker? After all, Miami had nothing to lose in the game the Nittany Lions were favored to win by at least four touchdowns.

The plan clicked as a poised Kelly hit 18 of 30 passes for 280 yards and three touchdowns in a stunning, 26-10 victory before 77,532 fans at Beaver Stadium. The Hurricanes had driven for a touchdown, recovered the ensuing kick, and scored a field goal for a 10-0 lead before the Nittany Lions ran a play. Moreover, the Hurricanes won while rushing for only 66 yards and starting three freshman recruits—tight end Andy Baratta and defensive end Greg Zappala, both Pennsylvanians recruited by Penn State, and center Don Bailey of Hialeah-Miami Lakes.

Flanker Jim Joiner caught six passes for 177 yards and two touchdowns. And the defense, which blanked the Nittany Lions in the second half, was led by linebacker Scott Nicolas (26 tackles) and end Tim Flanagan (25 tackles). The victory evened the record at 4-4, but more importantly it earned Miami a shot on national television the following week at top-ranked Alabama.

The Hurricanes again went with Kelly and their virtual pass-on-every-down offense, but Bryant had scouted Miami well. Also, Kelly suffered a rib injury in the first quarter and never returned in the 30-0 loss.

A few hours after the game, it was sayonara Tuscaloosa,

hello Tokyo. But why go 7,000 miles to play a "home" game that originally was scheduled for the Orange Bowl?

The idea began several months earlier at Notre Dame. For years, a Japanese automobile firm had been sponsoring a game named after one of its models (Mirage) and featuring American college football teams, and it coveted a visit by Notre Dame. Football was only about a dozen years old in Japan, only a few high schools played it, and there were no pro teams. But the Japanese nevertheless were intrigued by the game and its pagentry and bands. In fact, the Miami and Notre Dame bands received equal billing with the football teams throughout the week, as they made numerous appearances at parades and concerts.

Notre Dame balked at moving one of its home games to Tokyo but wondered about seeking a switch with Navy, which played the Irish at neutral sites every other year, or with Miami, which had drawn poor crowds when the Irish visited in recent years. *South Bend Tribune* sports editor Joe Doyle mentioned this in a column, and this book's author picked it up for a story in the *Herald*.

Elliott, then the athletic director, originally shrugged the idea off because he did not want to move any more games out of town. That would mean Miami would have only four home games for the second straight year, hardly a way to attract more fans. But Saban was intrigued by the thought of playing a game in Tokyo—it would be a recruiting tool, it would earn national publicity, and it would generate more revenue than a game in the Orange Bowl. Mirage Bowl sponsors not only picked up the UM's $75,000 in travel expenses but guaranteed each team $200,000.

In the end, the trip may have generated publicity, earned money, and been an educational experience for players and band members, but it was no way to prepare to play Notre Dame; never mind the fact that Dan Devine's Irish were "struggling" with a 6-4 record.

At 5:45 a.m. on Tuesday before the game, 55 players; 200 band members; and 71 coaches, school officials, and members of the media boarded a Japan Air Lines 747 jumbo jet at Miami International Airport. But the plane fumbled the opening kickoff, so to speak. There was a flat tire, which meant all 326 bleary-eyed passengers had to leave the plane and return to the terminal. The flight finally left nearly two hours late at 7:32 a.m.

Eight hours later, following a very bumpy descent around

mountains, the plane stopped to refuel at Anchorage, Alaska. To keep the players' blood circulating and avoid cramps, Schnellenberger ordered his team to walk a mile and a half through the terminal.

The Anchorage-to-Tokyo leg lasted another eight hours, then it took three hours to get through customs and bus 25 miles from the airport through rush-hour traffic in Tokyo, where it was Wednesday afternoon. Total travel time from UM campus to hotel room: 24½ hours.

Notre Dame was already there and had grabbed up the better of the practice fields, though that was not saying much. One field had a blade of grass every few inches, the other resembled a giant mud pie.

"It looks like a reclaimed rice paddy," groaned Schnellenberger as he wiped rain from his brow. The weather was dreary, drizzly, and 40 degrees every day the teams were in Tokyo.

The game, which drew 62,674 to the Olympic Stadium, was no contest. Hurricane backs suffered from fumbleitis and Kelly suffered another rib injury and departed early. The Irish won, 40-15.

As the Hurricanes headed for their return flight, UM radio announcer Ron Harrison joked that the Tokyo airport security guards were wasting their time searching the team for terrorists. "Obviously they didn't see the Notre Dame game," he said.

During the long trip home, Harrison's football network sidekick, Jim Gallagher, wrote "An Ode to the Hurricanes" in a tone a la Muhammad Ali:

We played in the land of the rising sun, and the sun never rose.
We played against Syracuse in Buffalo, and nearly froze.
We played twice in Tallahassee. Why? Nobody knows.
When you're the Miami Hurricanes, that's the way it goes.

The Irish had ended their season, but the Hurricnes still had to hustle back to Miami to prepare in just four days for their bitter rivals, the Gators. Some wags suggested that Miami would need only four hours to get ready this time for the Gators, who were only 0-9-1 in their first season under Charley Pell.

Before 28,051 in the Orange Bowl, the Hurricanes finally met a team they could run on as they rushed for 207 yards. They passed for 165 more yards as Kelly hit 10 of 17 passes. After rolling to a 27-10 lead, they held on for a 30-24 victory.

That salvaged a 5-6 record and left hope for the future, because every starter on offense, nine on defense, and nearly all of the second-team players would be returning.

The off-season turned out to be a typical UM good-news bad-news routine. The good news was that four touted running backs signed the state letter of intent—Key West's Robert (Speedy) Neal; Miami Northwestern's George (Buster) Rhymes; Columbus, Ohio's Keith Griffin, brother of two-time Heisman Trophy winner Archie Griffin of Ohio State; and Miami Springs' Freddie Miles. The bad news was that only Neal and Griffin signed the national letter. Rhymes opted for Oklahoma, and Miles failed to graduate and had to enroll in a junior college.

Other bad news was that budget cuts forced promotions director Jim White and business manager Dave Highmark plus a couple of secretaries out of work. Good news was that Schnellenberger struck a deal with Roy Hamlin, a promotions man from Fort Myers, Florida, who agreed to work on a commission basis.

Further bad news was that defensive tackle Lester Williams quit the team after one day of spring practice, saying, "It's just got something to do with the coaches. I don't believe in them as I should." He considered transferring to Oklahoma. Quarterback Richt complained about student apathy toward football and said he would transfer. And center Chris Duffy, who was told by the team physician he was fit to play but was told by his family physician he was not fit because of a knee injury, was booted out of the football dorm.

The good news was that Williams, saying his real problem was depression over surgery for a wrist injury, decided to stay. And Richt apologized for "hot-headed" statements and also remained.

Before the 1980 season began, the UM announced that home games would move from Saturday night at seven-thirty to Saturday afternoon at four in an effort to attract more families. And the first professionally produced UM highlights film was released for promotional purposes. It was called "The Road to the National Championship," but some wags called it "The Long and Winding Road."

In July, Schnellenberger and administrative assistant Proulx flew to Gainesville to scout accommodations for the Florida game. Proulx's recollection of the trip gives insight into the forceful, demanding, never-miss-a-detail approach by Schnellenberger.

"At one motel," said Proulx, "he was so demanding about every little facility that I couldn't believe it. Here it was midsummer and he had on a three-piece suit and he was telling off the manager and Howard wasn't even sweating. He wasn't sweating because he simply refused to sweat."

Schnellenberger made a deal with the motel, but there was no restaurant there, so he and Proulx sought a place to eat on Friday night and Saturday morning. They went to a posh country club, where the manager said they had never had a football team eat there.

"That settled it for Howard," said Proulx. "We made the deal. Then, on our way out, he turned to me and said, 'Can you imagine what this place will be like when we come in here 10-0?' We didn't make it. But that's when it really sank in on me what kind of man he is. He has a lot of Bear Bryant in him."

Schnellenberger's penchant for detail carried to the point that during the first fall scrimmage in 1980, he had the Hurricanes practice how to stand at attention during the national anthem, how to run on and off the field at halftime, and how to assemble on the bench.

Meanwhile, players continued to wonder whether the 6-1, 230-pound, poker-faced man with the pipe and mustache ever had a sense of humor.

"It's hard to tell when he's kidding and when he isn't," said Scott Atwell, a student assistant in the sports information office. "You're scared to laugh and you're scared not to."

Added wide receiver Walker: "For a year and a half, I thought he was just a mean man, with all those rules he gave us. I thought I would never hear him tell a joke. But when he started smiling and joking around every now and then, we just didn't know he had another side."

The other side became more apparent as the Hurricanes worked their way through a 9-3 season, their best in 30 years. Toward the end of the season, Schnellenberger said he would like to "leave a legacy to posterity. A contribution like Jack Harding did."

One way would be to see fruition of a stadium on campus. "The hardest thing I've ever had to do in my life is to take a team into the Orange Bowl," he said. Then he pointed out the window of his office toward the practice field. "A stadium right out there would change all that. I'd like to develop a hell-hole out there. A tight little stadium with people hanging over the edges."

But late in May 1981, after spending $150,000 on feasibility studies and delaying a decision for 18 months, the board of trustees shattered Schnellenberger's stadium dream. The board voted not to build a stadium on campus because it was low on the priority list of incoming President Edward Thaddeus (Tad) Foote, because there was too little space available, and because there was a fear that the fund raising for the stadium would detract from other university fund raising.

Though the football program showed a slight profit for the first time in more than a decade, Stanford said the athletic department would finish the fiscal year approximately $1.3 million in the red. He acknowledged that would bring the loss during the past three years to $4.1 million.

The board also instructed its executive committee to study sites for a possible stadium within five miles of the campus, the most logical site being Metro-Dade County's Tropical Park Stadium, the former horse track that was being used for high school football, track, and soccer.

"Naturally, I'm disappointed," said Schnellenberger. "I don't think it's a step backward, but I don't think it's a step forward, either. We're right where we've always been" (in the Orange Bowl).

Several alumni and UM backers feared a negative decision might mean Schnellenberger would not stay through the remainder of his contract, which had three years left. "This will have no bearing on my future at the university," he said. "I'll remain here as long as the university wants me and as long as indications are that they want to pursue a big-league football program."

The Prototype

A former University of Miami football player looked at pictures of the 27 Hurricane All-Americans on the walls of the Hecht Athletic Center and shook his head in amazement.

"Some of those guys really weren't good enough to make All-American," he said.

A longtime UM football observer added, "I don't think any team with the number of mediocre records Miami has gone through has made as many All-Americans. And that's not just an accident."

It is said that behind every All-American there is a good sports information director (SID in trade talk), a publicist who cranks out press releases and woos the people who select the teams.

The man behind the All-Americans at the UM was George Gallet, a quiet, diminutive gent who never tired of seven-day work weeks despite 44 years on the job. Gallet, who once interviewed Knute Rockne and blew set point on reigning Wimbledon tennis champion Bobby Riggs, was the UM's first and only full-time sports information director until the day he died, June 10, 1981. At 72, he was the dean of the nation's SID's. And fortunately for the UM and Gallet, President Stanford allowed him to work seven years past retirement age.

As a newspaper reporter or as publicist, Gallet saw all but one of the first 54 UM teams. He missed the 1944 season because of World War II.

"Not many people in the world have worked as long and as hard at what they loved as George did," said Kichefski. "People in the field around the country respected him. If he said Miami had a player of All-American caliber, the player made the All-American

George Gallet.

team."

Luther Evans, who covered the Hurricanes for 27 years for the *Herald,* added: "Not many people could afford to work at the university in its early days. George would work there from nine to six, then work seven to midnight at Flagler Dog Track. They called him Galloping George because he was so fast.

"And he was always optimistic. Miami would get beat, 44-0, and he'd say, 'We've really got a shot this week.' George also was a diplomat. People said he should have been a politician. He believed in them and they in him."

Gallet was a native of New York City but was raised in Miami, where he was a reserve quarterback at Miami High. A UM graduate in 1932, he was a reporter with the *Miami News* before becoming the UM's SID in 1937. Wilbert Bach had started the sports information office as a part-time job in 1935. Bach has remained a part-time assistant ever since.

Gallet was modest in talking about his accomplishments as SID except to admit he originated the play-by-play sheets for writers that now are standard in every press box in the United States.

He was an expert in use of hyperbole and colorful phrases in his press releases. Before a big game, he would write, "This has all the earmarks of a titanic struggle," or "Obstacles of major proportion face the UM.''

The week before Miami's game at Notre Dame in 1980, Gallet wrote, "It's a lead-pipe cinch that two undefeated teams will meet" (Miami was 4-0 and had an open date while Notre Dame was 2-0 and heavily favored over Michigan State).

George Mira invariably was referred to as "the fabled George Mira." Ottis Anderson was "The West Palm Beach Cyclone." A hot streak was "a winning rampage," and the Hurricanes were known as "UMers" or the "pigskin eleven."

Describing tackle Lester Williams' knack for nailing quarterbacks, a release said: "There's a difference between a bagman and a sackman. However, a sackman does bag the opposition passer."

A visitor to Gallet's office might have wondered if someone had taken the contents of the filing cabinets and dumped them on the floor.

"He has a floor filing system," said Bach of the piles of papers stacked on and under chairs, tables, and desks. "It's fascinating. But he knows where everything is."

Despite the clutter, Gallet invariably would bark at his assistants: "Don't touch my desk! Don't put anything on my desk!"

Though Gallet oversaw publicity for all UM sports, he was busiest during the football season because there were no days off. After a Saturday night game, whether it was at home or on the road, he would be in the office Sunday morning at eight. By noon, he and his staff had all the statistics updated and three press releases ready to be mailed.

"When Miami used to play on Friday night, he'd have the releases to the Pittsburgh papers on Monday before I did, and I was Pitt's SID," said Beano Cook, now the publicist of CBS Sports. "It was unbelievable. Instead of loafing on Saturday, he got his releases out by 1:00 p.m. and everybody else got their stuff out by Wednesday.

"He was the old-fashioned type of guy who believed in the phone and typewriter and was very efficient at it. When I was at ABC and we were doing college games, he always kept in touch. In 1971, he kept calling about Miami and Florida State in the opening game. When Houston and Arizona State wouldn't move their game to the afternoon on that date, I thought of Gallet because he kept after me and we did the Miami game."

Clearly, there was no person better qualified to select the all-time UM football team through 1980 than Gallet. Here's the team he picked with each player's final year of play listed:

OFFENSE

Ends: Bill Miller (1962), Jim Cox (1967)
Tackles: Dennis Harrah (1974), Al Carapella (1950)
Guards: Ray Arcangelette (1951), Chuck Guimento (1939)
Center: Bill Kimbrough (1928)
Quarterback: George Mira (1963)
Halfbacks: Eddie Dunn (1938), Frank Smith (1951)
Fullback: Don Bosseler (1956)

DEFENSE

Ends: Ted Hendricks (1968), Bob Masterson (1937)
Tackles: Eddie Edwards (1976), Tom Kearns (1941)
Middle Guard: Rubin Carter (1974)
Linebackers: Ed Weisacosky (1965), Rick Liddell (1973)
Defensive backs: Jim Dooley (1951), Burgess Owens (1972),
                  Jimmy Dye (1967), Tom Beier (1966)
Punter: Harry Ghaul (1948)
Place-kicker: Dan Miller (1981)

Gallet's choice as the greatest UM player ever was Hendricks. "No question," he said. "He was a three-time All-American, the only one at Miami, and he finished high in the Heisman Trophy voting."

The best team ever? "The 1954 one that went 9-1, losing only to Auburn," said Gallet. "Quarterback Carl Garrigus had spent the night before the Auburn game in the hospital with the flu. But he played and was running for a touchdown that would have given us a three-touchdown lead. But he was exhausted and fell down before scoring. Auburn rallied and won, 14-13."

Here are Miami's top five victories of all-time, according to Gallet: "Number one, for sure, was the 20-14 triumph at Purdue in 1950 the week after Purdue ended Notre Dame's 39-game unbeaten streak at South Bend," he said. "That rocketed Miami into big-time football. We made the top 10 for the first time in history, and 100,000 jammed the roads to the airport to meet the team when it returned.

*George Gallet (left) and his
all-time star, Ted Hendricks.*

"Before the 1980 season, I thought the others were the 10-7 victory over Southern California in 1966, 20-15 over Texas in 1973, 28-21 over Notre Dame in 1960 for our only victory over the Irish, and the 26-10 victory at Penn State in 1979. But I think the 1980 victory at Florida, 31-7, belongs somewhere in there, because it was at Gainesville, they were going to a bowl, and it was our biggest margin of victory in the 42-year series."

Perhaps Gallet's crowning achievement in press guides was the unique, colorful, slick-paper one shaped like a peach that he produced for the Peach Bowl.

"I wanted a beautiful, commemorative press guide that would be a prototype for others to follow," said Schnellenberger. He got it from the man who was a prototype sports information director.

As Kichefski has often said: "George Gallet was an institution within an institution."

Appendix

Courtesy University Of Miami
Office Of Sports Information

MIAMI'S BOWL RECORD

Palm Festival, Jan. 1, 1933 — Miami 7, Manhattan 0
Palm Festival, Jan. 1, 1934 — Duquesne 33, Miami 7
Orange Bowl, Jan. 1, 1935 — Bucknell 26, Miami 0
Orange Bowl, Jan. 1, 1946 — Miami 13, Holy Cross 6
Orange Bowl, Jan. 1, 1951 — Clemson 15, Miami 14
Gator Bowl, Jan. 1, 1952 — Miami 14, Clemson 0
Liberty Bowl, Dec. 16, 1961 — Syracuse 15, Miami 14
Gotham Bowl, Dec. 15, 1962 — Nebraska 36, Miami 34
Liberty Bowl, Dec. 10, 1966 — Miami 14, Virginia Tech 7
Bluebonnet Bowl, Dec. 23, 1967 — Colorado 31, Miami 21
Peach Bowl, Jan. 2, 1981 — Miami 20, Virginia Tech 10

MIAMI FOOTBALL YEAR BY YEAR

1926
HOWARD BUCK, Coach
(Freshman Team)

7	Rollins	0
12	Fla. Southern	0
22	Mercer	6
20	Stetson	0
6	Loyola U.	0
23	Havana	0
23	Havana	0
9*	Howard	7
122		13

Won 8, Lost 0
*New Year's Game

1927
HOWARD BUCK, Coach
(First Varsity Team)

39	Rollins	3
46	Piedmont	0
0	Spring Hill	6
0	Stetson	36
0	Howard	52
0	Oglethorpe	13
7	Georgetown College	7
0	Millsaps	31
7	Louisiana College	0
7*	Furman	39
106		187

Won 3, Lost 6, Tied 1
*New Year's Game

1928
HOWARD BUCK, Coach

62	Havana	0
31	Rollins	0
18	Elon	21
0	Howard	7
6	Stetson	15
20	Louisiana College	0
7	Union	6
6	Wake Forest	13
13*	Fla. Southern	13
163		75

Won 4, Lost 4, Tied 1
*New Year's Game

1929
J. BURTON RIX, Coach

6	Fla. Southern	0
32	Rollins	0
0	S.W. Louisiana	14
0	Stetson	12
7	Howard	0
45		26

Won 3, Lost 2

1930
ERNEST BRETT, Coach

13	Fla. Southern	6
7	Bowden	0
0	Temple	34
0	Howard	24
6	S.W. Louisiana	0
0	Rollins	0
0	Stetson	19
0	W. Kentucky	19
26		102

Won 3, Lost 4, Tied 1

1931
TOM McCANN, Coach

7	Bowden	12
12	So. Georgia (Douglas)	13
7	Rollins	0
20	Fla. Southern	31
0	W. Kentucky	20
0	Murray Teachers	15
6	Middle Tennessee	25
0	Alabama "B"	16
9	Erskine	0
12	Parris Island	6
9	Norman Park	19
14	Jax. St. (Alabama)	13
96		170

Won 4, Lost 8

1932
TOM McCANN, Coach

6	W & M (Norfolk)	2
30	Piedmont	6
6	So. Georgia (Douglas)	19
0	Rollins	6
0	Murray Teachers	0
7	S.W. Louisiana	0
0	Middle Tennessee	7
7*	Manhattan	0
56		40

Won 4, Lost 3, Tied 1
*New Year's Game

1933
TOM McCANN, Coach

20	So. Georgia (Douglas)	0
71	Piedmont	6
48	Bowden	0
33	Louisville	7
18	Rollins	0
0	Tampa	0
0	Stetson	0
7*	Duquesne	33
197		46

Won 5, Lost 1, Tied 2
*New Year's Game

1934
TOM McCANN, Coach

26	S.E. Louisiana	7

26	Fla. Southern	6
42	Wofford	14
6	Stetson	6
0	Rollins	14
19	Oglethorpe	6
6	Tampa	7
25	Baltimore Univ.	6
0*	Bucknell	26
150		**92**

Won 5, Lost 3, Tied 1
*Orange Bowl Game

1935
IRL TUBBS, Coach

2	S. E. Louisiana	0
0	Georgetown U.	13
7	Tampa	13
12	Stetson	13
3	Wake Forest	0
29	Rollins	0
17	Boston U.	0
21	Oglethorpe	13
91		**52**

Won 5, Lost 3

1936
IRL TUBBS, Coach

44	Ga. St. (Statesboro)	0
0	Tampa	0
6	Bucknell	0
26	Rollins	0
7	Boston U.	7
20	Stetson	6
13	Mercer	0
0	Ole Miss	14
10	Georgetown U.	6
3	South Carolina	6
129		**39**

Won 6, Lost 2, Tied 2

1937
JACK HARDING, Coach

40	Ga. St. (Statesboro)	0
26	Spring Hill	0
6	Bucknell	6
0	Tampa	12

25	Stetson	13
21	Catholic U.	0
0	Drake	7
0	South Carolina	3
0	Georgia	26
118		**67**

Won 4, Lost 4, Tied 1

1938
JACK HARDING, Coach

46	Spring Hill	0
32	Tampa	6
19	Florida	7
6	Drake	18
19	Rollins	0
44	Oglethorpe	0
0	Catholic U.	7
21	Duquesne	7
19	Bucknell	0
13	Georgia	7
219		**52**

Won 8, Lost 2

1939
JACK HARDING, Coach

0	Wake Forest	33
32	Tampa	7
14	Rollins	6
0	Catholic U.	14
19	Texas Tech.	0
33	Drake	6
0	Florida	13
6	South Carolina	7
27	N.C. State	7
0	Georgia	13
131		**106**

Won 5, Lost 5

1940
JACK HARDING, Coach

19	Stetson	0
27	Tampa	0
18	Catholic U.	20
31	Elon	7
14	Texas Tech.	61
0	Rollins	7

6	Florida	46
2	South Carolina	7
7	Ole Miss	21
7	Georgia	28
131		197

Won 3, Lost 7

1941
JACK HARDING, Coach

38	Elon	0
20	Tampa	6
21	Rollins	0
19	Howard	0
6	Texas Tech.	0
34	W.V. Wesleyan	0
0	Florida	14
7	South Carolina	6
7	Alabama	21
10	V.M.I.	7
162		54

Won 8, Lost 2

1942
JACK HARDING, Coach

0	Jax Air Base	14
65	Tampa	6
31	St. Louis	6
21	Rollins	0
32	Furman	13
0	N.C. State	2
12	Florida	0
13	South Carolina	6
21	West Virginia	13
195		60

Won 7, Lost 2

1943
EDDIE DUNN, Coach

6	Jax NATTC	0
52	Camp Gordon	6
13	Charleston C.G.	6
0	Jax NATTC	20
32	Presbyterian	13
21	Ft. Benning ·	7
124		52

Won 5, Lost 1

1944
EDDIE DUNN, Coach

0	South Carolina	0
0	Ft. Pierce Amph.	38
0	Wake Forest	27
0	Florida	13
7	N.C. State	28
31	Presbyterian	12
19	Auburn	38
2	Tulsa	48
14	Texas A&M	70
73		274

Won 1, Lost 7, Tied 1

1945
JACK HARDING, Coach

27	Chattanooga	7
21	Georgia	27
21	St. Louis	0
7	Florida	6
27	Miami (Ohio)	13
7	Clemson	6
13	South Carolina	13
21	N.C. State	7
21	Michigan State	7
33	Auburn	7
13*	Holy Cross	6
211		99

Won 9, Lost 1, Tied 1
*Orange Bowl Game

1946
JACK HARDING, Coach

13	William & Mary	3
0	North Carolina	21
20	Texas Christian	12
20	Florida	13
33	Chattanooga	13
26	Villanova	21
20	Miami (Ohio)	17
7	Louisiana State	20
40	Washington-Lee	20
21	Detroit	7
200		147

Won 8, Lost 2

1947
JACK HARDING, Coach

7	Baylor	18
7	Villanova	7
6	Texas Christian	19
6	Rollins	0
28	Geo. Washington	7
0	South Carolina	8
7	Cincinnati	20
7	Vanderbilt	33
6	Florida	7
6	Alabama	21
80		140

Won 2, Lost 7, Tied 1

1948
ANDY GUSTAFSON, Coach

25	Rollins	0
10	Villanova	19
6	Detroit	0
21	Georgia	42
13	Maryland	27
36	Cincinnati	6
19	Chattanooga	0
13	Florida	27
5	Kentucky	25
6	Vanderbilt	33
154		179

Won 4, Lost 6

1949
ANDY GUSTAFSON, Coach

52	Rollins	13
26	Louisville	0
0	Purdue	14
13	Georgia	9
27	Detroit	6
13	South Carolina	7
28	Florida	13
6	Kentucky	21
0	Maryland	13
165		96

Won 6, Lost 3

1950
ANDY GUSTAFSON, Coach

21	The Citadel	0
18	Villanova	12
20	Purdue	14
34	Boston U.	7
28	Pittsburgh	0
42	Georgetown U.	7
13	Louisville	13
20	Florida	14
14	Iowa	6
27	Misouri	9
14*	Clemson	15
251		97

Won 9, Lost 1, Tied 1
*Orange Bowl Game

1951
ANDY GUSTAFSON, Coach

7	Tulane	21
35	Florida State	13
7	Purdue	0
32	Washington-Lee	12
20	Ole Miss	7
0	Kentucky	32
34	Chattanooga	7
21	Florida	6
19	Nebraska	7
7	Pittsburgh	21
14*	Clemson	0
196		126

Won 8, Lost 3
*Gator Bowl Game

1952
ANDY GUSTAFSON, Coach

45	V.M.I.	0
7	Alabama	21
7	Boston U.	9
41	Richmond	6
20	Marquette	6
0	Kentucky	29
0	Vanderbilt	9
35	Stetson	0
6	Florida	43
7	North Carolina	34
13	Georgia	35
181		192

Won 4, Lost 7

1953
ANDY GUSTAFSON, Coach

27	Florida State	0
13	Baylor	21
39	Clemson	7
16	Nebraska	20
0	Maryland	30
0	Fordham	20
20	Auburn	29
26	Virginia Tech	0
14	Florida	10
155		137

Won 4, Lost 5

1954
ANDY GUSTAFSON, Coach

51	Furman	13
19	Baylor	13
26	Holy Cross	20
27	Mississippi State	13
9	Maryland	7
75	Fordham	7
13	Auburn	14
23	Alabama	7
14	Florida	0
257		94

Won 8, Lost 1

1955
ANDY GUSTAFSON, Coach

6	Georgia Tech	14
34	Florida State	0
0	Notre Dame	14
19	Texas Christian	21
21	Pittsburgh	7
14	Boston College	7
46	Bucknell	0
34	Alabama	12
7	Florida	6
181		81

Won 6, Lost 3

1956
ANDY GUSTAFSON, Coach

14	South Carolina	6
27	Boston College	6
13	Maryland	6
7	Georgia	7
14	Texas Christian	0
20	Florida State	7
21	Clemson	0
18	West Virginia	0
20	Florida	7
7	Pittsburgh	14
161		53

Won 8, Lost 1, Tied 1

1957
ANDY GUSTAFSON, Coach

0	Houston	7
13	Baylor	7
13	North Carolina	20
0	N. Carolina State	0
48	Kansas	6
13	Villanova	7
40	Florida State	13
6	Maryland	16
0	Florida	14
28	Pittsburgh	13
161		103

Won 5, Lost 4, Tied 1

1958
ANDY GUSTAFSON, Coach

0	Wisconsin	20
14	Baylor	8
0	Louisiana State	41
2	Boston College	6
15	Vanderbilt	28
6	Florida State	17
14	Maryland	26
26	Houston	37
9	Florida	12
2	Oregon	0
88		195

Won 2, Lost 8

1959
ANDY GUSTAFSON, Coach

26	Tulane	7
7	Florida State	6
3	Louisiana State	27

23	Navy	8
6	Auburn	21
3	Kentucky	22
14	North Carolina	7
26	South Carolina	6
18	Michigan State	13
14	Florida	23
140		140

Won 6, Lost 4

1960
ANDY GUSTAFSON, Coach

29	North Carolina	12
6	Pittsburgh	17
21	South Carolina	6
7	Auburn	20
10	Boston College	7
25	Florida State	7
28	Notre Dame	21
14	Syracuse	21
0	Florida	18
23	Air Force	14
163		143

Won 6, Lost 4

1961
ANDY GUSTAFSON, Coach

7	Pittsburgh	10
14	Kentucky	7
25	Penn State	8
6	Navy	17
7	Colorado	9
10	North Carolina	0
32	Georgia	7
6	Tulane	0
10	Northwestern	6
15	Florida	6
14*	Syracuse	15
146		85

Won 7, Lost 4
*Liberty Bowl Game

1962
ANDY GUSTAFSON, Coach

23	Pittsburgh	14
21	Texas Christian	20

7	Florida State	6
3	Louisiana State	17
28	Maryland	24
21	Air Force	3
25	Kentucky	17
3	Alabama	36
7	Northwestern	29
17	Florida	15
34*	Nebraska	36
189		217

Won 7, Lost 4
*Gotham Bowl Game

1963
ANDY GUSTAFSON, Coach

0	Florida State	24
3	Purdue	0
10	Tulane	0
0	Louisiana State	3
14	Georgia	31
20	Kentucky	14
16	North Carolina	27
21	Florida	27
20	Pittsburgh	31
12	Alabama	17
116		174

Won 3, Lost 7

1964
CHARLIE TATE, Coach

0	Florida State	14
0	Georgia Tech	20
7	California	9
20	Pittsburgh	20
14	Indiana	28
10	Detroit	7
21	Tulane	0
30	Boston College	6
35	Vanderbilt	17
10	Florida	12
147		133

Won 4, Lost 5, Tied 1

1965
CHARLIE TATE, Coach

3	SMU	7

24	Syracuse	0
16	Tulane	24
27	Louisiana State	34
44	Houston	12
14	Pittsburgh	28
27	Boston College	6
28	Vanderbilt	14
16	Florida	13
0	Notre Dame	0
199		138

Won 5, Lost 4, Tied 1

1966
CHARLIE TATE, Coach

24	Colorado	3
20	Florida State	23
8	Louisiana State	10
7	Georgia	6
14	Indiana	7
10	So. California	7
10	Tulane	10
38	Pittsburgh	14
44	Iowa	0
21	Florida	16
14*	Virginia Tech	7
210		103

Won 8, Lost 2, Tied 1
*Liberty Bowl

1967
CHARLIE TATE, Coach

7	Northwestern	12
8	Penn State	17
34	Tulane	14
17	Lousiana State	15
58	Pittsburgh	0
7	Auburn	0
14	Virginia Tech	7
49	Georgia Tech	7
22	Notre Dame	24
20	Florida	13
21*	Colorado	31
257		140

Won 7, Lost 4
*Bluebonnet Bowl

1968
CHARLIE TATE, Coach

28	Northwestern	7
10	Georgia Tech	7
3	Southern Cal	28
30	Louisiana State	0
13	Virginia Tech	8
6	Auburn	31
48	Pittsburgh	0
7	Penn State	22
6	Alabama	14
10	Florida	14
161	Won 5, Lost 5	131

1969
CHARLIE TATE, Coach

14	Florida State	16
23	North Carolina St.	13
0	Louisiana State	20
13	Memphis State	26
14	Texas Christian	9
36	Houston	38
30	Navy	10
6	Alabama	42
49	Wake Forest	7
16	Florida	35
201		216

Won 4, Lost 6

1970
CHARLIE TATE (2 games)
WALT KICHEFSKI (9 games)

36	William & Mary	14
21	Georgia Tech	31
18	Maryland	11
14	Tampa	31
17	Pittsburgh	28
3	Florida State	27
16	Tulane	31
8	Alabama	32
16	Syracuse	56
14	Florida	13
3	Houston	36
166		310

Won 3, Lost 8

1971
FRAN CURCI, Coach

17	Florida State	20
29	Wake Forest	10
41	Baylor	15
0	Notre Dame	17
31	Navy	16
24	Army	13
7	North Carolina St.	13
3	Alabama	31
6	Houston	27
16	Florida	45
0	Syracuse	14
174		221

Won 4, Lost 7

1972
FRAN CURCI, Coach

14	Florida State	37
10	Texas	23
3	Baylor	10
24	Tulane	21
33	Houston	13
28	Army	7
51	Nevada (Las Vegas)	7
0	Tampa	7
17	Notre Dame	20
28	Maryland	8
6	Florida	17
214		170

Won 5, Lost 6

1973
PETE ELLIOTT, Coach

20	Texas	15
14	Florida State	10
20	Oklahoma	24
15	Boston College	10
7	Houston	30
34	Syracuse	23
14	West Virginia	20
19	Army	7
13	Alabama	43
7	Florida	14
0	Notre Dame	44
163		240

Won 5, Lost 6

1974
PETE ELLIOTT, Coach

20	Houston	3
28	Tampa	26
0	Auburn	3
35	Pacific	6
21	West Virginia	20
7	Notre Dame	38
14	Virginia Tech	7
14	Florida State	21
7	Alabama	28
14	Syracuse	7
7	Florida	31
167		190

Won 6, Lost 5

1975
CARL SELMER, Coach

23	Georgia Tech	38
17	Oklahoma	20
16	Nebraska	31
10	Colorado	23
24	Houston	20
7	Boston College	21
16	Navy	17
24	Florida State	22
9	Notre Dame	32
11	Florida	15
157		239

Won 2, Lost 8

1976
CARL SELMER, Coach

47	Florida State	0
3	Colorado	33
9	Nebraska	17
7	Duke	20
19	Pittsburgh	36
49	Texas Christian	0
13	Boston College	6
7	Penn State	21
27	Notre Dame	40
10	Florida	19
16	Houston	21
207		213

Won 3, Lost 8

1977
LOU SABAN, Coach

0	Ohio State	10
6	Georgia Tech	10
23	Florida State	17
24	Pacific	3
14	Kansas	7
17	Texas Christian	21
7	Penn State	49
10	Tulane	13
0	Alabama	36
14	Florida	31
10	Notre Dame	48
125		245

Won 3, Lost 8

1978
LOU SABAN, Coach

7	Colorado	17
21	Florida State	31
38	Kansas	6
17	Auburn	15
19	Georgia Tech	24
17	Utah State	16
0	Notre Dame	20
16	Tulane	20
16	San Diego State	14
21	Syracuse	9
22	Florida	21
194		193

Won 6, Lost 5

1979
HOWARD SCHNELLENBERGER, Coach

24	Louisville	12
23	Florida State	40
6	Louisiana Tech	0
13	Florida A&M	16
20	San Diego State	31
19	Boston College	8
15	Syracuse	25
26	Penn State	10
0	Alabama	30
15	*Notre Dame	40
30	Florida	24
191		236

Won 5, Lost 6
*Tokyo, Japan

1980
HOWARD SCHNELLENBERGER, Coach

24	Louisville	10
49	Florida A&M	0
14	Houston	7
10	Florida State	9
14	Notre Dame	32
31	Mississippi State	32
12	Penn State	27
23	East Carolina	10
24	Vanderbilt	17
26	North Texas State	8
31	Florida	7
20*	Virginia Tech	10
278		170

Won 9, Lost 3
*Peach Bowl Game

Miami's All-Americans

Year	Name	Position
1950	Al Carapella	tackle
1951	Jim Dooley	halfback
1952	Nick Chickillo	guard
1954	Frank McDonald	end
1956	Don Bosseler	fullback
1959	Fran Curci	quarterback
1960-61	Bill Miller	offensive end
1962-63	George Mira	quarterback
1963	Dan Conners	tackle
1965	Ed Weisacosky	defensive end

1966	Tom Beier	defensive back
1966-67-68	Ted Hendricks	defensive end
1971	Harold Sears	linebacker
1972	Chuck Foreman	running back
1972	Burgess Owens	defensive back
1972-73	Tony Cristiani	middle guard
1974	Rubin Carter	middle guard
1974	Dennis Harrah	offensive tackle
1976	Eddie Edwards	defensive tackle
1977	Don Latimer	middle guard
1978	Don Smith	defensive tackle
1980	Jim Burt	middle guard

ALL-TIME RECORDS

Records set in 8-game seasons carry symbol (+), 9 games (#), 11 games (*). All other records set in 10-game seasons. Postseason games not included.

TEAM — SEASON

Most victories: 9 in 1950.

Most defeats: 8 in 1931, 1958, 1970, 1976 (*), 1977 (*).

Longest period no defeat: 14 games, last part of 1955 and first part of 1956 (tie included).

Most successive wins with no defeats or tie (single season): 6 in 1950, 1954, 1967.

Most successive defeats: 7 in 1958.

Most successive losses overall: 8 at end of 1971, start 1972, also end 1977, start of 1978.

Most points: 258 in 1980, opp. 310 in 1970 (*).

Fewest points: 26 in 1930; opp. 26 in 1929.

Most shutouts: 5 in 1933, 1936, 1941.

Most times shut out: 5 in 1927, 1930.

Most first downs rushing: 135 in 1938; opp. 132 in 1979 (*).

Fewest first downs rushing: 53 in 1968; opp. 33 in 1938.

Most first downs passing: 117 in 1963; opp. 93 in 1969.

Fewest first downs passing: 11 in 1945; opp. 12 in 1935 (+).

Most first down penalties: 18 in 1979; opp. 18 in 1979 (*).

Fewest first down penalties: 1 in 1952 (*); opp. 3 in 1953, 1955, 1956.

Most first downs: 197 in 1963; opp. 215 in 1979 (*).

Fewest first downs: 77 in 1944 (#); opp. 59 in 1938.

Most rushes: 567 in 1957; opp. 587 in 1979 (*).

Fewest rushes: 318 in 1963; opp. 314 in 1954 (#).

Most net yards rushing: 2,558 in 1954 (#); opp. 2,492 in 1944 (#).

Fewest net yards rushing: 798 in 1968; opp. 692 in 1938.

Greatest avg. gain per rush: 5.11 in 1954 (#); opp. 6.35 in 1944.

Least gain per rush: 1.88 in 1968; opp. 1.89 in 1938.

Most passes attempted: 360 in 1970 (*); opp. 311 in 1969.

Fewest passes attempted: 65 in 1945; opp. 80 in 1935 (+).

Most passes completed: 173 in 1963; opp. 173 in 1969.

Fewest passes completed: 35 in 1935 (+); opp. 26 in 1935 (+).

Most yards on passes: 2,183 in 1963; opp. 1,918 in 1969.

Fewest yards on passes: 269 in 1945;

opp. 393 in 1938.

Most passes intercepted: 31 in 1950 (#); opp. 32 in 1944 (#).

Fewest passes intercepted: 4 in 1975; opp. 5 in 1950.

Most yards returned interceptions: 456 in 1954 (#); opp. 382 in 1970 (*).

Fewest yards returned interceptions: 11 in 1963; opp. 9 in 1954 (#).

Most yards total offense: 3,756 in 1980 (*); opp. 3,655 in 1979 (*).

Least yards total offense: 1,406 in 1944 (#); opp. 1,028 in 1938.

Most yards total offense per game: 346.5 in 1969; opp. 380.3 in 1954.

Least yards total offense per game: 156.2 in 1944; opp. 102.8 in 1938.

Most plays total offense: 822 in 1970 (*); opp. 826 in 1979 (*).

Fewest plays total offense: 527 in 1947; opp. 441 in 1938.

Most punts: 92 in 1939; opp. 102 in 1938.

Fewest punts: 30 in 1954; 40 in 1962.

Highest punting avg.: 42.3 in 1969; opp. 41.3 in 1980.

Lowest punting avg.: 32.4 in 1962; opp. 31.9 in 1945.

Most punts returned: 51 in 1942; opp. 50 in 1970 (*).

Fewest punts returned: 15 in 1966; opp. 11 in 1954.

Most yards punt returns: 672 in 1942 (#); opp. 575 in 1947.

Fewest yards punt returns: 90 in 1966; opp. 70 in 1954 (#).

Highest avg. punt return: 19.8 in 1954; opp. 14.6 in 1949.

Lowest avg. punt return: 4.9 in 1977 (*); opp. 5.4 in 1965.

Most punts blocked: 9 in 1945.

Most kickoffs returned: 53 in 1944 (#); opp. 47 in 1954 (#).

Most yards kickoff returns: 1,054 in 1970 (*); opp. 925 in 1954 (#).

Fewest yards kickoff returns: 218 in 1950; opp. 261 in 1944 (#).

Highest avg. kickoff returns: 24.7 in 1978 (*); opp. 25.8 in 1971 (*).

Lowest avg. kickoff returns: 15.2 in 1968 (*); opp. 11.7 in 1941.

Most fumbles: 49 in 1971 (*); opp. 46 in 1970 (*).

Fewest fumbles: 17 in 1961; opp. 15 in 1955 (#).

Most fumbles lost: 26 in 1972 (*); opp. 27 in 1970 (*).

Fewest fumbles lost: 8 in 1968; opp. 6 in 1955 (#).

Most penalties: 81 in 1941; opp. 73 in 1958 and 1980.

Fewest penalties: 27 in 1953 (#); opp. 27 in 1966.

Most yards penalized: 693 in 1976 (*); opp. 771 in 1955 (#).

Fewest yards penalized: 236 in 1953 (#) opp. 182 in 1937.

Most touchdowns rushing: 29 in 1954 (#); opp. 23 in 1975.

Fewest touchdowns rushing: 3 in 1977 (*); opp. 2 in 1966.

Most touchdowns passing: 14 in 1969; opp. 19 in 1970 (*).

Fewest touchdowns passing: 3 in 1947 and 1971 (*); opp. 0 in 1956.

Most touchdowns kick returns: 2 in 1954, 1970 (*), 1976 (*), and 1978 (*); opp. 3 in 1973 (*).

Most touchdowns interception returns: 5 in 1967; opp. 4 in 1970 (*).

TEAM — SINGLE GAME

Most points: 75 vs. Fordham, 1954; opp.: 70 by Texas A&M, 1944.

Most points scored in defeat: 36 vs. Houston, 1969; opp.: 24 by Maryland, 1962.

Most points scored one quarter: 25 vs. Piedmont, 1933; opp.: 28 by Syracuse and 28 by Houston, 1970.

Most first downs: 32 vs. Kansas, 1957 and Alabama, 1963; opp.: 29 by Alabama, 1969.

Most first downs rushing: 27 vs. Pacific, 1974; opp.: 24 by Auburn, 1944.

Most first downs passing: 18 vs. Georgia, Pitt, Alabama, 1963; opp.: 19 by Georgia, 1963.

Most first down penalties: 5 vs. Wake Forest, 1969; opp.: 4 by North Carolina, 1960; Penn State, 1979.

Most yards gained rushing: 498 vs. Pacific, 1974; opp.: 536 by Auburn, 1944.

Fewest yards gained rushing: -85 vs. Auburn, 1968; opp.: -47 by Florida A&M, 1980.

Most yards gained passing: 343 vs. Houston, 1969; opp.: 407 by Georgia, 1963.

Fewest yards gained passing: -6 vs. North Carolina State, 1957; opp.: 0 by Ole Miss, 1951; S.E. Louisiana, 1935; Auburn, 1974.

Most yards total offense: 582 vs. Elon, 1941 (493 rushing, 89 passing); opp.: 574 by Notre Dame, 1973 (448 rushing, 126 passing).

Least yards total offense: 22 vs. Kentucky, 1951 (7 rushing, 15 passing); opp.: -2 by Spring Hill, 1938 (-32 rushing, 30 passing).

Most passes attempted: 49 vs. Notre Dame, 1967; opp.: 52 by Florida, 1971.

Most passes completed: 25 vs. Georgia and Pitt, 1963 and LSU, 1965; opp.: 34 by Florida, 1971.

Most TD passes: 4 vs. Havana, 1928 and Houston, 1969; opp.: 5 by Florida, 1971.

Most passes intercepted: 7 vs. Georgetown U., 1950; Florida, 1978; and Charleston Coast Guard, 1943; opp.: 7 by Tulsa and Texas A&M, 1944.

Most yards gained on interceptions: 169 vs. Fordham, 1954; opp.: 143 by Florida, 1959.

Most yards returned punts: 130 vs. Furman, 1942; opp.: 187 by Vanderbilt, 1944.

Most yards returned kickoffs: 171 vs. Texas A&M, 1944; opp.: 222 by Tampa, 1942.

Most penalties: 14 for 170 yards vs. Chattanooga, 1945; opp.: 18 for 148 by Kentucky, 1959.

Most fumbles: 9 vs. North Carolina State, 1971; opp.: 8 by Boston College, 1955 and Houston, 1970.

Most fumbles lost: 5 vs. Holy Cross, 1954; Boston College, 1958; LSU, 1959; Indiana, 1964; Maryland, 1970; FSU and Army, 1972; opp.: 6 by FSU, 1962; Tulane, 1970; and Vanderbilt, 1980.

INDIVIDUAL — SEASON
Net Yards Gained, Rushing

Ottis Anderson (*)	1,266 in 1978
Chuck Foreman (*)	951 in 1971
Ottis Anderson (*)	918 in 1976
Woody Thompson (*)	802 in 1973
Ottis Anderson (*)	782 in 1977
Frank Smith	764 in 1951
Tom Sullivan (*)	761 in 1971
Don Bosseler	723 in 1956
Eddie Dunn (#)	714 in 1937
Eddie Dunn	683 in 1938

Best Average Gain Per Play
25 Or More Rushes

Jack Losch 9.06 on	47 tries, 1955
John Varone 7.04 on	46 tries, 1955
Harry Ghaul 7.00 on	25 tries, 1948
John Douglas 6.7 on	27 tries, 1938
J. Williams (*) 6.6 on	65 tries, 1973
Walter Watt 6.6 on	27 tries, 1941
Eddie Dunn 6.3 on	113 tries, 1937

Best Average, 25 Or More Punts

Pat Barrett	43.1 on 45, 1969
Howard Plasman	42.7 on 54, 1941

Harry Ghaul	42.1	on 57, 1946
Rob Rajsich	41.13	on 76, 1977
Harry Ghaul	41.1	on 63, 1945
Mike Burke (*)	40.7	on 53, 1972
Harry Ghaul	40.68	on 63, 1947
Greg LaBelle (*)	40.63	on 70, 1980
Pat Barrett (*)	40.54	on 81, 1970
Hank Collins	40.52	on 75, 1968

Most Yards, Returned Punts

Eddie Dunn	412 in 1938
Al Kasulin (#)	412 in 1942
Eddie Dunn (#)	405 in 1937
Eddie Dunn	367 in 1936
Jimmy Dye	281 in 1967
Bill Steiner	234 in 1939
Bill Steiner	227 in 1940
Frank Smith	223 in 1951
Gordon Malloy (#)	223 in 1954
Bryan Ferguson (*)	223 in 1976

Most Yards, Returned Kickoffs

Jim Joiner(*)	19 for 454 in 1979
Chuck Foreman(*)	22 for 435 in 1972
Chuck Foreman(*)	18 for 430 in 1971
Tom Sullivan (*)	14 for 402 in 1971
Mark Rush(*)	16 for 397 in 1980
Ottis Anderson (*)	12 for 395 in 1978
Tim Morgan	14 for 385 in 1975
Tom Sullivan	18 for 377 in 1969
Tim Morgan(*)	16 for 352 in 1976
Tom Sullivan(*)	15 for 342 in 1970

Most Passes Completed

George Mira	334 in 1963
Kelly Cochrane (*)	287 in 1970
George Mira	260 in 1962
David Olivo	248 in 1968
Kelly Cochrane	243 in 1969
Ed Carney (*)	209 in 1972
Jim Kelly (*)	206 in 1980
Mike Rodrigue (*)	201 in 1979
Fran Curci	195 in 1959
John Hornibrook (*)	179 in 1971

Most Passes Attempted

George Mira	172 in 1963
David Olivo	137 in 1968
Kelly Cochrane (*)	127 in 1970
George Mira	122 in 1962
Kelly Cochrane	121 in 1969
Jim Kelly (*)	109 in 1980
Fran Curci	100 in 1959
Ed Carney (*)	94 in 1972
Mike Rodrigue (*)	94 in 1979
Bob Biletnikoff	85 in 1964

Most Yards Gained Passing

George Mira	2,155 in 1963
David Olivo	1,727 in 1968
Kelly Cochrane	1,673 in 1969
George Mira	1,572 in 1962
Jim Kelly (*)	1,519 in 1980
Ed Carney (*)	1,399 in 1972
Kelly Cochrane (*)	1,348 in 1970
Mike Rodrigue (*)	1,197 in 1979
Bill Miller	1,114 in 1966
Fran Curci	1,068 in 1959
John Hornibrook (*)	1,006 in 1971

Most Passes Caught

David Kalina	45 in 1969
Bill Miller	43 in 1961
David Kalina	43 in 1968
Nick Spinelli	41 in 1963
James Cox	41 in 1966
James Cox	39 in 1967
Ray Bellamy	37 in 1968
Joe Schmidt (*)	37 in 1970
Chuck Foreman (*)	37 in 1972
Joe Schmidt	36 in 1969

Most Yards Pass Receivers

Joe Schmidt	651 in 1969
Bill Miller	640 in 1961
David Kalina	628 in 1968
James Cox	627 in 1966
Pat Walker (*)	625 in 1979
Larry Brodsky (*)	570 in 1980
Steve Marcantonio (*)	568 in 1973
Chuck Foreman (*)	557 in 1972

James Cox	552 in 1967
Ray Bellamy	549 in 1968
Joe Schmidt (*)	549 in 1970

Most Passes Intercepted

Gene Coleman (*)	9 in 1979
Whitey Rouviere (#)	7 in 1954
Racey Timmons	7 in 1960
Bryan Ferguson (*)	7 in 1977
Fred Marion (*)	7 in 1980
Jim Dooley	6 in 1951
John Bookman	6 in 1956
Jimmy Dye	6 in 1967
Arnold Tucker	6 in 1943
Eddie Dunn	5 in 1936
John Tobin	5 in 1941
Whitey Campbell	5 in 1946
Frank Smith	5 in 1948
Elmer Tremont	5 in 1951
Carl Garrigus (#)	5 in 1954
Gregory Perez	5 in 1969
Burgess Owens (*)	5 in 1971
Ernest Jones (*)	5 in 1973

Fumbles Recovered

LeeRoy Lewis	5 in 1965
Ted Hendricks	5 in 1968
Mike Barnes (*)	5 in 1972
Ted Hendricks	4 in 1967
Jim Simon	4 in 1962
Dick Sorensen	4 in 1968
Al Palewicz (*)	4 in 1971
Rich Griffiths (*)	4 in 1973
Bill Frohbose (*)	4 in 1973
Jim Burt (*)	4 in 1980

Most Yards On Interceptions

Gary Streicher (*)	148 on 3, 1972
John Bookman	137 on 6, 1956
Arnold Tucker (x)	132 on 6, 1943
Ken Corbin	125 on 2, 1967
Ronnie Lippett (*)	118 on 3, 1980
(x - 6 games played in 1943)	

Most Touchdowns

Eddie Dunn	14 in 1938

Harry Ghaul	13 in 1945
Ottis Anderson (*)	11 in 1978
Frank Smith	10 in 1950
Chuck Foreman (*)	10 in 1971
Frank Smith	9 in 1951
Eddie Dunn (#)	8 in 1937
Bob Biletnikoff	8 in 1964
Woody Thompson (*)	8 in 1973
Walter Watt (#)	7 in 1942
Whitey Campbell (#)	7 in 1949
Bill Steiner	7 in 1940
Gordon Malloy (#)	7 in 1954
Sam Scarnecchia	7 in 1956
Eddie Johns	7 in 1960

Most Points After Touchdowns

Gordon Watson	25 in 1950
Don Curtright	23 in 1965
Mike Burke (*)	23 in 1972
Harry Ghaul	22 in 1945
Burt Grossman (#)	22 in 1952
Jim Huff	22 in 1969
Chris Dennis (*)	22 in 1974

Most Consecutive Extra Points

Mike Burke (*)	23 in 1972
Chris Dennis (*)	22 in 1974

Most Field Goals

Dan Miller (*)	15 in 1980
Dan Miller (*)	14 in 1979
Chris Dennis	14 in 1975
Jim Huff	10 in 1968
Dan Miller (*)	9 in 1978
Chris Dennis (*)	9 in 1977
Ray Harris	7 in 1966
Mike Burke (*)	7 in 1972
Don Curtright	6 in 1965
Chris Dennis (*)	6 in 1976
Jim Huff	5 in 1969
Mike Burke (*)	5 in 1971

Most Points

Harry Ghaul	100 in 1945
Eddie Dunn	86 in 1938

Ottis Anderson (*)	68 in 1978	
Dan Miller (*)	64 in 1980	
Frank Smith	60 in 1950	
Chuck Foreman (*)	60 in 1971	
Dan Miller (*)	57 in 1979	
Frank Smith	54 in 1951	
Chris Dennis	53 in 1975	
Eddie Dunn (#)	51 in 1937	
Bob Biletnikoff	48 in 1964	
Woody Thompson (*)	48 in 1973	

Most Points Kicking Only

Dan Miller (*)	64 in 1980
Dan Miller (*)	57 in 1979
Chris Dennis	53 in 1975
Jim Huff	47 in 1968
Dan Miller (*)	46 in 1978
Mike Burke (*)	44 in 1972

Total Offense

Player	Year	Rush.	Pass.	Total
G. Mira	1963	163	2,155	2,318
G. Mira	1962	160	1,572	1,732
D. Olivo	1968	155	1,572	1,727
K. Cochrane	1969	41	1,673	1,714
Jim Kelly (*)	1980	36	1,519	1,555

Player	Year			Total
E. Carney (*)	1972	83	1,399	1,482
F. Curci	1959	260	1,068	1,328
K. Cochrane (*)	1970	-24	1,348	1,324
B. Bilentnikoff	1964	351	920	1,271
O. Anderson (*)	1978	1,266	0	1,266

Touchdown Passes Thrown

Kelly Cochrane	11 in 1969
Jim Kelly (*)	11 in 1980
George Mira	10 in 1962-63
Bill Miller	9 in 1965
David Olivo	9 in 1968
George Mira	8 in 1961
David Olivo	8 in 1967
Bill Miller	7 in 1966
Kelly Cochrane (*)	7 in 1970

Touchdown Passes Caught

Bill Miller	5 in 1960
Frank Smith	4 in 1950
Ed Lutes	4 in 1950
James Cox	4 in 1965, 1966, 1967
Jerry Daanen	4 in 1966
David Kalina	4 in 1968
Joe Schmidt	4 in 1969
Nick Spinelli	4 in 1963

All Purpose Running

Player	Year	Rush.	Pass. Rec.	Kick Ret.	Total Yds.
O. Anderson (*)	1978	1,266	47	395	1,708
Foreman (*)	1972	484	557	514	1,555
Foreman (*)	1971	951	72	444	1,467
Sullivan (*)	1971	761	198	402	1,361
E. Dunn (#)	1937	714	—	544	1,258
E. Dunn (#)	1938	683	32	496	1,211
F. Smith	1951	764	161	256	1,167
O. Anderson (*)	1976	918	121	—	1,039
O. Anderson (*)	1977	782	243	—	1,025
Spinelli	1962	73	458	493	1,024

Most Tackles, By Positions

End, Weisacosky	112 in 1965
Tackle, Carter (*)	98 in 1973
Middle Guard, Burt (*)	100 in 1979
Middle LB, Sears (*)	74 in 1971
Linebacker, O'Mahony	104 in 1962
Cornerback, Beier	73 in 1966
Safety, Reeh (*)	68 in 1971
Linebacker, Liddell (*)	64 in 1973
Cornerback, Malloy (#)	41 in 1953
Safety, Reeh (*)	40 in 1971

Most Assists, By Positions

End, Weisacosky	52 in 1965
Tackle, Carter (*)	49 in 1973
Middle Guard, Reynolds	50 in 1961

Total Tackles And Assists

Weisacosky (End)	164 in 1965
Carter (T) (*)	147 in 1973
Griffiths (LB) (*)	160 in 1973
Nicolas (LB) (*)	140 in 1979
Burt (MG) (*)	129 in 1979
Sears (MLB) (*)	117 in 1971
Hendricks (E)	114 in 1967
Beier (CB)	108 in 1966
Reeh (S) (*)	108 in 1971

INDIVIDUAL — SINGLE GAME

Total Offense

Year	Team	Player	Rush.	Pass.	Yds.
1963	Georgia	Mira	4	342	346
1962	Nebraska	Mira (Gotham Bowl)	6	321	327
1963	Alabama	Mira	23	301	324
1963	Pittsburgh	Mira	10	309	319
1969	Houston	Cochrane	28	343	315
1979	Louisville	Rodrigue	26	287	313
1969	Navy	Cochrane	22	283	305
1962	Maryland	Mira	6	288	294
1970	W&M	Cochrane	16	271	287
1979	Penn State	Kelly	6	280	286

Net Yards Rushing
(Tries in Parentheses)

S. Roan, 249 (33), E. Carolina, 1980
F. Smith, 182 (15), Chattanooga, 1951
W. Thompson, 180 (32), Boston College, 1973
E. Dunn, 175 (11), Georgia St., 1937
Ottis Anderson, 167 (31), Boston College, 1976
E. Dunn, 166 (19), Stetson, 1937
F. Smith, 164 (21), W&Lee, 1951
O. Anderson, 154 (19), Utah St., 1978
O. Anderson, 150 (22), Syracuse, 1978
O. Anderson, 149 (39), Florida, 1978
E. Johns, 149 (13), Air Force, 1960

Long Runs, Rushing

Jack Losch, 90 vs. Bucknell, 1955
Mike Vacchio, 87 vs. FSU, 1951
Harry Ghaul, 82 vs. Florida, 1947
Ottis Anderson, 80 vs. FSU, 1978
Joe Plevel, 80 vs. Villanova, 1957
Clive Shrader, 75 vs. Cincinnati, 1948
John Bookman, 74 vs. Furman, 1954
Jack Losch, 73 vs. Boston College, 1955
Eddie Dunn, 73 vs. Spring Hill, 1938
Whitey Campbell, 72 vs. Detroit, 1949
Don Bosseler, 72 vs. Florida, 1956
Vincent Opalsky, 72 vs. Georgia Tech, 1967

Long Pass Plays

Mark Richt—Larry Brodsky, 81, Florida A&M, 1980
Frank Smith—Al Hudson, 81, Georgia 1948
Bill Miller—James Cox, 80, LSU, 1965
Steve Marcantonio—Phil August, 80, FSU, 1974
Bob Schneidenbach—Ed Lutes, 78, Clemson, 1951 (Orange Bowl Game)
David Olivo—Ray Bellamy, 78, Penn State, 1968
Frank Glover—Witt Beckman, 77, FSU, 1974
Bonnie Yarbrough—Bob Rosbaugh, 77, Maryland, 1958

Kelly Cochrane—Joe Schmidt, 76, Houston, 1969
Coy Hall—Steve Marcantonio, 76, Alabama, 1973
Kelly Cochrane—Joe Schmidt, 75, Houston, 1969
Frank Glover—Larry Cain, 75, Pittsburgh, 1976

Long Runbacks Of Kickoffs

Ottis Anderson, 100 vs. Utah State, Tulane, 1978
Tim Morgan, 100 vs. Houston, 1975
Tom Sullivan, 99 vs. Army, 1971
Russell Coates, 96 vs. W. Virginia, 1942
John Bahen, 93 vs. Florida, 1961
Tim Morgan, 93 vs. Notre Dame, 1976
Joe Schmidt, 92 vs. Tulane, 1970
Mark Rush, 92 vs. Miss. St., 1980
Eddie Dunn, 87 vs. Georgia St., 1936

Long Runbacks Of Punts

Walter Watt, 87 vs. Texas A&M, 1944
Jack Brasington, 82 vs. Louisville, 1949
H. Johnston—V. Mell, 80 vs. LSU, 1946
Jimmy Dye, 79 vs. Florida, 1967
Joe Panker, 75 vs. Mercer, 1936
Gordon Malloy, 75 vs. Holy Cross, 1954
Rich Robinson, 75 vs. Pittsburgh, 1967
Tony Stawarz, 75 vs. Georgia Tech., 1970

Runbacks Of Interceptions

Paul Hefti, 98 vs. Fordham, 1954
Ed Injaychock, 96 vs. Chattanooga, 1946
Gary Streicher, 96 vs. Army, 1972
Al Hudson, 89 vs. Holy Cross, 1946 (Orange Bowl Game)
Art Knust, 85 vs. Marquette, 1952
Harry Ghaul, 82 vs. Auburn, 1945
John Bookman, 82 vs. Boston College, 1956
Claude Harrison, 82 vs. Ft. Benning, 1943
Ken Corbin, 80 vs. Florida, 1967

Eldridge Mitchell, 79, intercepted pitch-out vs. Oklahoma, 1973

Long Punts

Rob Rajsich, 79 vs. Kansas, 1978
Rob Rajsich, 77 vs. FSU, 1978
Harry Ghaul, 77 vs. Florida, 1947
Howard Plasman, 74 vs. Alabama, 1941
John Douglas, 73 vs. Florida, 1938
Harvey Foster, 71 vs. Georgia, 1961
Al Kasulin, 71 vs. Furman, 1942
Harry Ghaul, 70 vs. Kentucky, 1943
Rod Huffman, 70 vs. FSU, 1974

Longest Field Goal

Chris Dennis, 54 yds. vs. Navy, 1975

Best Average Gain Per Rush (4 or More)

Jack Losch, 39.3 for four vs. Bucknell, 1955
Walter Watt, 20.3 for six vs. St. Louis, 1942
Jack Losch, 16.3 for eight vs. Boston College, 1955
Eddie Dunn, 16.2 for eight vs. Spring Hill, 1936
Eddie Dunn, 15.9 for 11 vs. Georgia St., 1937

Most Touchdowns

Bill L'Italien, 5 vs. Piedmont, 1933
Three each:
Eddie Dunn vs. Georgia St. and Stetson, 1937; Florida, 1938
Charlie Wilkerson vs. Havana, 1928
John Oram vs. Havana, 1928
Joe Panker vs. Baltimore, 1934
Warren Rose vs. Oglethorpe, 1934
Gene Bogart vs. Elon, 1940
Howard Plasman vs. West Virginia Wesleyan, 1941
Peanuts Donahoo vs. South Georgia Normal, 1933
Harry Ghaul vs. Miami U. (Ohio), 1945
Frank Smith vs. Boston U., 1950
Harry Mallios vs. Richmond, 1952, and

Missouri, 1950
Joe Plevel vs. FSU, 1957
Woody Thompson vs. Texas, 1973

Most Field Goals

Dan Miller, 4 vs. North Texas State, 1980
Jim Huff, 3 vs. LSU, 1968; and North Carolina State, 1969
Chris Dennis, 3 vs. FSU and TCU, 1977
Chris Dennis, 3 vs. Nebraska and Navy, 1975
Dan Miller, 3 vs. Florida, 1978 and 1979
Dan Miller, 3 vs. E. Carolina, 1980
Jim Huff, 2 vs. Va. Tech. and Pitt, 1968
Brian Selmer, 2 vs. Army, 1973
Ray Harris, 2 vs. Indiana, 1966
Don Curtright, 2 vs. Boston Col., 1965
Mike Burke, 2 vs. Houston, 1972
Chris Dennis, 2 vs. Houston, 1974

Most Extra Points

Ray Harris, 7 of 7 vs. Ga. Tech., 1967
Jim Huff, 7 of 7 vs. Wake Forest, 1969

Most Touchdowns Intercepted Passes

Ken Corbin, 2 vs. Florida, 1967

Most Times Carried Ball

Ottis Anderson, 39 vs. Florida, 1978
Smokey Roan, 33 vs. E. Carolina, 1980
Woody Thompson, 32 vs. Boston Col., 1973
John Noppenberg, 31 vs. Tampa, 1939
Ottis Anderson, 31 vs. Bos. Col., 1976
Ottis Anderson, 30 vs. Ga. Tech., 1977
Vincent Opalsky, 30 vs. Ga. Tech., 1968
Ottis Anderson, 29 vs. San Diego St., 1978
Taylor Timmons, 28 vs. TCU, 1977
Jim Dooley, 27 vs. Florida, 1950
Bob McDougal, 27 vs. Florida, 1942
Pete Boney, 27 vs. Oglethorpe, 1935
Pete Banaszak, 27 vs. Florida, 1965
Terry Fox, 26 vs. Oglethorpe, 1938
Nick Ryder, 26 vs. Florida, 1962

Most 100 Yard Games

Ottis Anderson, 8 in 1978
Chuck Foreman, 4 in 1971
Ottis Anderson, 4 in 1976

Most Pass Completions

George Mira, 25 of 44 vs. Georgia, 1963
George Mira, 25 of 44 vs. Pittsburgh, 1963
George Mira, 24 of 48 vs. Alabama, 1963
George Mira, 24 of 46 vs. Nebraska, 1962 (Gotham Bowl)
David Olivo, 22 of 32 vs. Va. Tech., 1968
Kelly Cochrane, 22 of 42 vs. Alabama, 1969
George Mira, 21 of 31 vs. Florida, 1963
George Mira, 21 of 31 vs. Maryland, 1962
Kelly Cochrane, 21 of 32 vs. W&M, 1970
George Mira, 21 of 36 vs. Kentucky, 1963
Bill Miller, 21 of 39 vs. LSU, 1965

Most Yards Passing

Kelly Cochrane, 343 vs. Houston, 1969 (17 of 31)
George Mira, 342 vs. Georgia, 1963 (25 of 44)
George Mira, 321 vs. Nebraska, 1962 (24 of 46) Gotham Bowl
Mike Rodrigue, 313 vs. Louisville, 1979 (19 of 32)
George Mira, 309 vs. Pittsburgh, 1963 (25 of 44)
George Mira, 301 vs. Alabama, 1963 (24 of 48)
George Mira, 288 vs. Maryland, 1962 (21 of 31)
Kelly Cochrane, 283 vs. Navy, 1969 (16 of 27)
Bill Miller, 281 vs. LSU, 1965 (21 of 39)
Jim Kelly, 280 vs. Penn State, 1979 (18 of 30)

Most TD Passes Thrown

Kelly Cochrane, 4 vs. Houston, 1969
George Mira, 3 vs. Maryland, 1962; vs. Florida, 1963
Bill Miller, 3 vs. LSU, 1965
David Olivo, 3 vs. Northwestern, 1968
Kelly Cochrane, 3 vs. Navy, 1969
Ed Carney, 3 vs. Maryland, 1972
Jim Kelly, 3 vs. Penn State, 1979

Most Passes Intercepted

Jim Dooley, 4 vs. Clemson, 1951 (Gator Bowl Game)
Three each:
Joe Dixon vs. Catholic U., 1937
Bill Steiner vs. Georgia, 1940
Whitey Campbell vs. Chattanooga, 1946 and Rollins, 1947
Al Hudson vs. Michigan State, 1945 and Georgia, 1948
John Bookman vs. Boston Col., 1956
Larry DiGiammarino vs. Oregon, 1958
Gene Coleman vs. Florida, 1979

Punting Avg., 5 Or More Points

Harry Ghaul, 55.3 for 6 vs. Miami(Ohio), 1946
Mike Burke, 50.3 for 6 vs. Houston, 1972
Harry Ghaul, 49.2 for 5 vs. Georgia, 1948
Al Kasulin, 48.3 for 6 vs. Jax Navy, 1942
Harry Ghaul, 48.3 for 6 vs. Villanova, 1947
Pat Barrett, 47.8 for 11 vs. LSU, 1969
Rod Huffman, 47.8 for 7 vs. FSU, 1975
Harry Ghaul, 47.6 for 7 vs. Cincinnati, 1948

Most Passes Caught

Jerry Daanen, 11 for 127 vs. LSU, 1965
James Cox, 9 for 128 vs. Florida, 1966
Nick Spinelli, 9 for 108 vs. Pitt, 1963
Bill Miller, 9 for 96 vs. Northwestern, 1961
Larry Brodsky, 8 for 143 vs. N. Texas State, 1980
Joe Schmidt, 8 for 129 vs. W&M, 1970
Ed Weisacosky, 8 for 124 vs. Georgia, 1963

Walt Sweeting, 8 for 113 vs. Notre Dame, 1972
Bob Nolan, 8 for 92 vs. Georgia, 1952
David Kalina, 8 for 99 vs. Alabama, 1968
Ray Bellamy, 8 for 121 vs. Auburn, 1968
Mike Adams, 8 for 117 vs. Notre Dame, 1976
Dave Kalina, 8 for 77 vs. FSU, 1969

Joe Schmidt, 129 on 8 vs. W&M, 1970
James Cox, 128 on 9 vs. Florida, 1966
James Cox, 127 on 6 vs. Penn St., 1967
Jerry Daanen, 127 on 11 vs. LSU, 1965
David Kalina, 127 on 7 vs. LSU, 1968

Most Yards Pass Reception

Joe Schmidt, 186 on 5 vs. Houston, 1969
Pat Walker, 159 on 6 vs. Louisville, 1979
Larry Brodsky, 143 on 8 vs. N. Texas State, 1980
David Kalina, 140 on 7 vs. Northwestern, 1968
Chuck Foreman, 135 on 7 vs. Maryland, 1972
Steve Marcantonio, 134 on 6 vs. Syracuse, 1973
Ed Lutes, 130 on 4 vs. Ole Miss., 1951

CAREER RECORDS
Touchdowns

Eddie Dunn (1936, 37, 38)	25
Ottis Anderson (1975, 76, 77, 78)	22
Frank Smith (1948, 50, 51)	20
Harry Ghaul (1945, 46, 47, 48)	20
Chuck Foreman (1970, 71, 72)	17
Vincent Opalsky (1967, 68, 69)	16
Harry Mallios (1950, 51, 52)	15
Walter Watt (1941, 42, 43, 44)	13
Woody Thompson (1972, 73, 74)	13
Gordon Malloy (1952, 53, 54)	12
Pete Banaszak (1963, 64, 65)	12
James Cox (1965, 66, 67)	12
Tom Sullivan (1969, 70, 71)	12

Yards Gained Rushing

Ottis Anderson (1975, 76, 77, 78)	3,331 in 691
Eddie Dunn (1936, 37, 38)	1,778 in 344
Don Bosseler (1953, 54, 55, 56)	1,642 in 385
C. Foreman (1970, 71, 72)	1,631 in 345
Frank Smith (1948, 50, 51)	1,576 in 309
T. Sullivan (1969, 70, 71)	1,541 in 387
V. Opalsky (1967, 68, 69)	1,451 in 377
W. Thompson (1972, 73, 74)	1,338 in 327
Nick Ryder (1960, 61, 62)	1,197 in 240
Terry Fox (1938, 39, 40)	1,177 in 289
J. Vollenweider (1959, 60, 61)	1,169 in 262
Harry Ghaul (1945, 46, 47, 48)	1,108 in 252
Pete Banaszak (1963, 64, 65)	1,107 in 263
Bob McDougal (1941, 42, 46)	1,098 in 265
Chris Hobbs (1978, 79, 80)	1,062 in 293
Harry Mallios (1950, 51, 52)	1,033 in 238
Jim Dooley (1949, 50, 51)	1,029 in 200

Extra Points

Chris Dennis (1974, 75, 76, 77)	66
Harry Ghaul (1945, 46, 47, 48)	58
Dan Miller (1978, 79, 80)	53
Gordon Watson (1944, 49, 50)	42
Ed Oliver (1953, 54, 55)	41
Jim Huff (1968, 69)	39
Ray Harris (1966, 67)	36
Mike Burke (1971, 72)	35

Points On Kicking Alone

Dan Miller (1978, 79, 80)	167
Chris Dennis (1974, 75, 76, 77)	156
Jim Huff (1968, 69)	84
Mike Burke (1971, 72)	71
Harry Ghaul (1945, 46, 47, 48)	64
Ray Harris (1966, 67)	60
Al Dangel (1957, 59, 60)	51
Bob Wilson (1960, 61, 62)	44

Most Consecutive Extra Points

Chris Dennis (1974, 75, 76)	48

Field Goals

Dan Miller (1978, 79, 80)	38
Chris Dennis (1974, 75, 76, 77)	31
Jim Huff (1968, 69)	15
Mike Burke (1971, 72)	12
Dan Miller (1978)	9
Ray Harris (1966, 67)	8

Scoring Leaders

Harry Ghaul (1945, 46, 47, 48)	184
Dan Miller (1978, 79, 80)	167
Eddie Dunn (1936, 37, 38)	160
Chris Dennis (1974, 75, 76, 77)	156
Ottis Anderson (1975, 76, 77, 78)	134
Frank Smith (1948, 50, 51)	126
Harry Mallios (1950, 51, 52)	102
Chuck Foreman (1970, 71, 72)	102
Vincent Opalsky (1967, 68, 69)	96
Jim Huff (1968, 69)	84

Ed Oliver (1953, 54, 55, 56)	83
Nick Spinelli (1961, 62, 63)	82
Woody Thompson (1972, 73, 74)	78

Forward Passes

George Mira (1961, 62, 63)	368 of 745
K. Cochrane (1969, 70, 71)	266 of 576
David Olivo (1966, 67, 68)	230 of 453
Fran Curci (1957, 58, 59)	187 of 356
Bill Miller (1965, 66, 67)	178 of 359
Kary Baker (1973, 74, 75)	158 of 359
Jim Kelly (1979, 80)	157 of 310
Ed Carney (1972, 73)	135 of 303
Mike Rodrigue (1978, 79, 80)	148 of 328
Don James (1951, 52, 53)	121 of 219
Bob Biletnikoff (1964, 65)	113 of 211

Forward Pass Yardage

George Mira (1961, 62, 63)	4,623
Kelly Cochrane (1969, 70, 71)	3,241
David Olivo (1966, 67, 68)	2,812
Bill Miller (1965, 66, 67)	2,328
Jim Kelly (1979, 80)	2,240
Ed Carney (1972, 73)	2,057
Kary Baker (1973, 74, 75)	2,016
Fran Curci (1957, 58, 59)	1,937
Mike Rodrigue (1978, 79, 80)	1,776
E. J. Baker (1976, 77)	1,422
Jack Hackett (1949, 50, 51)	1,386

Passes Caught

Bill Miller (1959, 60, 61)	102
James Cox (1965, 66, 67)	97
Dave Kalina (1968, 69)	88
Nick Spinelli (1961, 62, 63)	80
Joe Schmidt (1968, 69, 70)	75
Frank McDonald (1951, 52, 53, 54)	68
Pat Walker (1977, 78, 79, 80)	66
Jim Joiner (1977, 78, 79, 80)	66
Larry Brodsky (1979, 80)	63
Jerry Daanen (1965, 66, 67)	61
Steve Marcantonio (1972, 73, 74)	61
Phil August (1973, 74, 75, 76)	61

Yards Gained On Passes Caught

	Yards Gained	Passes Caught
James Cox (1965, 66, 67)	1,464	(97)
Bill Miller (1959, 60, 61)	1,448	(102)
Joe Schmidt (1968, 69, 70)	1,231	(75)
Pat Walker (1977, 78, 79, 80)	1,165	(66)
Dave Kalina (1968, 69)	1,160	(88)
Phil August (1973, 74, 75, 76)	1,155	(61)
Nick Spinelli (1961, 62, 63)	1,104	(80)
Larry Brodsky (1979, 80)	1,065	(63)
Steve Marcantonio (1972, 73, 74)	982	(61)
Jim Joiner (1977, 78, 79, 80)	981	(66)
W. Beckman (1971, 72, 74)	928	(56)

Touchdown Passes Thrown

George Mira (1961, 62, 63)	28
David Olivo (1966, 67, 68)	21
Kelly Cochrane (1969, 70, 71)	18
Bill Miller (1965, 66, 67)	17
Jim Kelly (1979, 80)	16
Fran Curci (1957, 58, 59)	13
Jack Hackett (1949, 50, 51)	12
Ed Carney (1972, 73)	9
E. J. Baker (1976, 77)	9
Jack Del Bello (1948, 49, 50)	8
Hal Johnston (1946, 47)	8
Kary Baker (1973, 74, 75)	8

Touchdown Passes Caught

James Cox (1965, 66, 67)	12
Nick Spinelli (1961, 62, 63)	9
Jerry Daanen (1965, 66, 67)	9
Bill Miller (1959, 60, 61)	8
Ed Lutes (1950, 51)	7
Frank Smith (1948, 50, 51)	7
Dave Kalina (1968, 69)	7
Joe Schmidt (1968, 69, 70)	7

Forward Passes Intercepted

Whitey Rouviere (1952, 53, 54, 55) 13 for 55 yds.

Gene Coleman (1977, 78, 79) 13 for 103 yds.

Jim Dooley (1949, 50, 51) 12 for 129 yds.

Bryan Ferguson (1975, 76, 77) 11 for 142 yds.

Fred Marion (1978, 79, 80) 10 for 111 yds.

Whitey Campbell (1946, 47, 48, 49) 10 for 64 yds.

Eddie Dunn (1936, 37, 38) 9 for 97 yds.

John Bookman (1953, 54, 55, 56) 9 for 178 yds.

Jack Del Bello (1948, 49, 50) 9 for 139 yds.

Al Hudson (1944, 45, 47, 48) 9 for 105 yds.

Jimmy Dye (1966, 67) 9 for 100 yds.

Ernie Jones (1973, 74, 75) 9 for 56 yds.

Yards On Pass Interceptions

Greg Perez (1968, 69)	182 on 8
J. Bookman (1953, 54, 55, 56)	178 on 9
Gary Streicher (1972, 73)	148 on 3
Bryan Ferguson (1975, 76, 77)	142 on 11
Jack Del Bello (1948, 49, 50)	139 on 9
Arnold Tucker (1943)	132 on 6
Jim Dooley (1949, 50, 51)	129 on 12
Carl Garrigus (1952, 53, 54)	128 on 6
Art Knust (1951, 52, 53)	124 on 3
Ronnie Lippett (1980)	118 on 3
Ed Injaychalk (1944, 45, 46, 47)	118 on 6

Yards Returned Kickoffs

T. Sullivan (1969, 70, 71)	49 for 1,121
Tim Morgan (1973, 74, 75, 76)	43 for 1,036
C. Foreman (1970, 71, 72)	42 for 882
Nick Spinelli (1961, 62, 63)	31 for 637
R. Smith (1963, 64, 65)	28 for 630
J. Joiner (1977, 78, 79)	27 for 624
Joe Schmidt (1968, 69, 70)	19 for 527
Mark Rush (1979, 80)	21 for 474
M. Simmons (1977, 78, 79)	22 for 443
E. Dunn (1936, 37, 38)	13 for 406
O. Anderson (1975, 76, 77, 78)	12 for 395

Punt Returns

E. Dunn (1936, 37, 38)	91 for 1,153
A. Kasulin (1941, 42, 43)	42 for 548
B. Steiner (1939, 40)	37 for 461
F. Smith (1948, 50, 51)	29 for 420
W. Campbell (1946, 47, 48, 49)	28 for 405
N. Spinelli (1961, 62, 63)	43 for 385
B. Ferguson (1975, 76, 77)	47 for 351
A. Sixkiller (1964, 65)	27 for 322
Russell Coates (1940, 41, 42)	25 for 278
J. Dye (1966, 67)	23 for 312

All Purpose Running

Player	Yrs.	Rush.	Pass Rec.	Kick Ret.	Total Yds.
O. Anderson	(1975, 76, 77, 78)	3,331	539	395	4,265
E. Dunn	(1936, 37, 38)	1,778	32	1,666	3,476
Foreman	(1970, 71, 72)	1,631	732	992	3,365
Sullivan	(1969, 70, 71)	1,541	332	1,132	3,005
F. Smith	(1948, 50, 51)	1,454	372	515	2,341
Bosseler	(1953, 54, 55, 56)	1,642	78	610	2,330

		Tries	Rush.	Pass.	Total
Spinelli	(1961, 62, 63)	74	1,104	1,059	2,237
T. Morgan	(1973, 74, 75, 76)	831	148	1,036	2,015
Jim Joiner	(1977, 78, 79, 80)	259	981	745	1,985
R. Smith	(1963, 64, 65)	770	342	817	1,929

Total Offense

Player	Yrs.	Tries	Rush.	Pass.	Total
G. Mira	(1961, 62, 63)	934	502	4,623	5,125
O. Anderson	(1975, 76, 77, 78)	696	3,331	69	3,400
K. Cochrane	(1969, 70, 71)	694	19	3,241	3,260
David Olivo	(1966, 67, 68)	743	156	2,812	2,968
F. Curci	(1957, 58, 59)	644	830	1,937	2,767
E. Dunn	(1936, 37, 38)	500	1,778	727	2,505
B. Miller	(1965, 66, 67)	483	9	2,328	2,337
J. Kelly	(1979, 80)	361	89	2,240	2,329
E. Carney	(1972, 73)	462	192	2,057	2,249
M. Rodrigue	(1978, 79, 80)	465	105	1,776	1,881
F. Smith	(1948, 49, 50, 51)	318	1,576	188	1,764
K. Baker	(1973, 74)	394	430	1,254	1,684

Most 100-Yard Games

Ottis Anderson (1975, 76, 77, 78) 13
Eddie Dunn (1936, 37, 38) 5
Chuck Foreman (1970, 71, 72) 5

Fumbles Recovered

Ted Hendricks (1966, 67, 68) 12
Pete Mastellone (1948, 49, 50) 8
Mike Barnes (1970, 71, 72) 8
Walter Kichefski (1936, 38, 39) 6
Sam David (1948, 49, 50) 6
Dick Sorensen (1967, 68, 69) 6
Al Palewicz (1969, 71, 72) 6

Most Tackles, By Positions

End—Hendricks (1966, 67, 68) 227
Tackle—Nicolas (1978, 79, 80) 226
Middle Guard—Burt (1977, 78, 79, 80) 177
Linebacker—Corbin (1965, 66, 67) and Liddell (1972, 73, 74) 201
Cornerback—Beier (1965, 66) 120
Safety—Marion (1978, 79, 80) 117

Most Assists, By Positions

End—Hendricks (1966, 67, 68) 100

Tackle—Greaves (1956, 57, 58) 76
Middle Guard—Burt (1977, 78, 79, 80) 86
Linebacker—Griffiths (1972, 73, 74) 121
Cornerback—Beier (1965, 66) 57
Safety—Marion (1978, 79, 80) 66

Overall Participation In Tackle, Tackle Assists

End—Hendricks (1966, 67, 68) 347
LB-Nicolas (1978, 79, 80) 332
LB—Liddell (1972, 73, 74) 321
LB—Griffiths (1972, 73, 74) 308
T. MG—Carter (1972, 73, 74) 306
LB—Axson (1977, 78, 79, 80) 299
DE, LB—Weisacosky (1963, 64, 65) 297
LB—Corbin (1965, 66, 67) 295

MISCELLANEOUS U of MIAMI RECORDS

Most consecutive forward pass completions—10, Eddie Johns vs. Boston College and Florida State, 1960.

Most consecutive forward passes completed, one game, Mike Rodrigue, 9, vs. Tulane, 1978.

Most consecutive field goals kicked—7, Dan Miller, last two in 1978, first 5 in 1979.

Highest percentage of field goal attempts converted—Dan Miller, .786 in 1979, 14 of 17.

Most consecutive field goals, one season—6, Jim Huff, in 1968.

Most touchdown passes caught, one game, 2 by several players. Last by Jim Joiner vs. Penn State, 1979.

Most consecutive 100 yard games, rushing—4 by Ottis Anderson, 1978.

Most consecutive games in which passer gained 200 yards or more—5, Kelly Cochrane, 1970, vs. Houston (343), Navy (283); Alabama (256); Wake Forest (208) and Florida (223).

Most consecutive passes thrown without an interception, one game—George Mira, 42 vs. Florida, 1963.

Most consecutive passes thrown without an interception—George Mira, 116 vs. Kentucky, North Carolina, Florida, Pittsburgh, 1963.

Most consecutive games catching TD passes—Nick Spinelli, 4 in 1963.

Most consecutive games scoring a touchdown—Eddie Dunn, 6 in 1938.

Most fumbles recovered, one game—Jim Burt 4 vs. Vanderbilt in 1980.

SUPPLEMENTARY RECORDS

Opponents Best Individual Single Game
Performances Against Miami

Total off.: 414 yards (7 rush, 407 pass)
   Larry Rakestraw, Georgia, '63
Rushing: 308 yards (33 carries)
   Curtis Kuykendall, Auburn '44
Passing: 407 yards (25 of 38 tries)
   Larry Rakestraw, Georgia, '63
Best rush avg.: 18.3 (8 carries)
   Liston Bochette, Rollins, '49
Most times carried ball: 38
   O. J. Simpson, Southern Cal. '68
Most touchdowns: 4
   Curtis Kuykendall, Auburn, '44
   Joseph Scott, Texas A & M, '44
   Anthony Gabriel, Syracuse, '70
Longest run: 83 yards
   Carl Genito, Kentucky, '48

Longest pass: 81 yards
   Jeff Austin to Emery Moorhead, Colorado, '76
Longest kickoff return: 100 yards
   Gary Martin, Alabama, '63
   Bob Polidor, Villanova, '46
   Mike Esposito, Boston College, '73
Longest punt return: 96 yards
   Hal Griffin, Florida, '46
Longest interception runback: 99 yards
   Fred Biletnikoff, FSU, '63
Most field goals: 3
   Grant Guthrie, FSU, '69
   Billy Schott, Texas, '72
   David Jacobs, Syracuse, '78
Most extra points: 6

George Jakawenko, Syracuse, '70
Richard Franco, Florida, '71
Most TD passes thrown: 4
Gary Huff, FSU, '72
John Reaves, Florida, '71
Most passes caught: 15
Carlos Alvarez, Florida, '69
Most yards pass receptions: 237
Carlos Alvarez, Florida, '69
Most passes attempted: 50
John Reaves, Florida, '71

Most passes completed: 33
John Reaves, Florida, '71
Most passes intercepted: 3
Jack Eastwood, West Va., '73
Best punting average: 52.4 (on 5)
Bob Campbell, Penn State, '67
Longest punt: 88 yards
John Fritsch, Maryland, '56
Longest field goal: 55 yards
John Riley, Auburn, '67

Football Players And Coaches
In University Of Miami Sports Hall Of Fame

Bill Kimbrough
Denny Leonard
Bob Masterson
Walter Kichefski
Hart Morris
Tom Kearns
Harry Ghaul
Al Carapella
Andy Gustafson
Jack Hackett
Don Bosseler
George Mira
Larry Wilson
Frank McDonald
Bill Miller
Dan Conners
Gordon Malloy
Frank Curci

Rod Ashman
Nick Wolcuff
Eddie Dunn
Jack Harding
John Tobin
Al Rosen
Whitey Campbell
Frank Smith
Jim Dooley
Leo Martin
Jim Otto
Dave Wike
Chuck Klein
Art Saey
Ray Arckey
Armand Vari
Edward Cameron
Ted Hendricks

HURRICANES FORMERLY OR PRESENTLY IN THE PROS

Don Bosseler, Washington Redskins
Fred Brown, Los Angeles Rams, Philadelphia Eagles
Al Carapella, San Francisco 49ers
Nick Chickillo, Chicago Cardinals
Fran Curci, Dallas Texans
Charles Diamond, Dallas Texans
Chuck Foreman, Minnesota Vikings,

New England Patriots
Gary Greaves, Houston Oilers
Jack Johnson, Chicago Bears
Tom Kearns, New York Giants
Walt Kichefski, Pittsburgh Steelers
Jack Losch, Green Bay Packers
Bob McDougel, Green Bay Packers
John Noppenberg, Pittsburgh Steelers,

Cleveland Rams
Terry Fox, Philadelphia Eagles
Jack Novak, Green Bay Packers
Tom Pratt, (coach) Kansas City Chiefs,
New Orleans Saints
Walter Corey, Kansas City Chiefs,
(coach) Cleveland Browns, Chiefs
Nick Ryder, Detroit Lions
Jim Simon, Detroit Lions, Atlanta
Falcons
John Sisk, Chicago Bears
Bob Masterson, Washington Redskins
John Bookman, New York Giants
Walter Watt, Chicago Cardinals
Jim Dooley, Chicago Bears (player,
coach)
Mike Hudock, New York Giants
Tom Jelly, Pittsburgh Steelers
Jack Losch, Green Bay Packers
Russell Smith, San Diego Chargers
Dan Conners, Oakland Raiders
Ed Weisocosky, Miami Dolphins
Bob Worl, New York Jets
Pete Banaszak, Oakland Raiders
John Matlock, New York Jets
Eugene Trosch, Kansas City Chiefs
Tom Beier, Miami Dolphins
Tom Sullivan, Philadelphia Eagles
Dennis Harrah, Los Angeles Rams
Rubin Carter, Denver Broncos
Don Latimer, Denver Broncos
Don Smith, Atlanta Falcons
Gary Dunn, Pittsburgh Steelers
Woody Bennett, New York Giants,

Miami Dolphins
Woody Thompson, Atlanta Falcons
Ottis Anderson, St. Louis Cardinals
Mike Burke, Los Angeles Rams
David Olivo, St. Louis Cardinals
Mike Barnes, Baltimore Colts
Arnold Butkus, Montreal Allouettes
Bob Brown, British Columbia Lions
Rich Robinson, British Columbia Lions
Jimmy Dye, Toronto Argonauts
Greg Perez, Calgary Stampeeders
Eddie Edwards, Cincinnati Bengals
Larry Brown, Kansas City Chiefs
Bryan Ferguson, New England Patriots
John Turner, Minnesota Vikings
Ernie Jones, New York Giants
Bill Cesare, Tampa Bay Buccaneers
Jerry Daanen, St. Louis Cardinals
Mike Haggerty, Pittsburgh Steelers
Bill Miller, Oakland Raiders
George Mira, San Francisco 49ers,
Miami Dolphins
Bob Tatarek, Buffalo Bills
Ted Hendricks, Baltimore Colts, Green
Bay Packers, Oakland Raiders
Tony Cline, Oakland Raiders, San
Francisco 49ers
Vince Opalsky, Los Angeles Rams
Dave Kalina, Pittsburgh Steelers
Jim Vollenweider, San Francisco 49ers
Jim Otto, Oakland Raiders
Burgess Owens, New York Jets, Oak-
land Raiders

LETTERMEN

1927

Ashman, Rod
Bleier, Theodore
Carbonneau, Harold
Catha, Lawrence
Courtney, Cliff
Franklin, Alfred
Hauser, Francis
Kimbrough, William
Kidwell, Dale
Lindstrom, Evan
Lyons, Herman
McGuire, John
Mills, Austin
O'Brien, James
Solie, Lloyd
Stanton, Robert
Sutton, Otis
Thomas, William
Tuttle, Leonard
White, Phillip
Wignall, Fred
Wood, Hayes

1928

Ashman, Rod
Bleier, Theodore
Catha, Lawrence
Courtney, Cliff
Downes, Robert
Franklin, Alfred
Hansen, Louis
Harris, Grant
Hauser, Francis
Kavney, Hugh
Kimbrough, William
Lindstrom, Evan
Lyons, Herman
Mercurio, Marion
Mills, Austin
O'Brien, Jim
Oram, Hal
Solie, Lloyd
Sutton, Otis
Wignall, Fred
Wilkinson, Charlie
Williams, Reed

1929

Bleier, Theodore
Catha, Lawrence
Courtney, Cliff
Downes, Robert
Franklin, Alfred
Gerrard, Stephen
Hansen, Louis
Hauser, Francis
Jones, William
Kavney, Hugh
Lindstrom, Evan
Mercurio, Marion
Okell, George
Siler, Frank
Solie, Lloyd
Wignall, Fred
Wilkinson, Charlie
Williams, Reed

1930

Bates, Johnny
Bielinski, Henry
Crowe, Luke
Downes, Robert
Fenwick, William
Franklin, Alfred
Hansen, Louis
Hauser, Francis
Jones, William
Kavney, Hugh
Martens, Raymond
Mercurio, Marion
O'Day, John, Sr.
Okell, George
Ramsbotham, Ernest
Robertson, Cushman
Rostron, Fred
Siler, Frank
Smith, Norman
Solie, Lloyd
Sutton, Otis

1931

Alter, Foster
Bates, Johnny
Cronin, Joseph
Crowe, Luke
Dansky, Walter
Downes, Robert
Fogler, Floyd
Gracyk, Edward
Graney, Thomas
Heckman, Charles
Kavney, Hugh
Kimbrough, Stanford
Kozlowski, Adolph
Lee, George
L'Italien, William
Middleton, John
O'Day, John, Sr.
Peterniche, John
Phillips, Stanley
Puglisi, Frank

Reichgott, George
Siler, Frank

1932

Bates, Johnny
Dansky, Walter
Fenwick, Bill
Fogler, Floyd
Foote, Norman
Graczyk, Edward
Graney, Thomas
Greer, Wallace
Heckman, Charles
Henderson, James
Kozlowski, Adolph
L'Italien, William
Matherson, Paul
Middleton, John
O'Day, John, Sr.
Okell, George
Ott, John
Peterniche, John
Phillips, Stanley
Riesman, Albert
Reichgott, George
Sissman, Michael
Snowden, Olin
Sutton, Otis, B.
Thompson, Tommy

1933

Beusse, James
Bierkamper, Gwynn
Brion, Harold
Buck, Walter
Cook, Cecil
Dansky, Walter
Donahoo, "Peanuts"
Fahrney, Emerson
Gracyk, Edward
Heckman, Charles

Henderson, James
Kuder, Al
Leonard, Dennis
Lewis, D. G., Jr.
L'Italien, William
Ott, John
Petrowski, Pete
Reichgott, George
Sissman, Mike
Thompson, Tommy
Wilson, Reggie

1934

Baker, Charles
Beary, James
Beusse, James
Bierkamper, Gwynn
Boney, Fleeman
Brion, Harold
Cook, Cecil
Dansky, Walter
DelMastro, Salvadore
Gaiero, Augustus
Glogowski, Nat
Horton, Mallory
Kalix, Martin
Leonard, Dennis
Panker, Joe
Petrowski, Pete
Phillips, Stan
Pickett, Malcolm
Rose, Warren
Shinn, Charles
Sissman, Mike
Thompson, Tommy
Wilson, Reggie
Wolcuff, Nick

1935

Baker, Charles
Beusse, James

Boney, Fleeman
Cook, Cecil
DelMastro, Salvadore
Dicker, Jack
Glogowski, Nat
Gostowski, Henry
Grau, Erwin
Graves, Archie
Kalix, Martin
Leonard, Dennis
Masterson, Robert
Ott, John
Panker, Joe
Petrowski, Pete
Rose, Warren
Shinn, Charles
Wolcuff, Nicholas

1936

Bolash, John
Csaky, Andrew
DelMastro, Salvadore
Dicker, Jack
Dunn, Eddie
Glogowski, Nat
Gostowski, Henry
Kichefski, Walter
Masterson, Robert
Panker, Joe
Rose, Warren
Shinn, Charles
Vaccarelli, Anthony
Wolcuff, Nicholas

1937

Black, William
Bolash, John
Chesna, Lou
Condon, Thomas
Csaky, Andrew
Dixon, Joseph

Douglas, John
Dunn, Eddie
Guimento, Charles
Hanley, Augustine
Hayward, Harry
Jones, Carl
McCrimmon, Steve
Masterson, Robert
Noppenberg, John
Oespovich, John
Paskewich, Frank
Pittard, George
Poore, James
Raski, Stan
Salisbury, Don
Vaccarelli, Anthony

1938

Bolash, John
Borek, Matthew
Cohen, Alvin
Corcoran, John
Csaky, Andrew
Dixon, Joseph
Douglas, John
Duncan, Eugene
Dunn, Eddie
Fox, Terrence
Grimes, Robert
Guimento, Charles
Hamilton, George
Hayward, Harry
Jones, Carl
Kichefski, Walter
Kurucza, John
McCrimmon, Steve
Noppenberg, John
Paskewich, Frank
Pittard, George
Poore, James
Raski, Stan
Salisbury, Don

Sapp, Carl
Snowden, Crumpton
Stockdale, Grant
Steiner, William

1939

Arries, Verdun
Borek, Matthew
Corcoran, John
Dixon, Joseph
Fox, Terrence
Grimes, Robert
Guimento, Charles
Jones, Carl
Kearns, Tom
Kichefski, Walter
Krutulis, Joe
Kurucza, John
McCrimmon, Steve
Noppenberg, John
Oespovich, John
Paskewich, Frank
Pittard, George
Poore, James
Raski, Stan
Salisbury, Don
Sapp, Carl
Schemer, Mike
Snowden, Crumpton
Steiner, Bill
Stockdale, Grant
Tobin, John
Wike, Dave

1940

Arries, Verdun
Bogart, Eugene
Borek, Matthew
Broker, Nick
Carifeo, Paul
Coates, Russell

Cohen, Seymour
Douglas, John
Fox, Terrence
Gorman, Raymond
Harris, Reddic
Kearns, Tom
Krutulis, Joe
Kurucza, John
Lee, Hartford J.
Lehn, Frank
O'Neal, Maston
Robinson, Ray
Sapp, Carl
Snowden, Crumpton
Steiner, William
Tobin, John
Totterdale, Bill
Trobliger, Bernard
Wunder, Bill

1941

Adler, Alfred
Broker, Nick
Cameron, Edward
Carifeo, Paul
Coates, Russell
Dunn, Raymond
James, Harvey
Kasulin, Al
Douglas, Robert
Gagliardi, George
Gorman, Raymond
Johnson, James
Jupin, Eugene
Kaldor, Joe
Kearns, Tom
Kendall, Jack
Krutulis, Joe
Lehn, Frank
McDougal, Robert
Mooney, George

Petroski, Joseph
Plasman, Howard
Robinson, Ray
Ruzomberka, Edward
Sapp, Earl
Tobin, John
Trobliger, Bernard
Watt, Walter
Wunder, William

1942

Adler, Alfred
Boyd, Tyra
Chuprevich, Joe
Coates, Russell
Dixon, William
Dunn, Raymond
Ferrante, Lou
Kasulin, Al
Klein, Morris
Douglas, Robert
Gagliardi, George
Gorman, Raymond
Hlasnick, Edward
Jahn, George
Kolz, Bob
McDougal, Robert
Marzella, Sam
Mooney, George
Musante, Andrew
Nealon, Robert
Pollock, Richard
Ruzomberka, Edward
Schultz, Leon
Watt, Walter
Sapp, Earl

1943

Barwick, Bill
Carifeo, Paul
Carden, N. J.

Deas, Lonnie
Eisnor, Bill
Ferguson, Ralph
Harrison, Claude
James, Harvey
Kaplan, Phil
Klein, Morris
Kearns, Tom
Kinsey, John
Krutulis, Joe
Leavitt, James
Levitt, William
Rosen, Al
Schultz, Leon
Smith, Ray
Tucker, Arnold
Watt, Walter
Wright, Leon

1944

Barrington, Glenn
Bartemus, J. B.
Brown, James
Dielens, Gus
Hancock, Gene
Harrell, Robert
Hildreth, Paul
Hudson, Al
Injaychock, Ed
LeCompte, Max
Levitt, Bill
McCreary, William
Mell, John
Perrin, Tom
Pinckney, Vince
Procida, Sam
Settle, Cecil
Smith, Al
Sobeck, Joe
Thomas, Joe
Trathen, Dick
Watt, Walter

1945

Bowman, Bob
Cameron, Edward
Chappas, James
Corrigan, Phillip
DelGrante, Edward
DeMarco, Mario
Dermigny, John
DiBuono, Carl
Doyle, Keith
Frantz, William
Ghaul, Harry
Hagan, Arthur
Hancock, Gene
Hudson, Al
Injaychock, Ed
Jones, Don
Krasnai, William
Krull, Joseph
Levitt, William
Lipchick, Pete
Marler, Sylvan
Mazeika, Ernest
Mell, John
Moyer, Ed
Settembre, Ernest
Pinckney, Vincent
Smith, Al
Spinelli, Vincent
Vaccaro, Jim
White, Shelton

1946

Adler, Alfred
Newman, Bob
Campbell, Whitey
Carifeo, George
DeMarco, Mario
Dermigny, John
Doyle, Keith
Dunn, Raymond

Eldredge, Dave
Ferrante, Lou
Frantz, William
Ghaul, Harry
Hancock, Eugene
Hauck, Ed
Injaychock, Ed
James, Harvey
Johnston, Hal
Kaplan, Phil
Kennedy, Donald
Kendrick, Jay
Klein, Morris
Krasnai, William
Krull, Joseph
McDougal, Robert
Mazeika, Ernest
Mell, John
Mosso, Carl
Moyer, Ed
Novak, Andy
Saey, Art
Ruzomberka, Ed
Schuler, Harold
Settembre, Ernest
Snowden, Charles
Sutter, Robert
Wilson, Lee
Yovicsin, Tony

1947

Adler, Alfred
Bowman, Bob
Campbell, Whitey
Carifeo, George
Carroll, Robert
Cobb, Donald
Davies, Arthur
DeLonga, Leonard
DeMarco, Mario
Dermigny, John

Dixon, William
Doyle, Keith
Dunlop, Art
Fieler, Ralph
Flynn, Thomas
Frantz, William
Ghaul, Harry
Hauck, Ed
Hudson, Al
Injaychock, Ed
Johnston, Hal
Kasulin, Al
Kendrick, Jay
Krull, Joe
Mazejka, Ernest
Mosso, Carl
Moyer, Ed
Novak, Andy
Saey, Art
Shrader, Clive
Schuler, Hal
Settembre, Ernest
Sutter, Bob
Yovicsin, Tony

1948

Burney, Jack
Campbell, Whitey
Carapella, Al
Carroll, Robert
Cobb, Donald
Czaplinski, Richard
Davies, Arthur
David, Sam
DelBello, Jack
DeMarco, Mario
Fieler, Ralph
Flynn, Thomas
Ferguson, John
Ghaul, Harry
Hudson, Al
Konovalchick, Andy

Krull, Joe
Mastellone, Pete
Mosso, Carl
Moyer, Ed
Novak, Andy
O'Leary, Jack
Russo, Art
Saey, Art
Settembre, Ernest
Shrader, Clive
Smith, Elmer
Smith, Frank

1949

Allen, Harold
Arcangeletti, Ray
Buoyoucas, Ted
Brasington, Jack
Campbell, Whitey
Carapella, Al
Carroll, Robert
Cobb, Donald
Chwalik, Walter
Czaplinski, Richard
David, Sam
Davies, Arthur
DelBello, Jack
Dooley, Jim
Ferguson, John
Fieler, Ralph
Flynn, Thomas
George, Charlie
Hackett, Jack
Jelley, Thomas
Lyden, Joseph
Martin, Leo
Mastellone, Pete
McDonald, Dave
Novak, Andy
Shrader, Clive
Sunderland, John
Vacchio, Mike
Watson, Gordon

1950

Allen, Harold
Arcangeletti, Ray
Bartolovich, Joseph
Bouyoucas, Ted
Bow, Johnny
Boxx, Bernard
Carapella, Al
Castagno, John
Chwalik, Walter
Czaplinski, Richard
David, Sam
DelBello, Jack
Devereaux, William
Diamond, William
Dooley, Jim
Fieler, Ralph
Gaines, Robert
George, Charlie
Hackett, Jack
Jelley, Thomas
Lutes, Ed
Lyden, Joe
Mallios, Harry
Martin, Leo
Mariutto, Donald
Mastellone, Pete
McCloskey, Jack
Schneidenbach, Robert
Shiver, Rex
Smith, Frank
Sunderland, John
Stafford, Robert
Stolk, Wilfred
Tremont, Elmer
Vacchio, Mike
Vari, Armand
Watson, Gordon

1951

Aguilera, Ralph

Arcangeletti, Ray
Bow, Johnny
Bartolovich, Joseph
Buccilli, Eugene
Castagno, John
Chickillo, Nick
Constantino, Anthony
 (Pud)
Chwalik, Walter
Diamond, William
Dooley, Jim
Fisher, William
French, Norman
George, Charley
Hackett, Jack
Knust, Art
Lubas, Ted
Lutes, Ed
McCloskey, Jack
McDonald, Frank
Mallios, Harry
Mariutto, Don
Martin, Leo
Melear, John
O'Boyle, Leo
Pagley, Vincent
Payne, Mack
Schneidenbach, Robert
Shiver, Rex
Smith, Frank
Stolk, Wilfred
Tedder, Phil
Tremont, Elmer
Vari, Armand

1952

Aguilera, Ralph
Albrecht, Richard
Bucilli, Eugene
Carlstrom, Joe
Chickillo, Nick
Constantino, Anthony
 (Pud)

Della Valle, Robert
Festa, Frank
Fisher, William
French, Norman
Garrigus, Carl
Grady, Frank
Greenspan, Sidney
James, Donald
Knust, Art
LaRussa, James
Linus, James
Lubas, Ted
McDonald, Frank
Mallios, Harry
Malloy, Gordon
Mariutto, Donald
Melear, John
Mosketti, Robert
Mugler, Glenn
Nolan, Robert
Pagley, Vincent
Panno, Phil
Payne, Jack
Pepsin, Thomas
Piper, Wally
Presnell, James
Rodberg, Allen
Rouviere, Whitey
Schneidenbach, Robert
Schultz, Joseph
Shiver, Rex
Smith, William
Tassotti, Dan
Vari, Armand

1953

Bookman, John
Bosseler, Don
Bucilli, Edward
Bucilli, Eugene
Della Valle, Robert
Dorshimer, Donald

216

French, Norman
Hutchings, Charles
James, Donald
Johnson, Donald
Johnston, J. B.
Knust, Art
Kohut, Joseph
Krotec, John
Linus, James
Lowe, Jack
Lubas, Ted
McDonald, Frank
Malloy, Gordon
Martin, Sylvester (Furman)
Nardulli, Frank
Nolan, Robert
Oliver, Edward
Pepsin, Thomas
Pratt, Thomas
Rodberg, Allan
Rouviere, Whitey
Smith, William
Tassotti, Dan
Tobey, Ernest

1954

Bonofiglio, Mario
Bookman, John
Bosseler, Don
Cunio, Bob
Della Valle, Robert
French, Norman
Garrigus, Carl
Hefti, Paul
Hudock, Mike
Hutchings, Charles
Johnson, Donald
Kohut, Joseph
Krotec, John
Losch, Jack
McDonald, Frank
Malloy, Gordon

Martin, Sylvester (Furman)
Nolan, Robert
Pepsin, Thomas
Pratt, Thomas
Rodberg, Allan
Rouviere, Whitey
Shields, John
Stokes, John
Tobey, Ernest
Vasu, George

1955

Bennett, Phil
Bonofiglio, Mario
Bookman, John
Bosseler, Don
Cunio, Bob
Della Valle, Robert
DeVore, Charles
Hefti, Paul
Hudock, Mike
Hutchings, Charles
Johnson, Don
Johnson, Jack
Kohut, Joe
Krotec, John
Losch, Jack
Martin, Sylvester
Melwid, John
Nolan, Bob
Oliver, Ed
Pratt, Tom
Reeves, Gene
Rodberg, Allan
Rouviere, Whitey
Scarnecchia, Sam
Siegel, John
Bob Stewart
Varone, John

1956

Bennett, Phil

Bookman, John
Bosseler, Don
Cunio, Bob
DeTroia, Tony
DeVore, Chuck
Diamond, Charles
Dorshimer, Don
Geatz, Phil
Greaves, Gary
Hefti, Paul
Hudock, Mike
Hutchings, Charles
Johnson, Don
Johnson, Jack
Kochifos, Andy
Newcomb, Vester
Oliver, Ed
Plevel, Joe
Pratt, Tom
Sandie, Bill
Scarnecchia, Sam
Siebel, William
Shields, John
Stewart, Bob
Vasiloff, William
Varone, John
Wallace, Don
Yarbrough, Bonnie

1957

Blasko, Byron
Corey, Walter
Crawford, James
Curci, Fran
Deiderich, Harry
Diamond, Charles
Geatz, Phil
Greaves, Gary
Hayes, Bill
Hildebrant, Doug
Mirilovich, Jon
Moskos, Jim

Newcomb, Vester
Nodoline, Frank
Otto, James
Plevel, Joe
Poole, Bill
Stewart, Bob
Stewart, Terry
Vasiloff, Bill
Varone, John
Wallace, Don

1958

Bouffard, Frank
Costello, John
Coughlin, Dan
Crawford, James
Curci, Fran
Davis, Doug
Diamond, Charlie
DiGiammarino, Larry
Geatz, Phil
Greaves, Gary
Hayes, Bill
Hildebrandt, Doug
Linning, Charles
MacIntyre, George
Mirilovich, Jon
Mitchell, Theron
Novak, Jack
Otto, James
Plevel, Joe
Poole, Bill
Remmy, Fred
Rosbaugh, Bob
Wallace, Don
Yarbrough, Bonnie

1959

Babb, Larry
Bouffard, Frank
Brickman, Bill

Clark, Tom
Corey, Walter
Crawford, James
Curci, Fran
Dangel, Al
Davis, Doug
Diamond, Bill
Eggert, Robert
Fritzsche, Ron
Harrison, Mike
Heninger, Larry
Herman, Jack
Linning, Charles
Livingston, Charles
Markowski, Stan
Mayhew, Jon
Miller, Bill
Mills, Reuben
Mirilovich, Jon
Novak, Jack
O'Day, John, Jr.
Otto, James
Reinhart, Frank
Remmy, Fred
Rosbaugh, Bob
Savoca, Vic
Stanley, Joe
Vollenweider, James
Watts, John
Wilson, Larry

1960

Dangel, Al
Diamond, Bill
DiGiammarino, Larry
Dentel, Bob
Eggert, Robert
Fernandez, Sam
Fritzsche, Ron
Harrison, Mike
Johns, Eddie
Lardani, Ray

Linning, Charles
Livingston, Charles
Markowski, Stan
Miller, Bill
Mills, Reuben
Mayhew, John
O'Day, John, Jr.
O'Mahony, James
Reinhart, Frank
Reynolds, Jerry
Rizzo, Ben
Ryder, Nick
Savoca, Vic
Timmons, Racey
Verkuilen, Dave
Vollenweider, James
Watts, William
Wilson, Larry
Yanda, Charles

1961

Bahen, John
Bennett, John
Bruno, James
Conners, Dan
Dentel, Robert
Diamond, Bill
Eggert, Robert
Fernandez, Sam
Foster, Harvey
Hart, Robert, III
Lillimagi, Leo
Losego, Richard
Maulty, Stanley
Miller, Bill
Mira, George
O'Mahony, James
Parsons, Van
Reinhart, Frank
Reynolds, Jerry
Rizzo, Ben
Ryder, Nick

1965

Baker, Frank
Banaszak, Pete
Barth, Robert
Beck, Frank
Beier, Tom
Bender, Vic
Biletnikoff, Bob
Blanchard, Norman
Bodie, Larry
Cassidy, Fred
Chambless, Bill
Corbin, Ken
Coughlin, Tom
Cox, James
Curtright, Don
Daanen, Jerry
Dice, David
Haggerty, Mike
Hamilton, Tom
Howington, Joe
Hutchins, Ralph
Kraszewski, Ed
LaPointe, Larry
Lewis, LeeRoy
Liebel, Robert
Matlock, John
McGee, Doug
McMillan, Jerry
Miller, Bill
Mira, Joe
Mirto, Joe
Nock, James
Robinson, Richard
Russo, Don
Salemi, Nelson
Schirmer, Bill
Sixkiller, Andy
Smith, Russell
Smith, Steve
Smith, Phil
Stanley, Robert

Tatarek, Bob
Tocco, Tony
Trosch, Gene
Tucek, John
Wahnee, Jim
Weisacosky, Ed
Werl, Robert
Wilson, Rex
Yaffa, Bernie
Zachary, Art

1966

Acuff, John
Baker, Frank
Barnett, John
Beier, Tom
Bodie, Larry
Carew, Hal
Cassidy, Fred
Chambless, Bill
Corbin, Ken
Cox, James
Czipulis, Robert
Daanen, Jerry
Dice, David
Domke, Robert
Dye, Jimmy
Folkins, Allan
Haggerty, Mike
Hamilton, Tom
Harris, Ray
Hartsel, Paul
Heinly, Ray
Hendricks, Ted
Hutchins, Ralph
LaPointe, Larry
Liebel, Robert
McGee, Doug
McGuirt, Jimmy
Miller, Bill
Mira, Joe
Mirto, Joe

Olivo, David
Omiecinski, Tom
Pierce, Jerry
Robinson, Richard
Russo, Don
Salemi, Nelson
Schirmer, Bill
Smith, Phil
Smith, Steve
Stokes, Bob
Tatarek, Bob
Tocco, Tony
Triay, Jim
Trosch, Gene
Tucek, John
Urbanowicz, Hank
Wahnee, Jim

1967

Abbott, Bob
Acuff, John
Barnett, John
Bodie, Larry
Brandy, Don
Butkus, Arnold
Carew, Hal
Carlin, Bob
Chaltas, James
Cline, Tony
Chambless, Bill
Collins, Hank
Corbin, Ken
Cox, James
Czipulis, Bob
Daanen, Jerry
DeRoss, Bill
Dice, David
Dye, Jimmy
Folkins, Allan
Fullerton, Charles
Gonzalez, Oscar
Hamilton, Tom

Harris, Ray
Heinly, Ray
Hendricks, Ted
Hopgood, George
Kresl, Jim
LaPointe, Larry
McGee, Doug
McGuirt, Jimmy
Miller, Bill
Mira, Joe
Mirto, Joe
Olivo, David
Omiecinski, Tom
Opalsky, Vincent
Pierce, Jerry
Robinson, Rich
Russo, Don
Schneider, James
Smith, Phil
Smith, Steve
Sorensen, Dick
Stawarz, Tony
Tatarek, Bob
Taylor, Rod
Teal, David
Tracy, Phil
Triay, Jimmy
Trout, Bill
Turner, Mike
Urbanowicz, Hank

1968

Abbott, Bob
Acuff, John
Barnett, John
Bellamy, Ray
Best, Bobby
Brandy, Don
Butkus, Arnold
Carlin, Bob
Chaltas, James
Chauvet, Jack

Cline, Tony
Colip, Tom
Collins, Hank
Czipulis, Bob
DeRoss, Bill
Folkins, Allan
Fullerton, Chuck
Golmont, Van
Gonzalez, Oscar
Heinly, Ray
Hendricks, Ted
Hopgood, George
Huff, Jim
Kalina, Dave
Kresl, Jim
Majewski, Bill
Olivo, David
Opalsky, Vince
Parker, Charles
Perez, Greg
Pierce, Jerry
Pytel, Lew
Schaap, Steve
Schmidt, Joe
Schneider, James
Seely, James
Sorensen, Dick
Stawarz, Tony
Stone, Dean
Stransky, Fred
Strawbridge, Rick
Taylor, Bob
Taylor, Rod
Thompson, Gary
Tracy, Phil
Trocolor, Bob
Trout, Bill
Turner, Mike
Woolum, Kerry

1969

Barrett, Pat

Bates, Junior
Bellamy, Ray
Best, Bobby
Butkus, Arnold
Chaltas, James
Chauvet, Jack
Cline, Tony
Cochrane, Kelly
Erwin, Lou
Golmont, Van
Gonzalez, Oscar
Griffin, Kevin
Haviland, Jim
Henson, Steve
Hopgood, George
Huff, Jim
Johnson, Dan
Kalina, David
Kresl, Jim
Lawrence, Wayne
MacDowell, Buz
Majewski, Bill
Matthes, Dieter
Matthews, Wiley
Mick, Gary
Opalsky, Vincent
Palewicz, Albert
Parker, Charles
Perez, Gregory
Pytel, Lew
Richard, Chuck
Riley, Mike
Schapp, Steve
Schmidt, Joe
Schmitt, Paul
Schneider, James
Schottenheimer, Kurt
Seely, James
Sorensen, Dick
Stone, Dean
Stransky, Fred
Strawbridge, Rick
Sullivan, Tom

Liddell, Rick
Marcantonio, Steve
Mitchell, Eldridge
Owens, Burgess
Palewicz, Al
Riley, Mike
Reynaud, Alan
Ritchie, Wilmore
Ross, Fred
Ruel, Golden
Sears, Harold
Smith, Tom
Streicher, Gary
Sweeting, Walt
Thompson, Woody
White, Ken
Williams, Johnny

1973

Altheide, Gary
Archer, Mike
August, Phil
Baker, Kary
Barone, Steve
Beasley, Eric
Brasington, Jack
Cain, Larry
Camut, Bert
Cardoso, Silvio
Carney, Ed
Carter, Rubin
Corker, Clarence
Corrigan, Phil
Cristiani, Tony
Daly, Mike
Demopoulos, George
Dunn, Gary
Frohbose, Bill
Gonzalez, Jose
Griffiths, Rich
Haines, Roger
Hall, Coy

Harrah, Dennis
Horschel, Paul
Ingram, Greg
Iredale, Phil
Just, Jim
Kryzak, Ed
Lanham, Bill
Latimore, Mike
Liddell, Rick
Looram, Kevin
Marcantonio, Steve
Mitchell, Eldridge
Morgan, Tim
Pinkston, Jim
Pisani, Dominic
Radford, Henry
Reynaud, Alan
Ritchie, Wilmore
Ross, Fred
Scavella, Steadman
Selmer, Brian
Streicher, Gary
Sweeting, Walt
Sydnor, Dave
Thompson, Dave
Thompson, Woody
Williams, Johnny
Wohleb, Bruce
Wysock, Joe

1974

Archer, Mike
August, Phil
Baker, Kary
Bates, Larry
Beckman, Witt
Breckner, Dennis
Cain, Larry
Campoli, Sam
Camut, Bert
Capello, Greg
Capraun, Bill

Carter, Rubin
Corker, Clarence
Daly, Mike
Demopoulos, George
Dennis, Chris
Duggan, Bob
Dunn, Gary
Edwards, Eddie
Ely, Bruce
Fetrow, Mike
Glover, Frank
Golding, Steve
Gonzalez, Jose
Griffiths, Rich
Harrah, Dennis
Horschel, Paul
Huffman, Rod
Iredale, Phil
Jackson, Dennis
Jenkins, Willie
Jones, Ernie
Kryzak, Ed
Lanham, Bill
Latimer, Clarence
Latimer, Don
Latimer, Mike
Liddell, Rick
Looram, Kevin
Ludwig, Steve
Marcantonio, Steve
Martin, Don
Morgan, Tim
Palmer, Jeff
Pinkston, Jim
Pisani, Dominic
Reynaud, Alan
Ritchie, Wilmore
Robinson, Oscar
Scavella, Steadman
Selmer, Brian
Streeter, Ron
Sullivan, Jim
Sydnor, Dave

Tezanos, Ralph
Thompson, Dave
Thompson, Woody
Turner, Johnny
Wallick, Gregg
Williams, Johnny
Wohlleb, Bruce
Wysock, Joe

1975

Adams, Mike
Anderson, Ottis
Archer, Mike
August, Phil
Baker, Kary
Bates, Larry
Bettencourt, Joe
Breckner, Dennis
Brown, Larry
Cain, Larry
Camut, Bert
Claud, Charlie
Cosden, Graig
Demopoulos, George
Dennis, Chris
Duggan, Bob
Dunn, Gary
Edwards, Eddie
Ferguson, Bryan
Ganong, Ray
Glover, Frank
Golding, Steve
Halas, George
Hill, Glenn
Iredale, Phil
Jackson, Dennis
Jenkins, Willie
Jones, Ernie
Kryzak, Ed
Latimer, Don
Latimer, Mike
Looram, Kevin

Ludwig, Steve
Makarevich, Frank
Martin, Don
Mason, George
Mathews, Gralyn
McGriff, John
Mitchell, Eldridge
Morgan, Tim
Monroe, Earl
O'Gara, Bob
Palmer, Jeff
Pinkston, Jim
Roberts, Kevin
Scavella, Steadman
Selmer, Brian
Sharpe, Bill
Smith, Donald
Sydnor, Dave
Thompson, Dave
Tokarski, Gary
Turner, John
Valerio, Rich
Walker, Ronnie
Wallick, Gregg
White, Mike
Wilson, Larry

1976

Adams, Mike
Anderson, Ottis
August, Phil
Azrak, Fred
Baker, E. J.
Bennett, Woody
Bettencourt, Joe
Bloxsom, Charles
Boyle, Ralph
Breckner, Dennis
Brown, Larry
Browning, Jim
Cain, Larry
Claud, Charlie

Cosden, Craig
Dennis, Chris
deShaw, Ricou
Edwards, Eddie
Evans, Johnny
Fenton, John
Ferguson, Bryan
Ganong, Ray
Glover, Frank
Golding, Steve
Halas, George
Hill, Glenn
Jackson, Dennis
Jackson, Dusty
Jenkins, Willie
Johnson, Ken
Kreuger, Don
Latimer, Don
Makarevich, Frank
Maler, Jim
Mason, George
Matthews, Gralyn
McGriff, John
Miller, Phil
Miranda, Jesus
Mitchell, Eldridge
Monore, Earl
Monroe, Karl
Morgan, Tim
Nixon, Herman
O'Gara, Bob
Palmer, Jeff
Roberts, Kevin
Sedley, Tom
Selmer, Brian
Smith, Donald
Standifer, Jim
Stanley, Richard
Tezanos, Ralph
Timmons, Taylor
Tokarski, Gary
Turner, John
Valerio, Rick

Walker, Ronnie
Wallick, Gregg
White, Mike
Wilson, Larry

1977

Anderson, O. J.
Alvers, Steve
Axsom, Mozell
Azrak, Fred
Baker, E. J.
Bennett, Woody
Bloxsom, Charles
Brown, Larry
Browning, Jim
Claud, Charlie
Coleman, Gene
Cosden, Craig
Daniels, Johnnie
Dennis, Chris
Evans, Johnny
Ferguson, Bryan
Galente, Tony
Gonzalez, Barry
Griffin, McKinney
Halas, George
Hill, Glenn
Hobbs, Chris
Jackson, Herb
Joiner, Jim
Johnson, Ken
Latimer, Don
McGriff, John
McMillian, Kenny
Mason, George
Millican, Pat
Miranda, Jesus
Monroe, Earl
Monroe, Karl
O'Gara, Bob
Sedley, Tom
Simmons, Malcolm

Smith, Don
Stanley, Ed
Swain, John
Rajsich, Rob
Roberts, Kevin
Timmons, Taylor
Turner, John
Valerio, Rick
Walker, Pat
White, Mike

1978

Alvers, Steve
Anderson, Ottis
Arenas, Alvaro
Axson, Mozell
Azrak, Fred
Baker, E. J.
Barbarino, Clem
Bloxsom, Charles
Bolton, Broderick
Breckner, Gary
Browning, Jim
Brodsky, Larry
Burt, James
Coleman, Gene
Cook, Charles
Cooper, Mark
Daniels, John
Eastburn, Brian
Evans, John
Fenton, John
Flanagan, Tim
Frazier, Frank
Galente, Tony
Goedeker, Mike
Gonzalez, Barry
Griffin, McKinney
Hirschman, Chuck
Jackson, Herb
Jefferson, David
Johnson, Ken

Joiner, James
Kreuger, Don
Marion, Fred
McMillian, Ken
Miller, Dan
Millican, Pat
Monroe, Karl
Nelson, Bob
Nicolas, Scott
Pokorney, Jim
Rajsich, Rob
Rodrigue, Mike
Salinger, Jeff
Sedley, Tom
Smith, Don
Smith, Mark
Swain, John
Upperco, Pete
Valerio, Rick
Walker, Pat
Williams, Lester

1979

Axson, Mozell
Bailey, Don
Barbarino, Clem
Baratta, Andy
Brophy, Jay
Bolton, Broderick
Breckner, Dennis
Brodsky, Larry
Burt, Jim
Brown, Danny
Boone, Jim
Canei, John
Cook, Charles
Coleman, Gene
Chickillo, Tony
Daniels, John
Davis, Jeff
Evans, Leon
Fenton, John

Frazier, Frank
Flanagan, Tim
Grady, Steve
Goedeker, Mike
Gonzalez, Barry
Hays, Bob
Hobbs, Chris
Joiner, Jim
Jackson, Herb
Jefferson, David
Kehoe, Art
Kelly, Jim
LaBelle, Greg
Marion, Fred
Miller, Danny
Nicolas, Scott
Nelson, Bob
Pokorney, Jim
Roughen, Rick
Rodrigue, Mike
Roan, Lorenzo
Rush, Mark
Salinger, Jeff
Smith, Mark
Swain, John
Simmons, Malcolm
Stewart, Dave
Timmons, Taylor
Upperco, Pete
Walker, Pat
Williams, Lester

1980

Axson, Mozell
Bailey, Don
Baratta, Andy
Barbarino, Clem
Belk, Rocky
Bellinger, Rod
Boone, James
Breckner, Gary
Brodsky, Larry

Brown, Danny
Brown, Greg
Burt, Jim
Canei, John
Chickillo, Tony
Comendiero, Juan
Cook, Charles
Cooper, Mark
Daniels, John
Evans, Leon
Fenton, John
Ferguson, John
Fernandez, Jack
Flanagan, Tim
Frazier, Frank
Frederick, Anthoney
Goedeker, Mike
Griffin, Keith
Hirschman, Chuck
Hobbs, Chris
Jefferson, David
Joiner, Jim
Kelly, Jim
Kehoe, Art
LaBelle, Greg
Lippett, Ron
Llinas, Jim
Marion, Fred
Miller, Dan
Neal, Robert
Nelson, Bob
Nicolas, Scott
Peasley, John
Pokorney, Jim
Richt, Mark
Roan, Lorenzo
Rodrigue, Mike
Rush, Mark
Smith, Mark
Stewart, David
Swain, John
Thompson, Lawrence
Walker, Pat

West, Isaiah
Williams, Lester
Zappala, Greg

Attendance

Largest Home Crowds

Notre Dame (1967)	77,265
Notre Dame (1955)	75,685
Florida (1969)	70,934
Notre Dame (1965)	68,077
Florida (1965)	67,762
Notre Dame (1971)	66,039
Florida (1962)	62,441
Wisconsin (1958)	62,087
Florida (1951)	61,602
Alabama (1954)	61,423

Hurricanes vs. Dolphins

Year	UM Attendance Avg.	UM Record	Dolphin Attendance Avg.	Dolphin Record
1965	49,163	5-4-1	--	--
1966	39,471	8-2-1	26,041	3-11
1967	49,307	7-4	28,978	4-10
1968	38,892	5-5	30,854	5-8-1
1969	41,329	4-6	34,687	3-10-1
1970	25,857	3-8	62,877	10-4
1971	29,786	4-7	64,912	10-3-1
1972	22,113	5-6	76,000	14-0
1973	31,961	5-6	63,211	12-2
1974	21,177	6-5	65,395	11-3
1975	23,476	2-8	64,764	10-4
1976	17,236	3-8	51,259	6-8
1977	29,641	3-8	45,671	10-4
1978	20,978	6-5	50,029	11-5
1979	26,065	5-6	56,892	10-6
1980	24,001	9-3	47,553	8-8

University of Miami Stadium

AS WE yell ourselves hoarse, tear up a brand new hat, and hug each other in a frenzy of delight while the Hurricanes are marching down the field for another touchdown, we never realize that we are doing the same thing that has been done for three thousand years by the red-blooded youth of many nations. The Greeks and Romans, who were the first to recognize physical training as an important factor in a well-rounded life, adopted the elements of their athletics from the various sports cultivated many hundreds of years before the Christian era by the Egyptians and Asiatic races. The Olympic games of the Greeks were held in a huge stadium, and gala events they were, indeed!

And now, after many centuries since the Greeks began the Olympiads, the University of Miami is building a stadium in which to hold contests and events similar to those of the ancient Greeks. The Heads of the Department of Physical Education and the Director of Athletics formed a plan to construct a bowl which will seat 50,000 people. The bowl, according to specifications, will be in the form of a horseshoe, and will include a football gridiron, a soccer field, a baseball diamond, four basketball courts, and a cinder track with a 220-yard straightaway. The field will be excavated to the depth of five feet, and the dirt will be used for the foundation of the seats. The large gateway, which will be in the open end of the stadium, is to be a magnificent example of architecture, having giant pillars on either side surrounded by tropical trees, shrubs, and flowers. The enbankment, which will form the foundation of the seats, will be landscaped and will add much to the beauty of the surroundings.

The Fund Board, composed of a group of prominent citizens of South Florida, was authorized by the Board of Regents to carry out a campaign to raise enough money to build the stadium. J. Henry Helser, a graduate of Leland Stanford, suggested the plan on which to work, selling advance tickets for next year's football games as a means of raising the money necessary. Stanford successfully carried out a similar plan, and the University of Miami is capable of doing the same. J. Henry Helser, chairman, and Harry H. Provin, vice-chairman, are in charge of the campaign.

(Reproduced from 1927 *Ibis Yearbook*.)

HURRICANE